THE LIFE
Of
RAH

An Autobiography

Rahimah S. Phillips

ISBN 978-1-0980-0480-4 (paperback)
ISBN 978-1-0980-0483-5 (hardcover)
ISBN 978-1-0980-0482-8 (digital)

Christian Faith Publishing, Inc.
832 Park Avenue
Meadville, PA 16335
www.christianfaithpublishing.com

This is a true story, inspired by actual events (to the best of the author's recollection.) However, some names and identifying characteristics have been changed in order to protect the privacy of certain individuals. Any resulting resemblance to other persons living, or dead, is entirely coincidental and unintentional.

Printed in the United States of America

To my son, to whom I gave life and would give my last breath. I hope your truth brings you peace.

To all the mothers, who took the time to try and be a mother to me, when my mother wasn't there.

To all the young women, who are struggling with raising their sons from boys to men and their daughters from girls to women.

To all the "ride-or-die" chicks, who have had my back from Jersey to Cali and "the AZ" in between.

To all the early childhood coaches, who march to the beat of a different drum because they know young lives matter.

To my grandfather, who was the apple of my eye and the one person who truly loved me. He always encouraged me to be strong.

To my youngest aunt, who was the one person who truly understood me and fully appreciated the way I live my life—*The Life of Rah*.

To my mother, last but not least - because, if it were not for the challenging situations that we went through, I would not have a story to tell.

PERSONAL DEDICATION

To my precious granddaughters, who I hope will make everything right with the world again.
Look your best. Act your best. Be your best.
Peace and blessings!
Love, Grandma Rah-Rah

I know what it is to be in need, and I know what it is to have plenty. I have learned the secret of being content in any and every situation, whether well fed or hungry, whether living in plenty or in want. (Philippians 4:12 NIV)

Contents

CHAPTER 1

When I Was

Drops of snow hit my top lip. Each drop felt colder and wetter than the drop before. My lip burned from the combination of water, dirt, and blood. I looked over at my mother. She was shivering, while she squeezed my left hand tightly. Without a word, she let my hand go and bent down to pick up some snow from the ground. She then made a small snowball and rubbed it across my top lip. I continued to cry, as tears ran down my face, mixing with the blood and dirt oozing from my busted lip. My mother was pissed, and I knew it. As a matter of fact, everyone knew it!

My mother was known for three things. She could curse anyone out, in a matter of seconds; she could drink you under the table; and she loved her daughter. That day, my teacher got cursed out for the umpteenth time. I had fallen off the sliding board at my school and busted my lip. My mother didn't like my nursery schoolteacher because, on occasion, she would tape my mouth shut for cursing and tie me to my chair with a jump rope. That day (the day it snowed), I remembered that the melted snow on the sliding board was wet, cold, and white. Walking to the bus stop, I noticed that the snow on the ground was dirty and black. I went to Weequahic Daytime Nursery and my mother had just cursed out my preschool teacher for the last time! That was the first memory of my mother. I was three. Life would soon change. And that's how life was—when I was.

Looking at my pictures, I looked happy when I was three. It was the late 1960s, and my mother was about twenty years old. I don't have many memories of my mother, especially not when I was young, and she was actually trying to be a good mother. The thing that I remember most, when I was three, is that my mother would take me to the nursery school every single day (regardless.) That meant I went to school in the spring, summer, winter, and fall—whether it was sunny, rainy, freezing, or snowing outside.

We didn't have a car then and had to catch the bus everywhere we went. I hated being dragged to the nursery school in the freezing cold, but it was important to my mother because it was part of our daily routine and showed consistency. It showed that my mother was trying to be a good mother. It also meant that she loved me. This was a good memory. Now, those days are gone, and fifty years of my life crowd my brain. I am trying to remember everything. Some things were good and some things were bad (like the time when I was six.)

I was playing in the bathtub, with my little tugboat and called it a ship. *Wham!* My mother slapped me right across my face and almost knocked out my loose tooth. She thought that I cursed and said, "Shit!" She said, "Say it again!" My face hurt, but I rolled my eyes, sucked my teeth under my breath, and kept on playing. I was more worried about losing my taste buds than losing my loose tooth because my mother had a habit of saying, "I'm gonna slap the taste out your mouth!" I was used to being slapped and beaten. My mother beat me all the time and, sometimes, for no reason at all. Other times, she threatened to "slap the black off me!" I got the dumb look. *Slap the black off me? What the heck did that mean? On top of being beaten, was I going to wake up one day and be light-skinned?*

At first, I really wasn't worried about the beatings because everyone I knew got beatings. My mother got beatings from her boyfriends. My cousins got beatings from my youngest aunt. My friends got beatings from their mothers. The dogs even got beatings from my grandfather. One time, I saw my grandfather beat one of the Dobermans with my grandmother's shoe because the dog had chewed the other shoe. Another time, I saw my grandmother beat my little cousin. I remember hearing my little cousin yell, "Lordy! Lordy! Lordy!" My grandmother would say, "Don't call on the Lord now!" I laughed out loud in my head, but I was shocked. My grandmother didn't do a whole lot of yelling, screaming, or beating. She was the matriarch of the family. Everyone called her "Nana," which meant grandmother, godmother, nurse, or chief. I would later learn that everyone either feared, or loved, my grandmother. It was the norm—a family tradition. I was six. And that's how life was—when I was.

When I was seven, my mother and grandmother took me school shopping for "back-to-school" clothes. We would go to *Two Guys* department store downtown Newark, on the corner of Broad and Market. I was allowed to pick out two outfits. One outfit was for the first day of school and the other one was for the second day of school. I always had an eye for fashion and looked pretty cool when it was time to go back to school. The only other time that I dressed up was for Easter. I could always count on my grandmother, or one of my aunts, to either buy me a new outfit or make me a dress. Unfortunately, I looked quite the mess when the other 362 days of the year came around. *Yup, that was it. Easter and the first two days of school—those were my times to shine!*

I laughed out loud in my head, as I thought about my long, skinny, hairy legs sticking out from underneath my Easter dress. Memories of my mother also made me laugh. Sometimes, she would say the weirdest things to me. She would tell me not to worry about my long, skinny, hairy legs because men would find them sexy when I was older. I didn't care about my mother's "life lessons" back then and didn't want to hear about grown men finding me sexy because I was only seven. I cared more about the kids who teased me every day and were calling me "Skinny Minnie" and "Hairy Harry."

When I was seven, somehow I knew my life was about to change forever (and not in a good way.) By the time I was eight years old, I knew that I was different from most of the other girls my age. I tried to look like the girls in my neighborhood, but - deep down, I knew that I was different. I walked different. I talked different. I looked different. I hated my body and did whatever I could to look like some of the other girls. This one girl, Rhonda, already had boobs and was wearing a training bra. Little Miss Rhonda Clark was ten going on thirty. I, on the other hand, looked like an eight-year-old boy.

I often hid behind the door in the locker room because I didn't want anyone to see me undressing. I especially didn't want them to see me in that hideous blue gym suit, with the matching belt and big silver buckle. I was a sight for sore eyes. I was determined not to be seen (not me, the future queen of fashion.) At school, I would pray and ask God for bigger boobs and a butt - any kind of butt. By this time, I had graduated from halter tops to tube tops (clearly, to accentuate my flat chest.) I would walk around chanting, "*I must... I must... I must increase my bust!*" I would dream about the high heels that I would wear (when I was older) to make my butt and calves bigger - and the arches in my feet higher.

God must not have been listening because I was still tall and lanky, when I was nine - and all the neighborhood kids still made fun of me, except for Rhonda (because she had stayed back twice and always smelled like pee.) I often wondered why I was so much taller than everyone else in my family, except for my eldest aunt, who had legs up to the ceiling. Yes ma'am... My eldest aunt and I were what everyone referred to as a "tall glass of water."

There was another tall girl at my school, but she looked like a grown woman. She was what everybody referred to as a "brick house." She had legs up to the ceiling, like my eldest aunt, and wore a skirt and heels every day. Our English teacher would turn beet red and start salivating, every time she entered the classroom. I laughed out loud in my head because he always adjusted his tie and pants after she left. I couldn't understand why all the other girls my age looked so much different than me. We weren't even in high school yet! I tried my best to pick out clothes that made me look more mature.

I remember strolling down the fake "runway" in my dress and heels, at my first fashion show (when I was ten.) It was at my grandmother's church and I wore one of my Easter outfits. After that, I began doing weekend fashion shows at the Peppermint Lounge on Central Avenue in East Orange. When I was fifteen, I started doing catalog work and local hair shows. My eldest aunt had introduced me to the fashion world, and I was already auditioning for TV commercials and going on "go-sees" in Manhattan (by the time I was sixteen.) Being tall and lanky was finally starting to pay off, but - other than fashion, my eldest aunt and I didn't seem to have a whole lot in common.

I remember the time when she took me to the movies to see *Prince* in "Purple Rain". On the way home, she just came out of nowhere and asked me if I sweat during sex. This was her somewhat subtle attempt to get closer to me. I turned my head toward her and gave her the dumb look. *Did she really think that I was gonna spill the beans?* Shenanigans! I knew that my eldest aunt was just spying for my grandmother. *Yup, that was her job!* And there wasn't much else to say about her. We both liked to read, and she enjoyed theater and classical music. She and my grandmother had taken me to see *West Side Story* on Broadway, when I was younger. I suppose that was when I began to enjoy musicals like *Porgy and Bess, Grease*, and later *Dirty Dancing*. As it turns out, fashion wasn't my only passion. My passion for music also grew.

In the 1970s, I loved to listen to *Bob Marley* sing "No Woman No Cry." My mother would say that I had an "old soul." Sometimes, I would actually act like a child and sing the "ABC" song along with

The Jackson 5. Most of the time, I would count on *The Staple Singers* to keep us in a good mood by singing "Respect Yourself" and "Let's Do It Again." My best friends (Karen and Egypt) and I went crazy whenever "Car Wash" by *Rose Royce* came on the radio. Sometimes, we would *really* act crazy and pretend to be famous—singing "Ooh Boy, I Love You So" (in the mirror with our hairbrushes.) The world was dance-crazed back then.

Then, there were the soundtracks to Black cinema movies - like "Shaft" and "Claudine." On late summer nights, we couldn't get enough of *Isaac Hayes* and *Curtis Mayfield*. When I was alone, music began to take a backseat to television. I spent most Friday nights watching TV shows, such as "Charlie's Angels", "The Love Boat", "Fantasy Island", and "Baretta." Some nights, when my mother was still around, we watched our favorite movies and popped Jiffy pop-corn. I would always sit and stare at the foil getting bigger and bigger! And that's how life was—when I was.

During the day, when other mothers worked, my mother could always be found watching her "stories." She never missed an episode of *Erica Kane* on "All My Children", or *Asa Buchanan* on "One Life to Live." As I grew older, I started to recall each and every episode of my own life (when I was alone.) I began keeping a diary that I would write in every day after school. When my words flowed like poetry, I would write the poems in a "special" little book. My poetry book consisted of ten pieces of large index cards stapled together. I num-bered each page like real authors did when they wrote real books. I decorated two other index cards with pictures and stickers, colored them green, and wrote my name in large letters so that people would know who the author was. These were my cover pages for the front and back of my poetry book.

Although my diary contained my innermost thoughts and a few family secrets, it was not as special as my poetry book. My diary was pink and had a lock that only a very special and extremely small key could fit. It was certainly pretty and definitely personal, but it was not special! Maybe, it was the fact that my diary was store-bought and my poetry book was handcrafted by me! Either way, I could open up my books and drift away into a land of memories. Some of the memories were good, and some memories were not so good. And that's how life was—when I was.

In the 1980s (when I was becoming a young woman), everyone was falling in love with *Theo* and *Denise* on "The Cosby Show." It reminded me of how my mother and I watched "Soul Train" and "Good Times", when I was young. Times changed, when I was in high school and went to stay with my grandmother. When I was fourteen, my grandfather would chase the boys away with his gigantic, handcrafted African wooden spear. During the holidays, I loved to watch my grandfather put on his dress sweaters and dance like Bill Cosby at the beginning of the show. My grandfather was always so charming and funny, and he reminded me of *Cliff Huxtable*.

When I was in my twenties, all the "around the way" girls wore big earrings and tried to rap like *Salt-n-Pepa* and *Yo-Yo*. "U.N.I.T.Y." by *Queen Latifah* (who also went to Irvington High) and "Ruffneck" by *MC Lyte* made every young woman feel liberated. Then, all the ladies turned "crazy, sexy cool" and started sporting short haircuts like "T-Boz" from *TLC* and *Halle Berry* in "Strictly Business." It seemed like every girl I knew tried to rock the "asymmetrical" hairdo. And I was no exception. I must have gone to the beauty salon ten times to try and get Richard to style my hair the right way. I refused to put a weave in my hair, and he refused to cooperate by not cutting my hair to match T-Boz's picture!

By the 1990s, club music and "house" music had taken off. In between the chaos that was my life, my friends and I danced to hits like "Love Sensation", "Doctor Love", "I'm Caught Up (In a One Night Love Affair)", "I Was Born This Way", and "My Love is Free" - at *Club Zanzibar* and *Club 88*. I remember the first time that I came home from *Club Zanzibar* (back when I was sixteen.) Strolling in (like I was grown) - at 5:30 in the morning! My grandmother was already up and getting ready for church. She gave me this look like I must have lost my mind. I laughed out loud in my head…but I never did it again.

In the 1990s (when I was a young mother), I listened to the smooth voices of *Jodeci* singing "Come & Talk to Me", *Janet Jackson* singing "If" and "That's the Way Love Goes", and *Tony, Toni, Tone* singing "Lay Your Head on My Pillow." One of my favorite R&B songs was "Knockin' Da Boots" by *H-Town*. The hip-hop era had also taken off with cuts like "What's the 411" by *Mary J. Blige* and "You're All I Need" by *Method Man* and *Mary J.* My other favorite songs were "Doin' It" and "Mama Said Knock You Out" by *LL Cool J.* I also loved "One More Chance" by *Biggie Smalls*, and "Keep Ya Head Up" and "Dear Mama" by *Tupac*. But we definitely can't forget about the "Jeeps, Lex Coups, Bimaz & Benz" by *Lost Boyz* and *Bone Thugs-N-Harmony* singing "Tha Crossroads." Another favorite was "O.P.P." by *Naughty by Nature*.

In the early 1990's, even the White boys got it in with *Color Me Badd*, singing "I Wanna Sex You Up." Back then, I would flip back and forth between WBLS, KISS FM, and Hot 97, tryin' to catch my favorite artists—like *Common* and *Lauryn Hill*. I was also always tryin' to catch the latest gossip from *Wendy*! Sometimes, I would just sit in my car and vibe to the lyrics of *Ice Cube's* "It Was a Good Day" and *Ahmad's* "Back in the Day." Somehow, those two songs always seemed to be the perfect start and finish of a perfect day.

By the mid-nineties, I was a Reggae fanatic and had started partying at *Club Eclipse* in Irvington. Every CD that I owned was by *Buju Banton*, or *Shaba Ranks*. Songs like "Action" by *Terror Fabulous* and "Murder She Wrote" by *Chaka Demus* rang through the streets. Then, the millennium came.

Life, when I was in my thirties, reminded me of life in my teens. One day, things were going good. The next day, things were going terribly wrong. One minute, I was up. Then, I was down. I was always trying to find solid ground. I didn't know who to trust and where to turn, but I tried my best just to maintain. I wished that I was young again. Back when I was young, I didn't have the best life. But it was my life. And that's how life was—when I was.

CHAPTER 2

School Daze

Whenever I was a young child, I felt like my life was passing me by. I often felt like I was in a daze. Some days were good, and some days were bad. Believe it, or not, the best days were when I was in school. That's because I was good at school. I had been taught the value of going to school and getting a good education at a very young age. Education would become my foundation. Without it, I would have nothing! I learned the importance of education early on, when I was about five years old. I remember the first time that I actually went to a "real" school like it was yesterday.

I was going to a "real" school. I was no longer in nursery school! I was going to "kinnygarden!" I sat in a daze on the edge of my mother's bed and watched her sleep. It was 8:15 in the morning. I think it was a Monday because it was the first day of school. Then again, it must have been a Tuesday because we always started school the day after Labor Day (which always fell on a Monday.) There were two main rules on the East Coast, and one of them was that no one could wear white before Easter. The other was that no one could wear white after Labor Day.

I was only five years old and the rules didn't matter much to me, but I followed them anyway. I finished eating my Cheerios and prayed that my mother would not wake up. I always ate Cheerios, or applesauce with milk. Besides my grandfather, those had become the constants in my life. I knew that I was running late for my first day of school, but I wanted to finish watching *The Flintstones*. They came on right after *Bugs Bunny & Friends* and *Casper the Friendly Ghost*. Sometimes, I even got up early enough to watch *Underdog* and *Magilla Gorilla*.

Just as the credits started rolling, I heard my mother yell my name. She always called me by my first and middle name, when she was mad. Then she yelled, "Girl, you better get yourself up and get ready for school!" The truth of the matter is that my mother should have been awake way before me and helping me get dressed for my first day of school. After all, I was only five years old! Instead, she did what she always did at night—fell asleep watching TV and drinking beer. That's why I had to wake up early and get myself ready.

It was my job to clean up after her and get myself ready for school. I changed out of the bell-bottom jeans and new T-shirt that I had picked out all by myself and put on the beautiful red dress my mother picked out for me. I was always dressing like a "flower child" (the Black version.) Every Saturday, I wore two-tone bell-bottom jeans and a halter top. My jeans were actually reversible. I could wear them on either side and pretend that I had two separate outfits. *Hideous!*

Sometimes, I wore a sundress. One thing that you could always count on was that I would wear my afro puffs, or a big afro with a headband. I was so grateful that my mother never made me wear ponytail holders, with those big colored balls, in my hair like other little girls. We always rocked our natural hair. Every now and then, my mother would use Vigorol to smooth out my edges and the naps in my "kitchen." I hated it because it stank up the whole apartment. Besides, I liked my afro and the naps that came with it. I also liked my mother's TWA (teeny-weeny afro.) I didn't put a full perm in my hair until after my son was born, when I was in college.

One time, when I was in high school, I tried a California curl. It was supposed to be the dry version of an "S" curl. I liked it because I didn't have to spray any activator on it. Everyone knows that curl activator was a hot, juicy mess! Reminiscing about the way I dressed and wore my hair made me think back to that first day of kinny-garden. I was only five years old, but I was serious about my hair and my clothes!

My red dress was gorgeous! It came right above my knees and had buttons straight down the center. Red was my favorite color. The dress had a ruffled collar with lace around it and elbow-length sleeves. I wore black, patent-leather shoes with a strap that went across my foot.

I wore ugly, little red socks to match my dress. The socks folded down and did not reach above my ankles. They were also trimmed with lace and were also hideous because they looked like "baby socks." In any event, I was ready to face the world and all the other kinny-garteners who were about to embark upon their first day of school.

I ran down two flights of stairs, bypassing the scary elevator. I bolted out the cracked glass front door of our apartment building. I looked out the window before leaving my mother's bedroom and saw my two best friends, Elly and Maddie. Elly's real name was Elizabeth. She was my age, but she acted a whole lot older. I didn't like her very much, but she was Maddie's little sister. Maddie's real name was

Madeline. She, on the other hand, was one year older than us and acted like she was an adult. She was very smart, and I liked her a lot.

My mother yelled my name, again. I could hear her calling out my first and middle name through her bedroom window. I looked up toward the second floor window and saw the look on her face. I went into prayer mode, like I had done earlier when I wanted to finish watching *The Flintstones*. I was no stranger to praying because my grandmother, who lived around the corner from us, dragged me to church every chance she got.

My mother and I glared into each other's eyes, with an all-too-familiar stare down. I moved my lips, but nothing came out. In actuality, I was silently pleading with my mother to stop embarrassing me in front of my new friends. Elly and Maddie lived in the apartment building across the street. They told me that they had previously lived in the building next to me and my mother, but had recently moved into their new building. I had never been inside their apartment before, but we played outside together all summer.

My mother obviously could not hear my lips moving because she continued to stare me down. Elly and Maddie began to walk ahead, but I asked them to wait for me. We were already running late, and I could tell that they were anxious to get to school on time. They walked ahead slowly and I could see them looking back for me, as I continued to plead with my mother. We were having an ongoing debate about whether, or not, I should be allowed to walk to school by myself.

I tried to convince my mother that I was not walking by myself, and pointed out that Elly and Maddie were waiting for me. My mother finally caved, after letting me know that she would be sitting in the window watching us. Walking to school with my new best friends on the very first day of school felt like the best day of my life. My mother trusted me, and I felt proud not to let her down. Elly, Maddie, and I reached the front doors of Chancellor Avenue Elementary School - and all was well with the world!

Even though summer was over, school days were fun because I was away from my mother for an entire day. I liked school, and I liked my teachers. I don't remember much about my kindergarten teacher. Most of my memories were of other teachers in my school and my neighborhood. After kindergarten, I transferred to Chancellor Avenue Annex (which was located just down the street.)

I would live in the same neighborhood until I was nine, when I was in the fourth grade. Although most of the people I knew were poor and lived in the projects or beat-up apartment buildings, there were actually some nice houses in Newark. They were on the side streets, near Weequahic Park. In fact, my grandparents owned one of those houses and lived in it—right behind my school.

My mother and I lived with my grandparents until I was five years old. My mother gave birth to me at the ripe young age of seventeen. She had not finished out the year at East Side High School and ended up taking night classes at Barringer High School so that she could receive her GED. Then, she took summer classes until she graduated and got her high school diploma. She then went on to college for two years and received an associate degree from Rutgers University in Newark. That's when I knew that I too would graduate from Rutgers.

Other than going to that horrid nursery school, I don't remember much of my childhood before turning five. I had seen photo albums and lots of pictures of me and my mother. I saw one picture of me sitting on her lap, with a big stuffed pink Easter bunny sitting next to us. She wore a navy blue dress with red buttons down the middle, and her hair was cut short. She had big, beautiful eyes and a smile to match. I saw another picture of her holding me in a beautiful white Christening dress. My mother was very pretty. It looked like she really loved me and enjoyed being a mother.

Other than a few birthday parties, I didn't see any pictures of me and my grandmother together. I thought this was very strange. In the commercials on TV, grandparents seemed to love their grandchildren more than the children's parents did. Clearly, this was not the case in my situation. My grandmother always put up a good front in front of other people, but she always seemed mean when she was alone with me and my mother.

When my mother and I moved out of my grandmother's house, we continued to live in the building on the corner of Wainwright Street and Chancellor Avenue for the next four years. My mother began to drink heavily, and I noticed that she never went to work like Elly and Maddie's mother, who was also single. They told me that their father died, but I heard that he just left. I didn't care one way, or another, because I had never even met my father. The only male role model in my family was my grandfather, and he was a godsend—an angel!

I needed one of God's angel's to look over me because the days of my mother watching over me from her bedroom window were long gone. My mother had become the child, and I was the adult. All

24

of a sudden, I had become the cook and the cleaning lady. Needless to say, this put a damper on my social life. I hardly saw Elly and Maddie anymore and spent most weekends at my grandparents' house.

I often wondered how my mother managed to pay the bills with no money. It turned out that we were on welfare. Our very mysterious orange car (which magically appeared in our parking lot one day) no longer worked. It had mismatch doors and an engine that looked like it had caught on fire. Without money and a car, I started to become suspicious of my mother's actions. *How were we living?* When I left for school and arrived home from school, my mother was always sleeping. She no longer cared about what I wore and how I got to school.

My mother could no longer pay the rent at our apartment in Newark. When I was nine, we moved to East Orange (to stay with my youngest aunt.) There were six of us (three adults and three children) living in a two-bedroom apartment. It was a nice house (a two-family) on Chestnut Street. My aunt had her own problems, and we only stayed there for about six months.

Then, my mother and I moved to a building on South Clinton Street in East Orange. By then, I had begun to see it all. Drugs and alcohol had taken its toll. I was sick of it all and just wanted to concentrate on getting out—out from underneath my mother and my grandmother. I also wanted to get out of my new neighborhood. I wanted to get away from my new building and away from my new life.

The apartment building was six stories high, and we lived on the fourth floor. The building was two stories higher than the one in Newark. There were six apartments on each floor, which gave me the potential to earn over $200 each week. I had it all figured out. I would charge each person fifty cents per bag to take out their garbage and another five to ten dollars per person to clean their apartment and iron their clothes for the week. It all depended on the number of people in each apartment and how many chores I did. Some days, I earned $50. Some days, I earned nothing at all.

Although we were farther away, I would still spend weekends at my grandmother's house (doing chores.) Unlike most children who were excited to spend time with their grandparents, my situation was a little different. I enjoyed seeing my grandfather and loved him very much. He was the apple of my eye. On the other hand, my only purpose in my grandmother's eyes was to clean her house. In return, I was given a home-cooked meal and an allowance.

I liked eating at my grandmother's house because she (like everyone else in the family) was a good cook. I especially liked her macaroni and cheese. She could make macaroni and cheese like nobody's business! I remember sitting at the kitchen table on Goldsmith Avenue and watching her grate the blocks of Kraft sharp cheddar cheese with a huge silver grater. She would mix in a perfect combination of milk and melted butter with the elbow macaroni, and put the glass dish in the oven. I would salivate, as she set the oven temperature to 375 degrees. It would be the longest forty-five minutes of my life! I couldn't wait until I was bigger and would make my macaroni and cheese just the same way!

My mother was a good cook too, but not like my grandmother. She could make some of the same things, but they didn't taste as good. I once read that if a person can read, he or she can cook. I was always taught that "real" cooking comes from the heart. A real cook doesn't need to measure the ingredients to a recipe. They just know the right amount is a pinch of this and a dash of that. A real cook can create something from nothing. A real cook can make a dish taste like it was made from scratch, when it wasn't. It's like knowing when a recipe says, "Just add water," you add milk instead. The dish will come out much creamier.

My mother's specialty was making breakfast, mostly because she never went to work and had a lot of extra time in the mornings. Her other specialty was chicken stew with large egg noodles and mixed vegetables. Unlike my grandmother, my mother never made anything for Christmas or Thanksgiving. Sometimes, she would make something special for Easter. One year, she cooked a duck. I didn't want to eat it, but she made me. I remember it being chewy.

After that Easter, I never wanted to eat a chocolate bunny again! The cooked duck reminded me of a rabbit. My mother must have felt bad. She bought me a bunny rabbit that same year. I didn't know if it was a boy or girl, but I named it Hoppy! She never cooked duck for dinner again and concentrated on teaching me how to make steak and eggs for breakfast. She had a special way of frying a T-bone steak with butter and onions. She could do the same thing with liver and make it taste just like steak! She also made the best lunch, a Pastrami and cheese sandwich, with lettuce, tomatoes, and Hellmann's mayonnaise. I remember that my mother was picky about her cheese. It had to be thin-sliced from the deli counter at the grocery store. She never bought processed cheese slices.

School lunch was never that great, but I always looked forward to my mother's sandwiches and seeing my grandmother's sister in the cafeteria. She worked at the Annex as one of the lunch ladies. I also looked forward to school trips because we could buy a "special" lunch, or bring lunch from home. Of course, my mother always made me her famous Pastrami sandwiches. I always made a special trip to the grocery store the night before a school trip. I would buy three dollars' worth of yellow American cheese, sliced thin. Then, I would pick out a head of Iceberg lettuce, three Jersey tomatoes, along with a juice, and a snack. I knew how we paid for the food, but I never knew how my mother paid for the trips because we never had any money. I was sure that she didn't use her food stamps. I was just glad that she was around to sign the permission slips. The only thing that I didn't like about school trips was that I never had enough money to buy a souvenir.

I loved going on school trips because I could hold hands and flirt with Patrick on the bus. Patrick and I were in all the same classes from the fourth to the sixth grade, and I had the biggest crush on him! Back then, I also had crushes on Trevor, Antoine, and Stephen. Antoine and Stephen were brothers, but it didn't matter to me because I wasn't old enough to have a boyfriend anyway. Antoine and Stephen lived in my building, but they didn't go to the same school as me, Trevor, and Patrick. It was the best of both worlds. I could see Trevor and Patrick every day at school, and see Antoine and his older brother when I got home. On my way home, I read the letters that I got from each of them. The words *"How's my chances?"* were followed by "Circle *Yes, No,* or, *Maybe*!"

Reminiscing about my school days made me think about all the "little" things that my mother and grandmother did (back in those days.) They both always had their own special way of doing things. My mother would pack my "brown bag" lunch and then disappear for days! My grandmother would attempt to compensate by buying me things. The only problem was that I hated the things she bought. One year, she bought me a pair of "Jellies." They were clear, plastic, and three sizes too big! They were the ugliest and cheapest shoes around ($2.99 a pair.) They cost $3.99, if you bought the ones with glitter.

On Christmas, my grandmother always bought me a huge jar of Vaseline. I didn't know which was worse—wearing Jellies, or getting Petroleum Jelly as a gift. Now that I think about it, the worse gift I ever received was a five-speed bike. It had tassels on the handlebars and came with a white basket. *How embarrassing!* Everyone else had a ten-speed. Besides, I hated the color brown! *Did she not know me at all?* I laughed out loud in my head. Later that year, I saw a navy blue ten-speed bike on sale at Valley Fair. I saved up my money and bought my own bike. When I was older, I asked my grandmother to give me money instead of buying me gifts. Now, I had two things to look forward to on Christmas—getting money and one of my grandmother's home-cooked meals.

My grandmother could sew and knit almost as well as she cooked. She would create the most hideous dresses for me. No one else that I knew wore crocheted dresses! I was often the laughing stock of the school because everyone could see through the knitted holes in my dress. I tried to compensate by wearing a full slip underneath the see-through dresses, which made things even worse because girls my age also didn't wear full slips. All I needed was a pair of my grandmother's taupe, opaque, old-lady stockings to complete my ensemble. I laughed out loud in my head—again. Nevertheless, I was somewhat grateful because I might not have had any clothes otherwise.

I never had new clothes anymore because my mother's addiction began to spin out of control. She drank beer and hard liquor constantly. I remember how, on the way to Weequahic Park, we would go into the corner liquor store and steal stuff. By stuff, I mean cans of Budweiser, bottles of Mad Dog 20/20, Wise potato chips, a pack of Juicy Fruit chewing gum, and a tube of ChapStick. This had become our normal regime on the way to the park.

My mother and I went to the park often and sometimes with my aunt. My mother had two sisters, one was older and one was younger. This definitely contributed to my mother's "middle child" syndrome. She was the "black sheep" of the family and I often wondered why she never screamed out, "Marsha! Marsha! Marsha!" like the girl from *The Brady Bunch*. Although I was not around when they were growing up, it was clear that my grandmother loved her other two daughters more than she loved my mother.

It seemed like my mother and grandmother didn't like each other at all. I was very surprised on the day that my grandmother showed up at our apartment with the police and threatened to send my mother's boyfriend to jail. For the first time in a long while, I was happy to see my grandmother. I was also happy to see the police because I too had threatened my mother's boyfriend. Just the day before, I hit him in the back with a two-by-four as I yelled for him to get off my mother.

My mother's brute of a boyfriend held her down on the bed, with his hands around her throat, and was raping her. She was screaming that he was hurting her and for him to turn her loose. He continued to pounce on my mother, until I clobbered him with the wooden beam. That's when I knew that I had to protect my mother for the rest of her life. Our roles had definitely shifted, and I had become the adult. Although she had the body of an adult, my mother seemed like a child to me because she was incapable of caring for herself and me.

I continued to cook breakfast in the morning, dinner at night, and clean the apartment every day after school. I took turns cleaning my grandmother's and eldest aunt's houses on weekends to earn extra money. Unlike the other children my age, I chose to save my money rather than spend it on penny candy from the corner store. I didn't eat a lot of candy but, like my mother, I loved "Chunky" candy bars and those little caramel square candies. I pinched pennies whenever I could because I knew that, in the long run, saving my pennies would become a means of survival.

As I thought about my future, visions of my life passed through my head. In addition to saving my pennies, I knew that education would be my savior. It would be my ticket out! I thought back to my third-grade teacher and the day that I handed my mother the long, white envelope from school. I wasn't sure what the letter said, but I knew that I had not done anything wrong. I was a straight "A" student, and all of my teachers loved me. The letter came from a White teacher who had taken a special interest in me. She wanted to know if she could meet with my mother. I wasn't sure why and was embarrassed for her to come to our apartment. She had asked to walk me home so that she could speak with my mother. She lied and said that it was because she was concerned for my safety.

I laughed out loud in my head, as I thought that the White teacher better be more concerned about her *own* safety. I must have come up with every excuse in the book to keep her from coming to our apartment, and it worked (or so I thought.) My mother literally laughed out loud, as she read the letter. She then became serious and curious at the same time. She wanted to know why this particular teacher was showing such an interest in me. I attempted to explain that I was a good student and the teacher thought I should do extra credit work as a tutor.

Imagine that! My teacher wanted me to help her "teach" other children! I would become a tutor for other students. This idea would become a common theme among most of my teachers throughout elementary, junior high school, and even college. I was confused by the devilish grin on my mother's face, as she read the letter. It did not look like a happy grin. My mother seemed jealous and genuinely unhappy for me. I, on the other hand, was ecstatic and was not about to let my mother ruin my happy moment!

I had never felt this feeling before, and I felt proud. My teachers believed in me! In all of my school years, there were only five teachers who I remember. First, there was my dreadful nursery schoolteacher (the one who taped my mouth shut for cursing and tied me to my chair with a jump rope.) She had also been the same one who my mother cursed out for letting me fall off the sliding board on that cold winter day (when I was three years old.) I wondered where Miss Williams was now and if she was still tying children to their chairs. Secretly, I hoped that she had been shunned from society and was being punished for her sins at a faraway reform school.

Next, there was my third-grade teacher (the nosey White woman who cared about me so much that she was willing to risk her life.) I thought for sure that she would die a tragic death at the hands of someone in our neighborhood, or at the hands of my mother! She seemed to take a special interest in me. I was surprised because this teacher was White. I often wondered what she was doing in a Black neighborhood and teaching at an all-Black school.

I wondered where she lived and whether, or not, she had a family. I remember thinking that I had never seen any White families in the neighborhood. Other than my third-grade teacher, I didn't recall seeing *any* White people in my neighborhood. At one time, Newark was considered one of the most dangerous cities in the United States. I've heard news reporters refer to Newark as "the murder capital of the world." Newark was also known as "Brick City" because of its housing projects. It was the scum of the earth and home of the lower-class Black folk. It would later become known as the "car theft capital of the world!"

There I was, with a White teacher, who was smack dab in the heart of Newark. She was in the middle of "my hood" and in the middle of my business. Then, there was my fifth-grade teacher, who praised and encouraged me simply because she believed in me. There was also my sixth-grade math teacher, who had a strange way of telling me to "shut my mouth!" He had a funny Southern accent, and it always sounded like he was telling me to shut my "math!" I laughed out loud in my head, whenever I heard Mr. Keeley's voice. Imagine a math teacher telling me to "shut my math."

Lastly, there was a sixth-grade Social Studies teacher, who was not actually "my" teacher. His classroom was across the hall from mine. But I would not have been able to deliver the sixth-grade graduation speech if it were not for him. I had been chosen as the valedictorian by "default" and got stage fright right before the ceremony began.

My friend Nikki, who lived around the corner from us with her grandmother, had not been to school in weeks. I wondered where she was. I had gone to her house several times and her grandmother said that she couldn't come out to play, and couldn't have company. I thought back to the last time that I spent the night at Nikki's house.

It was New Year's Eve, and we were dancing in the living room, waiting for the ball to drop! Just as the countdown began, the phone rang. It was the police! Nikki's mother had been involved in a car accident, a head-on collision. She was driving drunk. We later found out that she was driving on the wrong side of the Parkway and drove onto an exit ramp. She was killed instantly. Nikki had missed so many days of school since then, but I had hoped she would be at the graduation. She was the smartest girl in the whole school!

Victor and I were the next smartest. We had to duke it out by competing against each other in a spelling bee. I won. As I thought about my friend, I just stood there (looking stupid, in front of 350 students.) I froze. I couldn't speak. I couldn't move. I couldn't breathe! I wanted to run off the stage and out of the school as fast as I could, but I had nowhere to go! Once again, my mother had pulled one of her infamous disappearing acts and was "MIA." I couldn't remember a time, since kindergarten and third grade, when she showed some kind (any kind) of interest in my schoolwork. Now, I was about to start junior high school, and she was not at my graduation. She had been missing in action since we got evicted from our "deluxe" efficiency apartment on South Clinton Street.

The sixth-grade teacher, Mr. Evans, peeked from behind the curtain and tried to get my attention. I could hear him, but I was afraid to move. The other students sitting in the front row just below the stage stared up at me. No one said anything! Mr. Evans walked over to the podium and grabbed me by the arm. I thought that I was in trouble. When we got back behind the curtain, he asked if I was okay and told me to breathe.

He motioned to another teacher to bring me a glass of water. Two teachers, one of whom was my favorite fifth-grade teacher, returned with a cup of cold water and a box of tissues. I drank the cold water and wiped the tears from my face. Mrs. Moore, the fifth-grade teacher, hugged me and told me that everything would be okay. I loved her so much and wished she was my mother.

Mr. Evans told me to focus on one person only, instead of looking at everyone in the crowd. He told me to look down at the speech, which was written neatly on a piece of paper (if I needed to.) After a gentle nudge by Mr. Evans and a reassuring hug from Mrs. Moore, I dried my eyes and walked back onto the stage with a confidence that I didn't know I had. I delivered the sixth-grade graduation speech! I was no longer in a daze.

CHAPTER 3

The Color Of My Skin

The days of my life as a young child were gone. Life as I knew it was about to change. The people, places, and things that surrounded me would no longer exist. I started to notice things that I had not noticed before. I began to ask questions. *Why were my elbows, ankles, and knees so black?* A different color than the rest of my skin… That's the thought I had while I sat in the bathtub on the day my mother threatened to slap the black off me.

My mother claimed it was because I was dirty. I begged to differ! I laughed out loud in my head. I thought about how my grandmother had taught me all about education. I thought about how my eldest aunt had taught me all about fashion. But it was my mother who taught me all about life. And it was my youngest aunt who was my favorite because she was so full of life! So much so that she made my mother jealous. One day, my mother accused me of loving my youngest aunt more than I loved her because my aunt was light-skinned.

I stared at my mother in amazement. After all that I had done for her and all that we had gone through together, she had the nerve to say such a thing. I was truly hurt and realized that my mother had other problems, in addition to drinking. Clearly, her mental stability was now in question. Besides the fact that she stayed with a boyfriend who beat and raped her repeatedly, she was showing signs of paranoia. At the time, this was not something that I was familiar with or understood - so I chose to ignore it. However, it would rear its ugly head later in our lives.

I became curious about my mother's analogy regarding my feelings toward my aunt, and the color of people's skin. I knew that my mother had major hang-ups about White people. As a matter of fact, there was a whole list of things that she believed separated us (based solely on the color of our skin.) She would say White people eat pumpkin pie. We eat sweet potato pie. She said White people eat Northern fried chicken. Black people eat Southern fried chicken. They cook with Shake 'n Bake. We cook with flour. They like the meat. We like the skin. They like the white meat. We like the dark meat. They use lotion. We use baby oil. My head was spinning! I laughed out loud!

My mother and her two sisters grew up in Newark, in the 1950s and 1960s. It was during the civil rights movement. It was a horrible time for many Black people. I listened to stories my mother told about the riots and protests that happened on her way home from school. By the 1970s, things were peaceful. Things were good, until they weren't. My youngest aunt was the glue that held us all together.

She was only fifteen years older than me and very cute. As a matter of fact, everyone said that she was as cute as a button and sweet as pie! And she was indeed light-skinned. Light-skinned girls were always considered the pretty girls. My awareness of the color of my skin began way before my mother's idiotic statements about my youngest aunt. The first time that I saw *Uptown Saturday Night*, I was mesmerized by Calvin Lockhart's dark brown skin. Calvin Lockhart played the part of "Silky Slim," and his skin was the color of smooth, rich, dark chocolate.

I knew, from that point on, that I preferred dark-skinned men. My favorite part of the movie was when *Silky Slim* and his crew robbed "Madame Zenobia's." After busting up the joint, *Silky Slim* said, "Never have so few owed so much to so many." *Best line ever!* This affinity toward men of a darker complexion would later be affirmed, when I decided that I preferred Wesley Snipes as "Shadow" over Denzel Washington as "Bleek" in *Mo' Better Blues*.

Don't get me wrong… Denzel was fine and he can still get it! But there was something about "Shadow's" deep, dark skin that attracted me. My mother always said, "The darker the berry, the sweeter the juice." It's not that I was "color-struck." And I wasn't racist. I just didn't have any White friends growing up and had nothing to compare to. Most of my friends were my complexion, brown-skinned or the color of "brown sugar," as I like to say. My eldest aunt, along with my grandmother's youngest brother, his wife, and their children were dark-skinned. Their skin was the color of a Mounds chocolate bar, and their white teeth reminded me of the coconut.

On the other hand, my grandfather's relatives were extremely light. They all had "good hair" and hazel-colored eyes. My grandfather told me that his mother was part Indian. Although she had long, pretty hair, she didn't look like the Indians in the movies. She was more beautiful, and her face and neck were covered with little, black moles. I laughed out loud in my head at the fact that I somehow inherited the same little moles on my neck!

My grandfather's mother was very nice. I enjoyed spending time with my family very much because it made me feel like everything was normal. Then, the reality would set in. We weren't normal at all. My mother wasn't normal. I wasn't normal. My cousins thought that I was lucky because I was an only child. The reality was that they were the lucky ones. They would spend Christmas at our grandmother's house and then spend it again at their own house. My cousins would then visit their other grandmothers (the mothers of their biological father and of their stepfather.) I would never know what that was like. The reality was that I didn't have a brother. I didn't have a sister. I didn't have a father. I didn't even have a mother.

Although reality often set in, holidays were the only time that I saw my family and the only time that I felt like I belonged. It didn't matter about the color of our skin, or what we had and didn't have. This was a time for family to come together. And for a short while, I felt like I had a "normal" family. The only thing that was missing was my mother. She had gone off the deep end, and had been in and out of my life for some time. We had been evicted from so many apartments that I could no longer keep count. My mother and I would move back and forth between my grandparents and my youngest aunt for many years to come. The one constant was the animosity between my mother and grandmother, and between my grandmother and me.

I continued to focus on school and make new friends. Although I stayed in touch with Elly and Maddie, I rarely saw them because they moved to South Jersey. We were older now, and each of us was smarter in our own way. I caught the bus all by myself, just as I had walked to school by myself on that first day of kindergarten. The bus ride to Toms River seemed extremely long, but I didn't care because I was going to visit my friends. I had that same feeling of pride as Elly and Maddie's mother picked me up from the bus stop. Once again, I had done something on my own even though I'm sure that my grandmother had something to do with purchasing the bus ticket.

Elly and Maddie's new home was a far cry from the old, rat- and roach-infested buildings in Newark. Unlike my mother, who could never seem to keep a job, their mother always worked and had nice things even though she was single. I was jealous and wished that I lived in a house as beautiful as theirs. Elly and Maddie shared a bedroom with bunk beds. During my visit, they shared the bottom bunk, and I slept on the top bed. Other than eating dinner at the large dining room table with their mother, we played in the room and kept to ourselves. Elly and Maddie's mother didn't seem to like me very much, and I wondered if it was because of my mother.

Elly and Maddie seemed different to me. They had always been smart and acted older, but they were using words that I had never heard before. They talked and acted like White people. They didn't even act like my White teacher back in Newark. Elly talked through her nose and sounded like she had a cold. Maddie did the same and played with us a lot less than she did when we lived in Newark. They said that they were both planning to become nurses. They asked about my mother, and I told them that things were the same.

I couldn't bring myself to tell them that my mother was a full-blown alcoholic and drug addict, and that I was living off and on with my grandmother. Somehow, I was sure that information would not be surprising to Elly and Maddie's mother at all. Nevertheless, I kept my mother's secret as I had always done in the past and would continue to do. In the privacy of their bedroom, I showed Elly and Maddie some very adult games I learned while watching my mother have sex with her boyfriends. She had since broken up with the boyfriend who raped and beat her whenever he got drunk. She had since taken up with a bunch of new losers.

After observing my mother's inappropriate behavior on so many occasions, I began to imitate her. I watched myself in the mirror, as I made kissing faces and loud sex noises. I explored parts of my body and fantasized about being with a man. I knew that I was a child, but I wondered what sex really felt like. When she wasn't screaming like she was in pain, I heard my mother moan and groan in pleasure. Sometimes, I would listen unintentionally while wishing that I was somewhere else. That's when I knew my childhood days were over.

I rarely got the chance to play outside because I was always cooking, or cleaning, at someone's house. Whenever I cleaned at my grandmother's house, it had to be spick and span. The dishes had to be hand-washed and towel-dried, even though there was a dishwasher. The table had to be spotless and the floor swept. Every Saturday, the carpet in the living room and dining room had to be vacuumed. The bathroom and shower stall (the one that I often hid in) had to shine like new. Every dresser and knickknack in the bedrooms had to be dusted. I felt like I was Florence the maid in *The Jeffersons*.

At my eldest aunt's house, washing and ironing clothes had become a part of my cleaning routine (for which I was paid a weekly salary.) I saved every penny that I earned so that I could move away from Newark. We had moved from staying with my youngest aunt on Chestnut Street in East Orange by this time. But my mother and I were still living a very unstable life.

My youngest aunt had two sons and a daughter. Her oldest son was born with cerebral palsy and passed away at a young age. Her youngest son was one of my favorite people in the world. He followed me around like a little puppy. Her daughter and I were the closest of all. She was a middle child like my mother, and I loved her like a sister. My aunt did not marry the father of her three children—

her high school sweetheart. She lived with and later married another man, instead.

They too had a beautiful home and seemingly perfect life, which made me very jealous. Imagine my surprise, when I heard familiar noises coming from my aunt's bedroom one night. First, I heard my aunt and new boyfriend having sex. Then, I heard the all-too-familiar cries of pain. My aunt's boyfriend, and "soon-to-be" husband, was choking and punching her.

He had one hand wrapped around her throat, while he used his other hand to punch her in the face. My aunt screamed, as her boyfriend brutally beat her. The next day, she had a black eye and I wasn't sure what to do. In the past, I had helped my mother by beating her boyfriends off her with a two-by-four. This man was much larger than my mother's boyfriends, and I was afraid of him. Besides, I couldn't believe that this could be happening to my youngest aunt. She was the cute, sweet, light-skinned one... She was the person who my mother accused me of loving more than her. *Were they more alike than they thought?*

CHAPTER 4

My Mother's Child: A Motherless Child

Unlike my youngest aunt, my other aunt (the eldest one) didn't like me much. Deep down, I always believed that it was because I was my mother's child (her only child, a motherless child.) My eldest aunt sided with my grandmother about everything, including the war against my mother. Somehow, she was able to overlook the fact that I was my mother's child and found just enough compassion in her heart to allow me to spend time at her house on weekends. This was so that I could iron her clothes and clean her bathrooms.

She too owned a big, beautiful house (like Elly and Maddie's mother.) It was located in Hillside, the next town over from Newark. She was on her second marriage and had no children. My eldest aunt had graduated from a seamstress to a fashion model and school-teacher, and was probably the smartest person in our family. I never told my eldest aunt about the things that I witnessed at my youngest aunt's house.

The beatings continued. I never mentioned my youngest aunt's secret to my cousins, my mother, or my grandmother. I guess I was beginning to think that this was a normal part of life, at least in our family. As the years went by, I continued to move from house to house and longed for the holidays when our family seemed normal. Little did I know that those days would never come again.

I thought back and remembered how my mother had drilled me about my third-grade teacher's sudden interest in me. She was always putting my White teacher down. She blurted out insults and demanded to know what I had been doing at school. I assured her that I had nothing to do with my teacher choosing me and told her that other teachers also seemed to think that I was smart. In disbelief that her own child could be smart, my mother tried to convince me that the White woman was jealous of us.

I almost laughed out loud (just as my mother did when she first read the letter from my teacher.) It was such a ridiculous thought because we had absolutely nothing for my teacher to be jealous of. My mother continued to insist that White people were "secretly" jealous of Black people and, in actuality, wanted to be like us. I would later learn that this is sometimes true. But, back then, she sounded as crazy as she did when she accused me of loving my youngest aunt more than I loved her (just because my aunt was light-skinned.) Shenanigans!

I thought back to how my eldest aunt was a model and teacher, which had also become interests of mine. I loved children and thought about working in a school, but not as a teacher. When my fifth-grade teacher asked everyone what they wanted to be when they grew up, the other students wanted to become teachers, nurses, doctors, policemen, and firemen. When I told my teacher that I wanted to "run a school," she tried to clarify by describing the role of a school principal.

I explained that I wanted to work with little children and travel to different schools throughout the country. My teacher seemed as surprised as I was from this vision. At the time, I didn't know how I would do it, but I knew that I would find a way to make it happen. My teacher, Mrs. Moore, patted me on the shoulder and assured me of her confidence in me. She told me that I was someone special and that she had no doubt in her mind that I would succeed in life.

This was the best news that I had ever heard, and it made me excited to tell someone. I wanted to rush home to tell my mother, like I ran home with the envelope from the White teacher years ago, but no one knew where my mother was. This too had become the norm. My mother's frequent disappearing acts had become a normal part of my embarrassing life. The days of her watching me from her bedroom window were long gone. My mother had missed most of my school years and every important event in my life, thus far. That's when it hit me. I was a motherless child!

My mother had missed most of my childhood. Throughout elementary school, I had been chosen to work as a student tutor to help other students with math, English, and computers. Oddly, I got my love of working with computers from my mother and youngest aunt. The two of them received an associate degree from Rutgers University in Newark and had worked temporarily as data entry clerks. On occasion, my mother would talk to me about computers and her work.

I always hoped that my mother's joy of working with computers would help her to maintain a job, but that was not the case. Unfortunately, it was not the case for my youngest aunt either. They went through life without a care in the world as if it was one, big, nonstop party. My mother missed my State Spelling Bee competition, my sixth-grade valedictorian speech, and my high school and college graduations.

The one time that I remember my mother being there was when I sang in my school choir. I stood up in the third row. I was wearing a white blouse and navy blue, pleated skirt. I looked up and saw my mother and grandmother arriving late. It was the first and last time that I saw my mother at a school event. Things began to change well before then. It was 1977, and so many things happened (including the big blackout.) One hot, summer day, the lights had gone out all around the neighborhood.

The streets were pitch black! There was a major blackout in the tri-state area, which included New York and Jersey! It seemed to last forever, as I sat on the fire escape and watched Black people break into stores and steal from one another. I had never experienced anything like it before. I continued to reminisce about how things were back then. That was the year that I realized my mother was no longer my mother. I was no longer her daughter. I was a motherless child.

I remembered seeing the yellow piece of paper on the table where I did my homework and picking it up to read it. As I tried to decipher what the word "eviction" meant, I figured out that it had something to do with not paying the bills. Our electricity had been turned off once again, and my mother and I were eating by candlelight. I knew that we needed money. In addition to cooking and cleaning, I had graduated to "grocery shopper." I cooked, cleaned, and grocery shopped for everyone and anyone. Once a month, my mother would get a book of food stamps that was equivalent to real money.

The dollar bills were printed in colored booklets with different colored numbers to represent each dollar amount. The bills had to remain inside the stapled book and be torn out only in front of the store clerk. Once a bill had been broken, the change was given in the form of colored plastic coins, which I often used at the corner store to buy my favorite Wise Onion & Garlic potato chips. Although money was tight, my mother and I didn't skimp on name brands. We always bought Del Monte canned vegetables, Idaho potatoes, Schweppes Ginger Ale, Ritz crackers, Philadelphia cream cheese, and a five-pound bag of Domino sugar (just enough for a pitcher of red Kool-Aid.)

Jif and Peter Pan didn't make the cut because we were loyal to Skippy peanut butter and Welch's grape jelly. Once my mother began to sell her food stamps for cash, we could no longer afford the name brands because all of her money went to drugs. Peanut butter and jelly had become the meal of the month, and I had gotten pretty used to eating it every day. It got me through the day (all those times that I ran away.) Another favorite was Mott's applesauce mixed with milk. It was cheap, easy to make, and my mother had fed it to me since I was a baby. That's when I realized that some people and some things never change.

Another thing that never seemed to change was the lights in our apartment. They were always out, and we had to use Energizer "C" batteries to listen to the radio because we didn't have electricity. We were always in the dark. Buying batteries and cigarettes for my mother was another daily ritual that I had become accustomed to. My mother only smoked Kool cigarettes in the carton. They were hard times, but we always managed to see the light at the end of the tunnel until that dreadful day that the eviction notice came.

I continued to stare at the letters on the paper and tried to remember where I saw them before. I looked them up in the Webster dictionary that my grandmother gave me from her house. The dictionary was huge with a black leather cover and gold letters on the front of it. She also had a set of Encyclopedias, which I was not allowed to take from her house. "Eviction" meant that we were being thrown out of the apartment because my mother did not pay the rent, as usual.

I was tired of moving around and staying with random people. Just when I thought things were going okay, we were being forced to move again. Whenever she returned from one of her "mini vacations" or "disappearing acts" as I liked to call them, I asked my mother what she was going to do about the eviction notice. She had been MIA (missing in action) for three days and left me alone to fend for myself.

I kept on living, as if nothing was the matter. I woke up for school each day, packed a lunch, grabbed some change for a snack or in case of a real emergency, and came home to fix a peanut butter and jelly sandwich for dinner because my mother had sold our food stamps for drug money. One night, I tried to get creative and make rice pudding. I dumped a whole box of rice into a pot of boiling water. Suds were everywhere! Sometimes, I would eat at the neighbors' houses if they offered. Most of the time, I said, *"No, thank you"*—because I didn't want them in me and my mother's business.

After school, I did my homework and danced to the music on the radio. I hardly missed my mother, but always hoped that she was safe. When my mother returned, she responded to my question about the eviction notice by telling me to mind my business and to stay in a child's place. I thought that was a funny thing to say because I had never really been a child and would have loved to stay in a child's place, but I was a motherless child! Instead of staying in a child's place, I needed to worry about where I was going to lay my head for the next couple of days.

How dare her! My mother and I stared each other down-the same way we did on my first day of kindergarten, when she embarrassed me in front of Elly and Maddie. I didn't back down then, and I sure as hell wasn't going to back down now! I told my mother that I knew what eviction meant and that I wasn't going anywhere. She told me not to worry and that she would handle things.

I thought—*She has got to be kidding me!* As I scrambled to gather all of my savings and a few of my personal belongings, including my schoolbooks, I shook my head at my mother in dismay. I was no longer five years old, but things were the same, and she was still treating me like a child. I threw my stuff in a backpack, grabbed the jar of Skippy from the kitchen cabinet, and packed a large spoon. I went outside to play with my friends for a short while and came in early to see what my mother was doing to "handle" things.

Just as I suspected, she had drank herself into a stupor and was sound asleep. I kneeled by my bed and prayed to God. I asked Him to watch over us. The next morning, my mother was lying naked on her bed with a bag of weed, a cigarette, and a drink next to her on a small table. She did not wake up when I called out to her, so I checked to make sure she was breathing. I grabbed my backpack and went to school. Looking at my mother drunk and nearly comatose, reminded me of the time that I decided never to smoke or drink (back when I was seven.) I had made up my mind to never smoke, drink, or do drugs. Now, I knew I had to become an adult. Now, I knew I might never see my mother ever again!

When I arrived home from school, my mother and our things were gone. The black wooden door was chained and padlocked. A notice from the Sheriff's office was taped to the door. I pushed the door just enough so that I could see inside the apartment. I could see that the table where I did my homework still had the eviction notice on it. There were several large, black garbage bags sitting on the floor in the middle of the room. It was obvious that my mother had not "handled" things and did not have enough time to gather all of our belongings.

I was very glad that I gathered my savings and put what I needed in my backpack. I knew that, as long as I had my schoolbooks and my peanut butter, I would be okay. I sat on the stairwell outside of our apartment, whipped out my big spoon, and started eating peanut butter from the jar it was in. I removed my schoolbooks, did my homework, and used the rest of the books to sit on. I sat on the stairwell across from the scary elevator for two whole days, before people started to ask questions about my mother's whereabouts.

I lied and said that she was on her way home. I knew that they knew I was lying. Every now and then, someone offered me something to eat. I happily declined because I had my peanut butter and did not want to take a chance in missing my mother's possible return. Night had fallen, then day came, and night again! I had already missed one day of school.

I continued to stare at the elevator. I remembered how a month earlier, a six-year-old boy died. He had been playing in the elevator like we were told so many times not to do. Somehow, he got caught in between the elevator shafts as the elevator went down to the next floor. Since I was afraid of heights and never liked elevators, there was no chance of me ever being in danger of getting hurt by playing in one.

The summer before, one of my mother's stupid boyfriends thought it would be funny to dangle me in the air over a parking garage. Of course, my mother did and said nothing. We had ridden the elevator all the way to the top floor of the garage. Since that time, I have never liked parking garages or elevators. After letting my mind drift for a moment, I was immediately brought back to reality as the sound of pitter-patter feet ran past me sitting on the stairwell. School was out, and children were coming home.

I knew my mother was not coming back. I probably knew this from the morning that she did not wake up when I called out to her two days ago, but I had more pressing matters to think about. I needed to use the bathroom, and I needed to wash up because I was starting to stink. I tried to remember which neighbors were home at this time of the day. I was also trying to be careful about not telling our personal business.

I knew that certain information in the wrong hands could land me a place in foster care, a shelter, or a group home. I thought about my grandmother for a quick moment, but decided that I would rather stay where I was. I went upstairs to get something to drink from one of my schoolmates and to use the bathroom. I peed, washed in the usual areas, and thanked my upstairs neighbor. I sat back down on the stairwell.

I wished that I knew how to make myself disappear like my mother had done. She had a way of just up and leaving, when things got rough. When all else failed, she turned to drugs and alcohol to make her pain go away. I wished that I could make my pain go away.

I went next door to another friend's house. I knew that she and her mother would be home because her mother also did not work. My friend and I conspired in the privacy of her bedroom and bathroom. We concocted stories about how my mother had left town for a couple of days, leaving me without enough food to eat. We decided to ask if I could spend the night. The next night, we asked if I could spend another night. This went on until Friday when we asked if I could stay until the weekend was over.

Although partially true, my friend's mom became suspicious of me and Egypt's story. Her mother wanted to know if I knew when my mother was coming back. She was aware of my mother's addictions and the fact that my mother would probably not be returning any time soon. Egypt's mother suggested that we call my grandmother. I could only hear bits and pieces of the phone conversation. My grandmother would pay her $50 each week. When they were done talking, it was decided that I could stay with Egypt and her family for the time being. Egypt and I jumped for joy!

Egypt was one year younger than me, and we went to the same school. Over the past year, we had walked to and from school together every day. She had two younger brothers and a baby sister, who I absolutely adored. Her youngest brother and I were totally in love with each other. He was only two years old, but said my name with such emphasis and waited like a sick puppy for me to come home from school each day. He would run as fast as he could and jump into my arms. That's when I knew that I was meant to work with young children.

I often thought about how my fifth-grade teacher had patted me on the shoulder to reassure me that I would be successful in life.

She told me to follow my dreams no matter what. I hadn't realized it before, but I was getting pretty good at taking care of other people and myself. I thought about all the times that I had taken care of my mother when she was passed out from drinking, or whatever.

I remembered all the cleaning, cooking, washing, ironing, and shopping I had done over the years. Now, it was time to demonstrate my skills in taking care of children. I offered to take care of Egypt's younger siblings, while her mother looked for work. Like my mother, my youngest aunt, and many of my other friends' mothers, Egypt's mother was also in an abusive relationship. She was unemployed and getting beat up by her husband on a regular basis. This was nothing new to me, and I stepped in to take care of the household.

Although she was only one year younger, Egypt did not possess the "skills" that I did. Her only job was to go to school, while I cooked and helped her mother take care of the little ones. We agreed that I could stay indefinitely, at least through the rest of the school year and maybe even the summer. Before I knew it, almost two years had passed, and I was graduating from junior high school. After graduation, Egypt's mother decided that I should go and live with my grandmother.

I was devastated and quickly thought of another plan. Another friend, who did not live far from Egypt, told me that I could stay with her and her family. She said that her parents went to bed early and that there were so many people in and out of their house that no one would even notice me. Amy had three older sisters, and they each had husbands and children. Including her parents, family members, and the neighbors who frequently passed through, there were always about twenty people in Amy's house at any given moment.

It was very easy for me to get caught up in the mix. I came over every day after school and pretended to go home before Amy's parents went to bed. When I wasn't sleeping on the couch, Amy would hide me in her bedroom or the bathroom. It reminded me of the times when I would hide in the bathroom at my grandmother's house. Hiding in bathrooms was my solace. It became one of the things that I did on a regular basis, whenever I wanted to feel safe. Safe is something that I never felt, as my mother's child; a motherless child.

CHAPTER 5

My First Love

I longed to be loved, just like I longed to be safe. I longed for the love and security that some of my friends had. I wanted and needed someone to love and protect me (someone to keep me safe.) Then, someone new came into my life. He was more than a boyfriend. He was a lover, a brother, and a best friend. He was my protector and had stolen my heart. He was my savior!

Surprisingly, my grandmother agreed to let me stay with my "first love" and his mother. It was surprising because she seemed to hate us being together (with every fiber of her being.) I accepted the fact that my grandmother hated me, but I couldn't understand why she hated my new boyfriend at first. I wondered if it was because she caught us tongue kissing by that big, huge tree in Irvington Park. Maybe, she was just jealous of our love. All I know is that I never wanted to go back to living with her, or my mother, ever again.

Freshman year in high school was a lot of fun. During the summer, I worked at Kentucky Fried Chicken (on Elizabeth Avenue, across the street from Weequahic Park.) My eldest aunt's first husband knew the manager and was able to get me the job. I worked from 4:00 in the afternoon to midnight, three days a week and on weekends. Back then, I think we still called it Gino's. I hated getting off work at midnight and missing all the fun on the weekends. By my sophomore year, I was in love! I had plans to marry my new beau. He was everything that I dreamed of. He would drive me to school in the mornings and pick me up after school, every day. Then, he would drive me to work and pick me up after work, every night. I wished that I didn't have to go to work. I didn't really need the money anymore because my new boyfriend bought me everything my heart desired.

He and his mother constantly took me shopping for clothes and shoes. This time, I was allowed to buy more than two "back-to-school" outfits! He bought me my first pair of Lee jeans, my first Wrangler jean suit with a matching jacket, and a navy blue Members Only jacket. My new boyfriend even started buying me expensive jewelry. On graduation day, his mother threw me a big party in their back yard, and my boyfriend gave me a promise ring with my first initial on it. The promise was that we would be together forever. The ring was 14-karat gold, with a diamond-cut "R" that fit my middle finger perfectly. As usual, my mother was not there.

My grandmother attended my high school graduation, but she wasn't at the party. She had come to the graduation with my eldest aunt (who, of course, didn't let the day go by without her usual criticisms.) The band played "It's So Hard to Say Goodbye to Yesterday," the theme song from *Cooley High*. It reminded me of all the things I had gone through, and I began to cry. My aunt looked at me and said, "You're crying like this is the first time that you've heard this song." I gave her the dumb look and walked away. Before heading to the car, I gave my grandmother a hug. My boyfriend and his mother were waiting for me. I had a party to go to!

The party went off without a hitch, and life was grand! High school had been perfect until my new boyfriend cheated on me with my archenemy. I guess I should have known all along that he was cheating. There was that time when a girl from Egypt's and my junior high school in East Orange moved to Irvington. She started going to the high school, and I guess she met my boyfriend. Months later, I found out that he asked her for her phone number. Another time, a friend of mine told me that my boyfriend was trying to talk to her younger sister.

My new beau had always flirted with my friends and other girls I knew. Two of my cousins even told me that he asked for their phone numbers. I would soon find out that "my first love" knew no boundaries. I remembered how he had invited his ex-girlfriend to his twentieth birthday bash. Her older sister and I were the same age. She always wanted to fight me because my boyfriend was still screwing her little sister. Now, he had invited her little sister (his ex-girlfriend) to his birthday party!

All the signs were there, but I chose to ignore them. I loved this man to no end, and I thought he loved me! I tried to recall the day that we first met. I met "my first love" at my friend's going-away party. I had also seen him a few times at the basketball games. He seemed older than the rest of the students, and I never saw him with anyone. That's when Mikayla told me that my "soon-to-be" boyfriend had graduated four years earlier.

Mikayla was my new best friend and lived with her grandmother near the high school. Her mother was also on drugs. During our freshman year of high school, we were inseparable until she moved down South. Mikayla's mother was dying and wanted to see her daughter right away. Mikayla didn't finish the school year - but, before she moved, she introduced me to a guy at her going-away party. He was short and stocky, but extremely nice. We immediately took a liking to one another and began spending a lot of time together.

He was a construction worker and lived with his mother and sister near the high school. He was no longer in high school and drove a car. He drove a silver Thunderbird that looked like it was from the 1970s. He was a very stylish dresser, which made me a little confused about the car that he chose to drive around in. Later, he explained that the old car was his mother's and that he would be purchasing his dream car very soon. It would be a 5.0 red Ford Mustang GT, with black leather seats.

My new boyfriend picked me up every day from school and took me to his house. Before long, we asked his mother to call my grandmother to see if I could stay with them. I was surprised that my grandmother agreed because she had always threatened to call the cops on my boyfriend and said that he was way too old for me. Then, I remembered how I had reminded her of all that I had gone through. I guess her guilt was too much to bear.

I smiled, as I thought about our first date. I continued to see my new beau at the Irvington High basketball games. After Mikayla vouched for him (by getting his license plate number, social security number, street address, and a solemn promise that he would bring me back in one piece), I allowed "my first love" to take me out on a *real* date. It was a Friday night, and we went to McDonald's after the game. I ordered a number 5 from the menu (a Big Mac, a large fry, and a large Coke.) For the first time in a long time, I felt like I didn't have to worry where my next meal was coming from!

Although he was a little shorter than I was, I was mesmerized by his swag. I don't know if men had swag back then—but, whatever it was, he had it. He had all the right clothes, the right words, the right moves, and eventually the right car. My new boyfriend had stolen my heart! He was "my first love," and we were head over heels in love. We spent every waking moment together, and he took care of me like I had never been taken care of in my life!

My new boyfriend continued to buy me clothes for school and clothes to go out on the weekends. He dressed very fashionably and wanted me to do the same. Every day after school, I waited for him like a sick puppy dog. I imagined that I must have felt the same excitement that Egypt's little brother felt while waiting for me to come home from school. I remembered how he would run his little legs as fast as they could go and jump up into my arms, as I came down the street. It was the best feeling.

Every Friday, like a two-year-old, I waited anxiously for my new boyfriend to pick me up. Sometimes, we went to the movies at the broken-down Castle Theater on Springfield Avenue in Irvington Center. My new man would wear his brown leather bomber jacket and a beige Kangol hat. I would wear new jeans and a sweater that he bought me, along with the new shoes that his mother bought. One time, we were at the movies, and someone shot a gun at the ceiling and made the glass chandelier fall down. We had gone to see *Friday the 13th, Part 3*. Everyone ran for their lives, just like in the movie.

On Thursday and Sunday nights, we went skating at "Twin City." On Saturday mornings, my new boyfriend's mother cooked a big breakfast of scrambled eggs, grits, sausage, and biscuits. She always made me a separate dish with turkey sausage, or beef bacon, because I didn't eat pork. Although we were boyfriend and girlfriend, we never kissed or flirted around his mother. We acted like best friends, until his drunken aunt blurted out that she heard us having sex. Of course, she said this during Saturday breakfast, right at the kitchen table in front of everyone! We just looked at each other and kept eating.

Saturday nights were reserved for walking around on 42nd Street and taking pictures together. The pictures were taken by random dudes on the street with a Polaroid camera and a variety of backgrounds. The choice of backgrounds consisted of a large wicker chair surrounded by the New York City skyline, or a bunch of guys huddling together as they represented their "hood." Of course, my new boyfriend and I always chose the background with the NYC skyline so that I could sit on his lap in the wicker chair. It was so romantic, and we were so in love.

We were so much in love that we spent Saturday afternoons at the Galleria Motel in Irvington. It should have been called the "Gonorrhea" Motel because of all the prostitutes that came in and out of there. But we were so blinded by love that we didn't care at the time. My boyfriend would buy me a single red rose and bring a boom box with a cassette of all our favorite slow songs. We could only rent the room for a maximum of four hours, but that was long enough for us. Our night of passion was followed by a drive to White Castle on Elizabeth Avenue in Newark. This soon became our weekly ritual.

Time was flying by. Four years had passed, and I had gone away for the weekend to visit the campus at Rutgers University in New Brunswick. My mother and youngest aunt went to Rutgers, and I wanted to graduate from there as well. I was determined to get a four-year degree and a good job—something my mother never did. My new boyfriend was opposed to the idea of me going to college and working, after I graduated high school. He had this crazy idea that I would be a stay-at-home mom. He had expressed on many occasions that he made enough money to take care of us.

Although that may have been the case, I learned at a very young age that I should always be in the position to take care of myself. I had always been taught to be independent. I thought about the number of times that my mother said that she would "handle" things, and the number of people (including myself) who I had to take care of just to stay alive. There was no way that I was going to put my life into another person's hands (especially not the hands of my new boyfriend, who was already cheating on me.)

The cheating finally stopped with his ex-girlfriend. He had found a new conquest! Goldie was short, light-skinned, and—as much as I hated to admit it, she was cute. I hated her and wished she looked like a troll. She was considered a "redbone," which is what all the boys liked back then. She was a cheerleader and had become my archenemy. Everybody adored her (including my new boyfriend.) I had been cleaning up his bedroom after school one day and found a gift box under the bed. The box was large and wrapped in green, shiny paper with a small, red bow around it. It had already been opened but, obviously, not properly hidden.

I looked inside the box and saw three hideous, dress shirts with a Christmas card. I read the card and saw that it was from Goldie! My boyfriend didn't even wear dress shirts. Shenanigans! I had been suspicious because the phone would often ring when I was alone (waiting for my boyfriend to come from work.) He and his mother had given me a key to the house so that I could come and go as I pleased.

Most days, I came to the house right after track practice. Running track made me feel good inside. I was used to running because I had done it all of my life. On the track field, I would pretend to close my eyes and let my long, lanky legs run wherever they would take me. I wanted to run away from everybody and everything. Sometimes, I secretly wished I was running toward "the light." That never really worked because—when I opened my eyes—the big, bad world was still there!

Running track reminded me of those days (when I was a young child hiding behind the basement door in my blue gym suit.) And let's not forget those gym shoes. You know the ones…Everyone had their choice of navy blue, or white, pumpkin seed sneakers. I hated those sneakers just as much as I hated gym. I didn't mind getting a "Zero" for the day, and I couldn't understand why my gym teacher just wouldn't let me get an "F" in gym. I had no intentions of wearing that gym suit with those sneakers.

I couldn't climb that stupid rope to the ceiling, or jump over the hurdles. Then, I finally found something that I was good at in gym. I could run like the wind. My track coach would say, "Pump your arms, Rah!" Sometimes, I could hear him shouting my boyfriend's name as I ran around the track. I always wore a T-shirt with my boyfriend's name on the back of it (like I was his property.) It sounds corny now - but, back then, I was proud to let everyone know that I was his girl and he was "my man." It made me feel good inside.

However, having my suspicions confirmed did not make me feel so good inside. One day, I answered the phone and the person on the other end hung up. I knew it was *her*! It was around this time that I suddenly became interested in getting to know one of the basketball players at my high school a little better. I figured "what's good for the goose is good for the gander." I was infatuated with my new basketball star... But I *loved* my new boyfriend and wanted him to know how much he had hurt me. I thought about the first time "my first love" and I made love. It was his twentieth birthday and he had a basement party at his mother's house, on 21st Street in Irvington.

After everyone left the party, we went upstairs to his bedroom and locked the door. My boyfriend pushed the "Play" button on his boom box cassette recorder, and I turned out the lights. As I began to get undressed, he asked me to put the lights back on so that he could see. I wore a white button-down blouse and navy blue gauchos. I closed my eyes and sat on the edge of the bed.

My new boyfriend helped me slowly unbutton my white blouse. It was taking forever, and I was so nervous. My hands were sweating, and I didn't want him to know. So I clinched the blanket on his bed tightly and held my breath. Then, he stood me up and slid down my gauchos. He reached around my back to unhook my bra. All I heard was, "Daaaamn!" "Lord, have mercy!" I laughed out loud in my head, *Yessss!* God had finally answered my prayers! I had inherited my mother's nice boobs! My "girls" were lovely and finally ready to make their first appearance. We started kissing, as we lie on the bed. When I opened my eyes, it was all over. The room was spinning, and I saw stars!

Now, four years had passed and we were breaking up. I had just finished my freshman year at Rutgers. Just like so many other people, my boyfriend had hurt me. With nowhere else to go, I returned to my grandmother's house. For some strange reason, I was lying on her bed. I cried, as I thought about losing my new boyfriend and the fact that my life had just passed before my eyes. Without so much as a hug, or a kiss, my grandmother attempted to comfort me. She stood in front of her dresser mirror and said, "Once a man cheats, he'll always cheat!" That's when I knew I could never trust anyone, ever again.

He was now my ex-boyfriend, but he was going to kill me. We had only been broken up for six months. Even though he had been the one to break *my* heart, he was going to be heartbroken by my news! I always thought that we would get married. My ex had been my savior and the love of my life. I often wondered what my life would have been like, if he had not shown up at Mikayla's going away party that first year. We were together for over four years, and it seemed like a lifetime. He exposed me to so many things and gave me the chance to be loved by a real family.

His family had problems just like everybody else's, but they stuck together (at least everyone except his sister.) His sister and I had fought like cats and dogs, since the time I entered their lives. Our love-hate relationship was confusing because she would often pay me a dollar to grease her scalp and go to the corner store for her. Sometimes, she would even pick me up from the school nurse's office when I had cramps. The next day, she was acting like she hated me again. She was mean-spirited and seemed jealous of the relationship that I had with their mother.

I would later realize that my ex's sister and I fought like two children vying for the attention and love of a mother. My ex-boyfriend's mother was a godsend. I had never asked to become a part of their family—but, somehow, I was brought into their lives because that's what I needed at the time. I thought about how I would tell my ex-boyfriend and his mother the news. *Who was going to be my savior now?* I was about to go through it!

CHAPTER 6

Going Through It

Have you ever wanted to turn back the hands of time? That was my wish… I wished that time could stand still just long enough for me to understand what had happened over the past five years. *What was I about to go through? What had I already gone through?* I thought back to a time when I was really going through it.

I thought back to how I had been a motherless child. I had bounced from house to house (staying with this friend and that friend.) I had even stayed with my ex-boyfriend and his family. Although my youngest aunt had her own struggles, she would often let me stay with her. I even had a key to my grandmother's house. I wondered if maybe (just maybe) she had given me a key to her house because she actually loved me and wanted me to feel safe.

Deep down, I knew the harsh reality was that my grandmother had given me a key so that I could come and clean her house after school. Most times, I hid there while no one was home because I thought I would be safe from my mother. I would stand in the shower stall and pray that no one would find me because I had promised myself I was never going back to live with my "crazy" mother! One day, my grandfather found me.

My grandmother was determined to bring me and my mother back together, once again. I couldn't believe that she had gone and found her. When my mother arrived at the house, she banged on the door like a crazy person. Then, she began yelling and screaming.

She accused my grandmother of kidnapping me. I laughed out loud in my head to keep myself from crying. I knew that my mother's accusations wouldn't go over well because my grandmother had a "reputation" to uphold.

At first, my grandmother wouldn't let her in. It had been almost five years since I last saw my mother (sleeping like she had taken a Quaalude, while we were being evicted.) In spite of everything, I had made it through junior high school without her. Now, I was determined to make it through the rest of high school. I was a motherless child, and I didn't need my mother in my life anymore!

My mother went across the street to use the payphone. I watched her from the window in my grandmother's dining room. I could see her standing in front of Untermann Field. She must have realized that she didn't have any money because I could hear her pleading with my grandfather's cousin on the second floor to let her use the phone. When the police arrived, they said that the situation had to be resolved in family court. My grandmother gave me up without a fight. I was shocked by the next thing that happened. My grandfather threatened to leave my grandmother, if she made me go back. She just stood there while my mother took me. She had the audacity to say that she couldn't get involved! My grandfather was appalled. He knew that my mother was an addict and that she had beaten me before. They were all fighting over me. We were all going through it.

That day (at my grandmother's house) wouldn't be the first time that the police became involved in one of our "family matters." It also wouldn't be the last. I began to go through the same story with the unfamiliar White woman that I explained to the police officers. The White woman, who appeared to be in her mid-thirties, walked toward me with a clipboard. The police officers, who arrested me, and the one at the "check-in" desk were also White. I hadn't really noticed it before, but all the police officers were White. Most of my teachers at Irvington High School were White too, unlike my teachers in elementary school who were Black (except for my third-grade teacher who came to my apartment that one time.)

The White woman sat in the chair next to mine and began writing on her clipboard. I could see from where I was sitting that my name, street address, and age had already been entered. The woman began asking me questions, and I wondered why she was asking questions that she already had the answers to. Once again, I was reminded of that dreadful conversation with my mother about the "ulterior motives" of White people. My mother was convinced that all White people couldn't be trusted because they had a hidden agenda and were out to get us.

We never went to family court and my grandfather didn't leave my grandmother. Instead, I was sent to live with my mother. That is, until the big fight. Thinking back, it must have been my youngest aunt who called the police that day. I realized that they hadn't rung the bell to the third-floor apartment where my mother and I lived. My younger aunt must have called and let them in. I was mortified at this thought! I wondered if my youngest aunt was no longer an ally and whether, or not, I should consider her the enemy. After all, she was siding against me with the enemy. After three hours of listening to me tell her the same story over and over again, the White woman collected her clipboard and walked away from me. I watched her and all the other White people scurry about throughout the small, brick building.

The two police officers returned to the room and escorted me to a smaller room, in the back of the building. There, I met with the same White woman and a younger White man. He was kind of cute. Other than Robert Redford and Clint Eastwood, I didn't really find White men attractive (especially not after all my mother's hang-ups about the "color of our skin".) Somehow, after seeing him in *The Good, the Bad, and the Ugly*, I managed to keep the major crush that I had on Clint Eastwood a secret.

I would walk around the apartment humming the music from the movie; "Wah, Wah, Wah…Wah-Wah-Wah…" Then, I would pretend that I was riding on the back of Clint's horse. Clint looked so cool, with his shawl, cowboy boots, and that cigar dangling from the corner of his lips. I thought that he should have been the one they called "Angel Eyes," instead of "Blondie." I laughed out loud in my head. Who knew that my crush on Clint Eastwood would later cause me to develop crushes on other White men, like Kurt Russell from *Tequila Sunrise* and Brad Pitt from *A River Runs through It*. They both had the bluest eyes and cutest dimples I had ever seen! My mother was wrong. All White people weren't bad! I laughed out loud in my head (again.)

However, this cute White man standing in front of me was different. He smiled at me and stood up from his chair. He was casually dressed in dark gray slacks, a gray-and-white-striped business shirt, cheap shoes, and did not wear a tie. I noticed his smile because I had a thing for a nice smile and white teeth. Although my mother was hardly ever around, she kept up with my dental appointments when she was able. I remember Dr. Roberts, my dentist, very well! He was young, Black, and cute. He reminded me of Richard Roundtree in the movie *Shaft*.

My mind began to wonder again and I thought back to when I was ten years old. My mother and Dr. Roberts decided that I needed braces. My life was already ruined (so I thought.) *Why did my mother want to make things worse by putting braces in my mouth right before junior high school?* My mother paid for my new braces with her Medicaid card, which was what people used for insurance when they didn't have enough money to pay for their medical and dental bills with cash.

The subject of braces wouldn't come up again, until after I had been living next door with Egypt and her family over the next two years. I remember telling Egypt's mother that the dentist was in a big, blue building on Central Avenue. I even remembered that Dr. Roberts' office was on the tenth floor. I had two full rows of silver, metal tracks installed in my mouth two days before "picture day." The only other thing that could have gone more wrong was that the enormous red pimple on the tip of my nose would burst just as I smiled and said, "Cheese."

The thought of pus from my busted pimple running down the tip of my nose and onto my ugly braces made me laugh out loud in my head. I looked up and smiled back at the cute, young, White man (who was waiting patiently for me to shake his hand.) He introduced himself as Mr. White, and I laughed out loud in my head (again)—a White man called Mr. White. I told him my name, which I knew that he knew from the White woman and the sheet on the clipboard.

Mr. White explained that he was a counselor who worked with teens in challenging situations. Once again, I thought back to my mother's assumption that all White people had a hidden agenda. I decided that I would share my "life story" with Mr. White. The three of us (Mr. White, the White woman, and I) sat and talked for hours. I did most of the talking, while they listened.

All my life, I had wanted someone to listen to me. I had wished and prayed for someone to hear my cries and my screams, and to understand what I was going through. Unfortunately, that had not happened before now. Two complete strangers, who had no idea of who I was and where I had come from, were listening to me. They cared about what I had to say and the things I was going through. I wasn't sure where I should begin. I started telling the story about how my youngest aunt must have called the police; and how my mother had walked toward me and attempted to hit me while I stared out the window.

Mr. White and the White woman prompted me to start from the beginning of my childhood. I shrugged my shoulders in disapproval, as I thought - *This could take a lifetime!* Although I wanted someone to hear my story and understand the things I was going through, I was still unsure as to whether or not I could trust White people. I thought again about how my mother had always tried to convince me that they were jealous of us. This notion still did not make sense to me, especially since she (and other Black people) were the source of all my troubles.

My mother had been the knife in my back, the thorn in my side, and the brunt of all the things I was going through. Ironically, she would be the one who I could not trust. She would go off the deep end and begin destroying everything and everyone in her path. This would include threatening my grandmother with a kitchen knife. There would even come a time, while I was in college, when my grandmother would call *me* of all people to protect *her* from my mother.

Here I was, deciding whether or not to trust two total strangers (White people) with my life story. Until now, everything had seemed as though it happened just yesterday. I could always recall each and every time that my mother called me by that other name. I could count the number of times that I had run away—like that time when I was ten on South Clinton Street. I could still see some of the welts that covered my arms and legs from the belt beatings.

I think the thing that I feared most (as my mother walked toward me on the day that my aunt called the police) was that she would beat me with that huge, heavyweight championship belt again. Unlike our apartment on South Clinton Street, there was no walk-in closet on the third floor of my grandmother's new three-family house. There was nowhere to run, nowhere to hide. I would have to take the beating. I would never allow myself to be beaten, or locked in a closet, again.

I continued to tell Mr. White and the White woman all about the fight (and my childhood.) I shared with them that my mother became pregnant with me during her high school years, at the young age of sixteen. I told them that we lived with my grandparents until my mother was twenty-two years old and I was five. They seemed intrigued to hear about my first day of kindergarten and the way my mother watched me from her bedroom window.

Although they tried to hide their feelings, Mr. White and the White woman became emotional as I explained that my mother was not always the way she was. I attempted to clarify what I meant by adding that I remember my mother taking me to and picking me up from nursery school when I was three years old. I recalled the day when it was snowing and my mother made a snowball from dirty snow to sooth my busted lip. I told how I had fallen off the sliding board on the playground of the nursery school, and my top lip was bleeding. I also told how my mother was mortified when she picked me up from the nursery school that day and had cursed out my pre-school teacher!

I remembered how, that same year, my mother had cursed out everyone in the school because my teacher tied me to a chair and taped my mouth shut. I had a habit of cursing because my mother and youngest aunt did it so often around me. I told about the time when I was six years old and my mother slapped me because she thought I said, "Shit!" I talked more about how my mother had often beat me with the huge leather belt and locked me in the walk-in closet on South Clinton Street. Sometimes, she would grab whatever was in her reach, like an extension cord or a "switch" from outside on the street. Before that, she had only slapped me.

We didn't really start going through it until she started drinking herself into oblivion. She looked for jobs, but would come home and drink because she couldn't find work. I continued to tell Mr. White and the White woman about the things I had been going through. Life—in the beginning—seemed good. I couldn't recall any memories with my grandmother, other than the yearly birthday parties at her house behind Weequahic High School in Newark. I talked about how I had seen pictures of me with other relatives and friends at those same birthday parties. That's how I knew that the parties happened. There seemed to be over a hundred pictures, in various photo albums, of a loving family. I tried and tried, but could not remember any of those times (only the times when I started going through it.)

Mr. White shifted his body in the chair and gave a look to the White woman. I wondered what they were thinking and what that look meant. *Had I said too much?* I sat up straight in my chair and paused before continuing my story. I talked about my childhood friends, Elly and Maddie. I told Mr. White and the White woman about the White teacher who came to the apartment because she thought I was a good student. I told them that I had not known any White people before meeting my third-grade teacher. Now, here I was, surrounded by White people!

I began to describe the abuse that I was subjected to, most of which came from my mother's boyfriends. She dated the most god-awful men! I will never forget this one guy named Will, which might have been short for William (but I never really knew.) He was around for a while. I don't know when my mother met him, but I first saw him lying on top of my mother soon after I started kindergarten. He went to the park with us every now and then. He is also the one who started my mother stealing (at least to my knowledge.)

That's when we would go to the corner liquor store before going to the park or movies, and I would watch them steal everything from gum and candy to beer, potato chips, and bottles of hard liquor.

I hated Will! By the time we moved to South Clinton Street, my mother was no longer cheating with the Muslim man that managed the store beneath our building. Will came with us, and he was like a piece of ugly furniture that we just couldn't get rid of. It had been five years, and he was still around.

My mother spent most of her time attempting to beg, borrow, and steal. I, on the other hand, tried to act civilized. Despite the chaos around me, I was determined to be a good person. I was a true believer of "when you know better, you do better!" One day, on the way home from the movies, I found a ten-dollar bill on the ground. We were walking home from the movie theater on Main Street in East Orange, when I saw the bill lying on the sidewalk. My mother told me that the bill was probably counterfeit.

I laughed out loud in my head, as I thought - *"Who would know better than her?"* Nevertheless, I picked up the ten-dollar bill and put it in my pocket. When we arrived at our apartment on South Clinton Street, my mother started negotiating with me. Like a true hustler, she tried to convince me that I should give her half of my money. I hadn't decided whether, or not, I was going to keep the money. The truth is that I didn't know how to go about returning it, and I didn't know who to return it to.

Still, the money belonged to me until I decided otherwise. There was no way on God's green earth that I was giving my mother a dime! She had taken enough money from me already. The next day, I put the ten-dollar bill in an empty wallet that I had also found and put the wallet in a mailbox on the corner of our apartment building. I continued my story about my mother's shenanigans and told how she would spend the next years in and out of jail and "hustling" on the street.

Mr. White and the White woman continued to ask questions about my mother and wanted to know if Will had ever touched me in an "inappropriate way." Mr. White clarified the question by asking if Will had ever hurt me "down there." I told them that I had never been sexually abused. They gave each other that all-too-familiar stare. It was the same look I gave my mother, when I knew she was lying about something.

I changed the subject and began talking about school. Most people who passed through my life were impressed by my "vernacular." All the time that I spent in school was paying off, and I definitely had a way with words. In the midst of all the chaos, I had been able to focus my attention on my studies rather than the things I was going through. I had mastered the English language and most of my other school subjects. I decided that English and math were my favorite subjects. I always brought home an "A" in each of my subjects. Things started to get a little harder in high school - and there were many distractions, such as a new boyfriend. Will wasn't around during my high school years because my mother had apparently graduated to much more successful losers.

Mr. White and the White woman continued to remain intrigued, as they listened to me go through the minutia of my life's events. I told them that, in spite of everything, my mother and grandmother had taught me the value of getting a good education. My grandmother hated me and my mother nearly killed me—but they felt that it was important for me to have a successful future.

I laughed out loud in my head (again.) But, this time, I actually smiled and Mr. White smiled back. We had made a connection. The White woman looked at us curiously. I went back to the part of the story where I talked about my mother's boyfriends abusing her. One night, I lie across my bed-as I often did when I was alone in my room. I heard my mother yelling for Will to stop hitting her. When I got close enough to see, I saw Will on top of her. That was not the unusual part because that was an everyday occurrence.

I told how my mother was lying on her back, and Will was kneeling on the bed with one knee on each side of her. She was screaming, as he continued to choke her. That night, I ran back into my bedroom and picked up the two-by-four that was hidden behind my doll house. I held it with both hands and swung as hard as I could. It reminded me of the time that I hit Andre in the back of the head because he made me trip and fall on a Coca-Cola bottle in the parking lot of our building. He was such a little punk and so was Will (for beating up on women.)

Will rolled off my mother and onto the side of the bed. I threw the bloody two-by-four down on the floor. I wasn't sure where it came from or why I had it, but I was glad that I did. I checked my mother to see if she was breathing. Reluctantly, I took a few coins and went to call my grandmother from a payphone on the next corner. I decided not to use the payphone in front of the infamous liquor store that we had stolen from on so many occasions.

Instead, I walked to the next block and called my grandmother from the payphone in front of the cleaners and beauty salon on Chancellor Avenue. It seemed safer at the time. My grandmother arrived minutes before the ambulance. My mother begged her not to call the police, as my grandmother threatened that she would do the next time Will put his hands on my mother. But it was too late! I was in total shock of all the events that were taking place. No one seemed to care that I had clobbered Will with a two-by-four, or that I had witnessed my mother getting raped (for the first time.)

My mother's abuse continued from one boyfriend to the next. She drank more heavily and took her frustrations out on me. We were smack-dab in the middle of going through it together. That was the key word, "together!" No matter what, we were a team and had never been apart, until my mother started disappearing.

At first, she would come home late from work, once she finally found a job. Every other day, my mother's boss would call and ask if she was coming to work. We had a phone in the apartment by then and even managed to keep the lights on, every now and then. I thought things were getting better, but I guess we were still going through it.

The tables had turned, and I started to wonder if my *mother* would be home before the streetlights came on. Each night, she would arrive home later and later. Then, she started to miss more and more nights, until she didn't come home at all! I wasn't sure whether to be happy, or sad, about my mother's frequent disappearing acts. I guess I was relieved, when she finally decided not to come home for good.

Mr. White and the White woman also seemed relieved. Maybe, they were happy for me! I couldn't quite read the expression on their faces, which I was pretty good at doing most of the time. I still wasn't sure if I could trust White people, and I had no idea what was about to happen to me. Each of us shifted in our chair, and I waited for a sign to continue my story.

Mr. White offered me some water. I told him, *"No, thank you"*—even though I was dying of thirst. Maybe, it was because of the whole "don't trust White people" thing that my mother had instilled in me. I felt bad not accepting the water because I was sure Mr. White knew that I did not trust him. I refocused my attention on my mother. I wondered where she was and what she was doing while I was being held here in this small, brick building, down the street and around the corner from my grandmother's new three-family house.

The White woman and Mr. White seemed to be more focused on my past life (my childhood) than my current adventures. I was only concerned with the here and now. It was getting late and I was tired. I wanted to go home, but didn't know where home was. I wondered if I would have to spend the night in jail. Then, it became apparent that the police officers were able to see straight through my mother's lies. She had tried to convince them that I attacked her when, in fact, it was the other way around.

My mother had been unable to explain how I attacked her if I was staring out the window with my back turned toward her. They wanted to know why my mother had taken the hinges off my bedroom door. When it came down to it, she was in more trouble than I was because she could not give a reasonable explanation for her actions.

More importantly, my mother had endangered the welfare of a child—her own child! Unfortunately, there was no one to corroborate either one of our stories. My youngest aunt had only seen me knock my mother over the couch, but I wasn't worried about having proof because I knew that I was telling the truth. After all, I was only a child and had no reason to lie.

I would soon find out that there would be a price for telling the truth. I would find out that I always need proof! The small, brick building that I had spent the majority of my day in was actually a group home. Mr. White, the White woman, and the police decided that my mother was a danger to herself and to me. They told my mother that she would have to go to family court to get me released back into her custody.

Of course, my grandmother and eldest aunt did nothing - and I ended up staying at the group home. As time passed, I thought about what I would do when I got out. The group home wasn't jail, but I was not free to go. I had to be released into the care of an adult. *Where was my youngest aunt?* I couldn't reach her. I called my boyfriend and explained what happened (but he didn't come.) I continued to beg Mr. White (the child and family counselor), but he said that I could not have visitors. I didn't understand why... All I knew is that I was definitely going through it!

CHAPTER 7

Abandoned

I felt all alone. I thought about my life, over and over, again. I reminisced about my ex-boyfriend (my first love)—and all the things I had gone through. I thought about my new news and all of the people who had come before it. I continued to recall the chain of events that got me to this point. I remembered hiding in the bathroom of my grandmother's house. I remembered my grandfather saying that he would not let my mother take me. I remembered having to go back to the third-floor apartment with my mother. After that, everything went black.

I remembered that my mother and I had gotten into a huge fight and nearly beat each other to death. I was lying on my bed (with nowhere to go) fully dressed in jeans, a T-shirt, and the red shoes that my boyfriend's mother bought for me. "Do What You Feel" by *Denice Williams* and "Touch a Four Leaf Clover" by *Atlantic Starr* played back-to-back on the radio. They were two of my favorite songs and always reminded me of weekends with my boyfriend. As a matter of fact, every song that played on the radio reminded me of my boyfriend and our newfound love.

I often felt like I had no one to love and no one to love me. The past year that I spent at my grandmother's house was horrific! I had to get up an extra hour earlier just to get to school on time. I walked from Goldsmith Avenue in Newark to the border of Newark and Irvington on Chancellor Avenue just to catch the bus at Valley Fair.

The bus took me to Irvington Bus Terminal, which was a couple of blocks from the high school. Every now and then, my grandmother took pity on me and gave me a ride. She would drop me off by the Parkway. When we weren't arguing the whole way there, we spent thirty minutes being absolutely silent in the car. It was probably a good thing that we road in silence—because my grandmother drove like a bat out of hell and might have killed us otherwise.

I longed for the days when my boyfriend would pick me up and take me to school on his way to work. I knew that this meant he too had to get up an extra hour earlier so that neither one of us would be late. Songs, such as "I'm in Love" by *Evelyn Champagne King* and "Forget Me Nots" by *Patrice Rushen*, always made me think of him. The year was 1983, and I had finally made it through my junior year of high school. I should have been super excited about becoming a high school senior and being "in love!"

Instead, I was stuck in this godforsaken room listening to my mother yell my name. She still called me by that other name that I hated. Unfortunately, the music coming from the radio had not drowned out the sound of her dreadful voice. "Do you hear me calling you?" "Girl, you better answer me." My mother came storming through the doorway of my bedroom. I looked at her like she was crazy. We looked at each other with that all-too-familiar stare that we had become accustomed to. This particular time, we stared at each other much longer than usual. I got up from my bed and stood still. I watched my mother walk toward me with anger in her eyes. I tried to remember the last time I saw that look.

Ah, yes! It was all coming back to me. It was the day that I ran away from home, back when I was a young child on South Clinton Street. It was right before my mother went MIA on one of her disappearing acts. I had just turned ten years old, and I was best friends with Karen, who was eleven. Our birthdays were on the same day, in July. Our mothers were born on the same day, in January. We were "blood sisters" and we cut our thumbs to prove it!

Karen and her mother had already been living in the building on South Clinton Street, when my mother and I moved there. Karen was kind of strange and very loud. The other children seemed afraid of her because she was somewhat of a bully. I too was a little afraid of her, but we became friends anyway.

I told Karen my deepest, darkest secrets. She knew all about my mother. She knew all about the alcohol, the drugs, and the beatings. Like Elly and Maddie's mother, Karen's mother also worked. It seemed like my mother was the only mother who didn't work for a living. In fact, she had gone from smoking cigarettes to smoking weed; the beer had been replaced by hard liquor; and the stare downs had changed to beatings! We had no electricity, no food, and no money. My grandmother would drop by every now and then to bring by some groceries. Sometimes, she would stop and stare at my bruises—but wouldn't say anything.

I often wondered how a grandmother could turn her head to such abuse. I had never heard of such a thing. All the other grandmothers were so nice and loving. Although we rarely spoke, I continued to clean my grandmother's house on the weekends. I hated going there, but it was a chance for me to see my grandfather and to get away from my mother. I thought about all the reasons why I wanted to get away from my mother. It was a Thursday, and it was a hot, summer day. I needed to use the bathroom to do "number two." We didn't have any toilet tissue, and I had asked Karen if she could bring me some from her apartment.

When she knocked on the apartment door with the tissue, my mother was furious. My mother always yelled at me for telling other people our business. I guess my mother didn't let Karen in with the tissue because I never got it. Instead, she told me to use my wash rag to wipe my butt. It was the same rag that I used to wash my face and body all week. Reluctantly, I folded the brown wash cloth and wiped my behind with it. I felt dirty and embarrassed. I flushed the toilet, washed the rag in the sink, and washed my hands with dish liquid. The whole time, all I could think about was what I would say to Karen.

I knocked on Karen's door softly, hoping that she wouldn't answer. She opened the door to her apartment and smiled at me shyly. I think that we were both embarrassed, but it was always hard to tell with her. Sometimes, she looked like the cat that swallowed the canary! I couldn't decipher if she was happy, sad, or what truth lie behind those smiling eyes. Nevertheless, she had become my confidant, and I told her everything. She opened the door, hugged me, and yelled to her mother that we were going outside to play.

Once we were outside, Karen asked me what I did without the tissue. I told her that I used a washcloth and washed it out. Strangely, she asked me if I was going to use the same rag to wash up again. Although it was an awkward conversation, I pondered the same question. I shrugged my shoulders and claimed I didn't know. Then, she said the most surprising thing. She suggested that we pack our backpacks and run away together. I had plenty of reasons to run away, but I couldn't figure out why Karen wanted to leave her mother.

It was summer, and full backpacks would be a dead giveaway because we were not in school. We pretended to play outside, as we devised our plan to run away from home. We were in the middle of a game of hide-and-seek with some of the other kids from the building. I couldn't concentrate because thoughts of running far away from home consumed me. A huge rock across the street from the building had been designated as home base. Whether we played tag, freeze, hide-and-seek, house, or doctor—the huge rock was our "meeting point." It was home plate… Our safe place… Once we made it to the rock, we were safe (no matter what!)

We could sit on it - lie down on it - lean against it. It didn't matter… We would be out of breath, but we would find the strength to convene at the big, huge rock. Sometimes, we would just sit and chill—eating our *Rock Candy, Pixy Stix, Fun Dip,* and *Bomb Pops* (against the big rock.) Aah…the memories. But now was not the time to take a stroll down memory lane. Karen and I had bigger plans. Bigger than the big rock!

The other kids were all gathered at the rock, which meant that Karen and I needed another place to meet and discuss our plans to run away. We decided to meet underneath the porch of Egypt's house next door. We crouched down and crawled under the wooden porch. Karen had made up her mind that we needed backpacks to carry food and clothing. I agreed, as I listened to the other kids continue to play hide-and-seek.

I could overhear them asking each other what happened to the other two girls. That day, I spent most of my time leaning against the huge rock. Unlike the other children who were running around frantically to find a hiding place, Karen and I walked and talked. She was the only one who knew my big secret. The big secret was that we were running away from home because my mother beat me so severely that my body was covered with welts. I could barely walk, let alone run.

The same day that we ran out of toilet tissue and I had to use the brown wash cloth to wipe my behind, my mother made me strip down and remove all my clothes. She beat me because I told Karen that we didn't have any money and toilet tissue. My mother was embarrassed and infuriated! She took her anger out on me by beating me with a huge black leather belt. I always referred to the belt as a "heavyweight championship belt" because it was wide and covered with jewels. The belt was an odd shape and could never fit through those small loops on a normal pair of pants.

After the beating, my mother locked me in her huge walk-in closet for over two hours. The size of the closet seemed odd because the apartment was so small. My mother and I shared an efficiency apartment, which meant that we lived in one, large room with a separate kitchenette. It was called a kitchenette because it could not fit a table and chairs. The kitchenette was only large enough for the sink, stove, and refrigerator. The walk-in closet was larger than the kitchenette.

Sometimes, when I was locked in the walk-in closet, I would look through my mother's things. She kept odd things in the closet, such as old albums, pictures, and a red jewelry box. The jewelry box contained one of my mother's front teeth, a pair of my baby shoes, a locket with a picture of me and her on my first Easter, packs of funny-looking paper to roll her joints, and a small bag of marijuana.

I looked at the clock on the table by my mother's bed, when she opened the door to the walk-in closet. My legs were sore from crouching down on the floor, and they hurt from the beating. I walked slowly to my side of the room, which was separated from my mother's side of the room by a bookcase. I attempted to lie across the bed. I waited silently and patiently for her to say something. I had spent two hours locked in the walk-in closet, and it seemed like an eternity.

I was sitting on the edge of the bed in a daze, when I heard my mother's voice. Surprisingly, she was telling me that I could go outside to play. I thought—*What a dumb time for me to play outside.* I walked slowly past my mother and into the bathroom where I had left my clothes on the floor. I walked back to my side of the room and began to get dressed. My body was sore and tears ran down my face. I couldn't walk down the stairs and decided to take the scary elevator.

When Karen opened the door, I told her about the horrible beating and the walk-in closet. She smiled weirdly and didn't seem surprised. After devising our plan during the game of hide-and-seek, we separated to retrieve our backpacks from the apartments. My mother was asleep on the bed. I grabbed some shorts, a T-shirt from the hallway cabinet, and the jar of peanut butter from the kitchenette. I was almost out the door when I remembered that I needed a spoon. My mother shifted her position on the bed, and I was scared she would wake up. I heard her ask where I was going, just as I was closing the apartment door.

I told my mother that I had used the bathroom again and was going back outside. I didn't wait for a response and headed toward the scary elevator. I heard my mother yelling my name, as she reminded me to be in by the time the streetlights came on. There were streetlights on every corner, but the ones in front of our building were missing a bulb. The lights always flickered, and we often used that as an excuse to stay outside longer.

The plan was to run away to Main Street. We would be long gone before the streetlights came on. Karen knew that I was in pain and promised to take care of me because she was the oldest. I was so happy that she decided to run away with me because I was afraid. It was getting dark outside, and we had been gone for hours. I was pretty sure that the streetlights were on in front of the building. Whenever I wasn't home by the time they flickered, my mother would scream my name from the window of our fourth-floor apartment.

I wondered what my mother was doing. Karen and I had eaten the peanut butter that I brought along. We were tired, scared, and lost. Karen suggested that we go back home. I knew that this was a bad idea because my mother was going to kill me. Somehow, we found our way back to our apartment building. My mother was standing in front of the building with the "heavyweight championship" black leather belt, which she used unsparingly to beat me with all the way up the stairs to the fourth floor.

I regretted coming back home and stared at my mother all night, with tears in my eyes. The feeling that I had when she came storming through my bedroom door was the same feeling I had the night that I ran away, when I was ten years old. I thought back to how the fight started. I remembered how I had gotten up from the bed and stood staring at my mother. I walked slowly toward my bedroom window, looking over my shoulder at my mother. She had an angry glare in her eyes and stared me down, as she often did. I was almost as scared as I was when I returned home from "running away" with Karen that day on South Clinton Street.

Only, now, things were different. I was a teenager, and wasn't afraid of my mother anymore. I decided at that moment that I was too old for beatings. We lived on the third floor of a three-family house owned by my grandmother. It was a one-bedroom apartment, and my mother made the living room into her bedroom. My grandparents still lived in the house behind Weequahic High School, but they had recently purchased this house in Irvington.

When we first moved to Irvington, White people came out onto their porches and stared. It was an all-White neighborhood and there was only one other Black family, who happened to live right next door. It was the 1980s and the first time that I had seen so many White people at one time. It made me wonder what the high school would be like. I could tell that it would be very different than Weequahic High School in Newark.

My mother had returned from the longest disappearing act ever and needed a place to live. No one had heard from, or seen, her since she left South Clinton Street. My mother had abandoned me while I waited for two days on the stairwell for her to return. That was two months after the infamous beating and my attempt to run away, which happened when I was almost eleven years old. She never came back, and I lived next door with Egypt and her family for two years. After that, I stayed with Amy, off and on, in East Orange for one year, until I went back to live with my grandmother in Newark.

Memories began to cloud my brain, as I listened to my mother continue to yell my name. She stood in the doorway of my bedroom. I ignored her and continued to stare out my bedroom window. I could see her walking toward me from the corner of my eye. There was nowhere to run and nowhere to hide. The apartment didn't have a walk-in closet. Whatever was about to happen would happen right here and right now!

My mother raised her hand to hit me, but the strangest thing happened. I put my arm up to block the blows, and she fell against the wall. I didn't help her and turned my back to my mother. When she gained her balance, my mother attempted to hit me again. This time, we were face-to-face and were staring into each other's eyes. We wrestled, and she fell again. My youngest aunt, who lived on the second floor of the three-family house, heard the commotion and came running upstairs.

My aunt yelled my name and pulled me off my mother. I walked back to my bedroom window and continued to stare out of it. I longed to be anywhere else but here. I prayed for my boyfriend to rescue me, which he had done so many times before. I was convinced that my grandmother and my mother were jealous of him. They destroyed everything he bought me and were intent upon destroying my relationship with him as well. Two of the things that they took from me were my boom box and trimline phone.

I thought about the beige trimline phone that my boyfriend bought me. He had paid for the line to be installed so that we could talk on the phone all night without being interrupted. Now, I couldn't even call him. The boom box was similar to the one that my mother and Egypt's mother had back in the day. I used it to listen to all our favorite love songs that we taped on cassette. We "ingeniously" labeled the cassette tapes "Slow Songs." Now, that was gone too.

There was a knock on the door. The police came and arrested me for assault. My mother told them that I attacked her! The police officers took a report and took me away. I told the officers the truth about how my mother stormed into my room and tried to hit me from behind, as I stood near the window. I explained how I had to defend myself and told the officers about the previous abuse that I suffered from at the hands of my mother. My youngest and favorite aunt remained silent.

I was somewhat shocked at my aunt's silence. I couldn't figure out if she was silent because she was afraid of my mother, or because she thought I had done something wrong. I had never seen her and my mother argue. They were like twins, except for the color of their skin. I thought back to that dreadful conversation with my mother, when she accused me of loving my youngest aunt more than I loved her because my aunt was "light-skinned." Shenanigans!

The truth was that I did love my youngest aunt more than I loved my mother (but not because of the color of her skin.) It was because she had always seemed more like an older sister to me rather than an older aunt. After all, she was only fifteen years older than I was, and she was so tiny that we were practically the same size. I was just taller. It was always mind-boggling how all the women in my family were barely five feet tall and bowlegged—except for me and my eldest aunt, who stood nearly six feet tall.

Although my youngest aunt had never come in between me and my mother, there would definitely be "another" fight if she decided to jump in the middle of this fight. I thought back to how the police officers decided that the situation warranted some investigating. They handcuffed me and took me away, like a criminal. It was not the same police station that I had gone to when I got arrested for jaywalking, during my freshman year.

This building looked more like an office building, and there was no cell with bars. It was a small, brick building located down the street and around the corner from my grandmother's new three-family house in Irvington. I noticed that it had two, or three, floors. I wasn't sure because we took the stairs, and I was in handcuffs. As I looked up, I could see that the stairwell continued to the next floor.

The stairwell reminded me somewhat of the stairwell that I sat on while waiting for my mother for those two days (after we had gotten evicted on South Clinton Street.)

Although we had only walked up two flights of stairs, it seemed to take forever. One of the police officers walked me to a desk and told another officer to check me in. As I stared at the sheet of paper with my name, street address, and age written on it, I began answering the officer's questions. I thought - *This can't be happening to me!* I thought about how my mother had made my life a living nightmare from the time I was five years old.

Once again, here she was making my life miserable. She had disappeared (vanished from the face of the earth) for almost five whole years. Now, she was back and wreaking havoc in everyone's lives. I wondered how my youngest aunt could let this happen. *Where had she been?* It didn't bother me that my eldest aunt and my grandmother were not there to defend me. They had never really been by my side—at least, not in my eyes. But my youngest aunt had always been there for me. I looked around and, this time, she was not there. Like everyone else in my life, my youngest aunt had abandoned me.

CHAPTER 8

The Doberman Family

I thought about the one person who had never abandoned me—
my grandfather. Although I felt abandoned, I knew that he was
the one person I could still count on—no matter what, because
he loved me. I thought about the things that made me happy! I
thought about the constants in my life. And crazy as it may sound,
these were my grandfather, Lava soap, and Dobermans. That's what
came to mind. I remembered how my grandfather would wash his
hands with green Lava soap every time he came home from a long
trip. I would stand at the bathroom door and watch him wash his
hands.

The dirt would pour off like mud. I wondered where he had
been. *Why was he so dirty? Why were his hands so black? Why were
his clothes stained with oil? Did he work at a gas station? Had he been
on an actual farm, where he had to pick his own fruits and vegetables?*
Thinking about a farm made me think about that time when my
cousins and I went down South.

It was the time when we broke their grandmother's glass dish
while singing the theme song to *The Jeffersons*. It was the time when
we had to pick our own fruits and vegetables! We had gone down
South for the entire summer - for ten whole weeks! While we were
"moving on up," a glass dish went up into the air and hit the floor
with a bang. Glass was everywhere! My cousins and I stopped dancing and just stood there, staring at one another. We were speechless

and couldn't move! We knew that there would be hell to pay. We had been in trouble since we arrived.

We all had to sleep in the same bed, and my youngest cousin kept peeing in the bed. Their grandmother wasn't happy about that. My other cousin burned her leg on a motorcycle that she had no business being on in the first place. Their grandmother wasn't happy about that either. It was my first time leaving New Jersey. I wasn't happy about that! I complained about things that could only happen in the South. I hated getting up at the crack of dawn, when the roosters crowed. I hated shucking corn and milking the cows. I was used to my milk coming in a red and white carton, from the corner store. I hated "fetching" water from the well, in the back of their grandmother's house. Most of all, I hated the "Piggly Wiggly" store down the road. They rarely sold beef and there weren't even any sidewalks that led to the road.

I just wanted to go back home—back to Jersey—and back to East Orange. But no one was leaving before my cousins' grandmother determined which one of us broke her glass dish! I only lasted for two weeks and begged to go back home. I laughed out loud in my head. Still, I couldn't figure out why my grandfather was so dirty. We didn't live down South, on a farm. His army-green work shirt was always stained with oil and mud. His matching work pants were just as dirty. It didn't really matter to me where he had been. I adored my grandfather and stared at him intently. I watched his every move. Sometimes, he would come in from work all dirty and sit right down at the kitchen table. It would take him a long time to wash up, so my grandmother would insist on us saying the grace right away.

Normally, we would say:

"Gracious, Lord, make us truly thankful for what we are about to receive, for the nourishment of our body, in Christ's sake. Amen!" When we were really hungry, my cousins and I would say, "God is good. God is great, and we thank him for this plate!" My grandfather would always say, "Good God, good meat, now thank the Lord and let's eat!"

My cousins and I would look at each other from the corner of our eye and then stare down at the table to keep from laughing.

My grandmother would blow a gasket! Then, my grandfather would kick off his brown leather shoes and leave them on the floor. They would be lying right there, underneath the kitchen table for hours. My grandmother hated that! If she hated it, I loved it! My grandfather didn't even bother to untie his laces. He just used his toes to push each shoe off the back of his heels. Then, he would unbutton the top two buttons of his shirt and walk to the bathroom.

He would open a fresh bar of green Lava soap and scrub his hands together. Dirt would fall under the running water, and the sink would turn black. Mud would be everywhere! *Was he a pig, or had he been out slaughtering one?* I laughed out loud in my head (again.) I thought about the soap and how harsh it was. It was as abrasive as the Ajax I used to clean the bathtub. This was his routine, whenever he came home from a trip.

The only other time my grandfather used the Lava soap was when he washed his hands after caring for the dogs. *Yup, Lava soap and Dobermans!* It sounds funny when I say it aloud, but those had become the constants in my life. It had been a life of turmoil where I needed someone, or something, that was consistent. Someone or something like my grandfather, the Lava soap, and our Dobies.

My mother was always gone (in and out of my life.) My eldest aunt was always taking the side of my grandmother. Now, my youngest aunt was betraying me. She had sided with my mother and had abandoned me. Up until now, I had been able to depend on my youngest aunt. Now, she was gone. She too was in and out of my life (starring in disappearing acts just like my mother.)

I only had two things that I could really count on—the Dobermans and my grandfather. My grandfather truly loved me, and I knew one day that he would save me! The dogs loved me too! Before he had gotten sick, my grandfather told me that he would never let me live with my mother again. My grandfather was more than a constant in my life. He was the breadwinner and the protector of the family. He set the pace that determined how we functioned as a unit. The unit fell apart when he died. I tried not to think about that. I wanted to remember the times when he was alive.

When I was a child, I remember staring up at him like he was larger than life. My grandfather stood six feet three inches tall and weighed well over two hundred pounds. Sometimes, the last button at the bottom of his army-green shirt was unbuttoned, and I could see his big belly hanging out. Sometimes, the hairs on his chest peeked out from the top of his undershirt. Every now and then, he would take his shirt off at the kitchen table and walk around in a sleeveless T-shirt (with his belly hanging out.) My grandmother hated when he did that (just like when he kicked his shoes off under the table.)

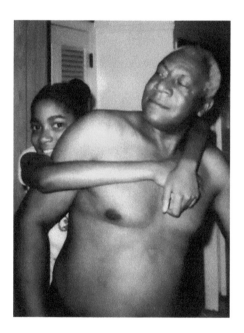

My grandfather was big and strong, and I was proud to be his granddaughter. Although my grandmother and my mother had taught me all about education and life, my grandfather was the one who taught me about strength and resilience. Through that resilience, I was taught to shun away fears and not show too much emotion. In my grandparents' eyes, displays of emotion were a sign of weakness. I guess that is why they never showed me much affection. Come to think of it, I never saw my grandparents hug or kiss each other.

Come to think of it, no one in my family ever showed much emotion. I can remember all the times that my mother yelled at me, screamed at other people, or threatened to "beat someone's *ass*"—But I don't ever recall her telling me that she loved me. She never took the time to sit with me and read a story, or tell me that things would be okay. Even after she got beat up by her boyfriends, she tried not to cry in front of me. It was as if crying was something that wasn't tolerated.

I remembered the time when one of my grandmother's brothers died. We were on our way home from the funeral. Another car hit my grandfather's blue Lincoln Continental, a Mark IV from the 1970s. Before my grandfather could even get out of the car, the driver of the other car was rolling up his window and trying to pull off. My grandfather was yelling and cursing (like my mother had done with my preschool teacher.) I felt afraid for the man. My grandfather yelled, "Your horn works. Now, try your breaks!" I laughed out loud in my head.

When we got home, my grandmother started yelling at my grandfather. I had never heard her yell before. The next thing I knew, she was in the bathroom crying. My grandfather was banging on the bathroom door for her to let him in. He promised not to hurt her, if she opened the door. I had never seen him hurt her before, and I was confident that he wouldn't hurt her now. She stayed in the bathroom, crying. I had never seen her cry before.

This was the only time that I had seen either of them show emotion. My grandfather—like my grandmother—never really hugged and kissed me, but I knew that he loved and adored me. I knew this because he always took the time to talk to me. Sometimes, we would sit at the kitchen table and talk for an hour. Other times, we would sit in his truck and talk. I thought back to the first time that I sat in his truck. I was coming from the candy store around the corner, and I saw the truck coming down Leslie Street.

My grandfather's truck was the biggest and most beautiful truck I had ever seen! It was an eighteen-wheeler, with a semitrailer. The cab was dark green and looked larger than life! My grandfather stuck his head out the window and tooted the horn. I loved when he did that! I forgot all about my Onion & Garlic potato chips and ran across the street. As soon as the truck reached the corner, I would climb in. I always felt so proud when I was with my grandfather. Everyone knew and loved him. But he had a special love for me. I was his baby girl—his granddaughter, his pride and joy, just like his truck and just like the Dobermans!

We had no secrets from each other, and we shared everything! I remember the first time my grandfather showed me how to change a flat tire. He also showed me how to drink from a canteen. I also remember the first time he taught me how to tie a tie. He told me to hang it around his neck unevenly. Then, I would fold the longer end over the shorter end. Next, I would wrap the longer end twice around, creating a loop. Lastly, I would bring the longer end through the loop and pull until a knot formed. I have only had to tie a tie once since my grandfather taught me, but I'm glad that he taught me how.

I knew about the Playboy magazines that he kept hidden under the newspaper, on his nightstand - and the tin can of Katydids that he hid under his side of the bed. I was sure that the tiny silver key that turned the tin can was sure to fit my diary. I laughed out loud in my head. I knew just where to look for his eyeglasses, when he said they were lost. I knew where he kept his coin and stamp collections.

One day, my grandfather even showed me the gun that he kept hidden on the shelf in his bedroom closet. He said it was to keep his truck and the Doberman puppies safe because people were always trying to steal them. Then, he showed me his favorite paring knife that he used to slice vegetables and fruit. I felt so special, when he gave me his Swiss Army knife. It was complete with a nail file, small magnifying glass, scissors, a can opener, and knives with different types of blades. It was my favorite color (red!) He said that I should carry the knife around with me at all times for protection. I knew that my grandfather cared about my safety and loved me dearly.

During the summer months, he would give me his loose change so that I could play the games at the carnival in the school playground across the street. I never rode the rides, but I always had enough spare change to buy the biggest bag of pink cotton candy to share with my grandfather. His loose change always amounted to five, or ten, dollars - Sometimes, even twenty dollars. I knew that because I would help him roll his pennies and other coins into those tight paper sleeves that the bank gave him. I was his special helper, his confidant.

Unlike my grandfather, my grandmother rarely asked me about what was going on in my life. Usually, the only time she opened her mouth was to criticize me. Other than that, it seemed like the only time we spoke was to talk about *Dynasty* (when Krystle Carrington slapped Alexis and they both fell into the swimming pool.) Sometimes, we would also catch up while trying to figure out who shot J.R. Ewing on *Dallas* and who stole Val's twins on *Knots Landing*. But the relationship between me and my grandmother was nothing like the one between me and my grandfather. My life changed drastically, after my grandfather's truck accident.

When my grandfather became ill, he and I were inseparable. I would rush home from school and watch *Barnaby Jones* with him because it was his favorite show. He hated the commercials and would scream at the TV whenever *Crazy Eddie* came on the tube. I would laugh out loud in my head, when he cursed at the TV. Sometimes, I could hardly wait for my grandfather to fall asleep so that I could change the channel. I would watch *The Six Million Dollar Man* - and pretend to be the "Bionic Woman", with Napoleon (our Doberman) as the bionic dog. Oftentimes, my grandfather would have wandered off before I arrived home. I would comb the streets of Newark looking for him (much like the times when I would look for my mother when she would go missing.)

I would usually find my grandfather near the corner of Bergen Street and Lyons Avenue, walking toward Weequahic Park. He always said that he was trying to get to work. The funny thing was that he no longer worked! Once we were home safe, I would help him wash up. He didn't need the green Lava soap anymore. I would cook and help him get ready for dinner. Like most of my relatives, I had been cooking since I was a young child. I was a very good cook and house cleaner by the time my grandfather became ill. I tried to remember a time when it wasn't like this—a time when my grandfather was in charge. But things were different now.

My grandfather was sick, and my mother was back. And there I was, looking around at this new house that my grandmother bought for us to live in. All of a sudden, my grandmother had the urge to "keep the family together." I laughed out loud in my head at the thought that my mother and I were expected to live on the third floor, in this one-bedroom apartment that had been converted into two bedrooms. The living room served as her bedroom, and I slept in the other room. It was pretty much the same as our apartments in Newark and East Orange, except that it wasn't an apartment building.

I didn't want to go back to the "same" old thing. I wanted—needed—something different. Now that my grandfather was ill, I wondered how long I would have to stay here and how long it would be before one of my mother's boyfriends came and took over. My youngest aunt lived downstairs on the second floor with her children and the same boyfriend that I saw beating her up some years ago. Only now, he was her husband.

I hated my family by this time and had no desire, or intention, to stay in that house. My mother threatened to put me in a group home, if I ran away again. I couldn't understand why my grandmother was now siding with my mother. My mother and I got into fights every day, and I ran away again. All I ever heard was, "Don't do this, and don't do that!" I tried to think positive, but in the midst of our family's dysfunction, "all things don't" seemed to revolve solely around me. It was no wonder that I was so miserable.

There were definitely more "don'ts" than "do's." My grandmother would say, "Don't be like your mother. Don't drop out of school, and don't have a child out of wedlock." I laughed out loud in my head at the fine example my mother was setting…and after all of her preaching about education, my grandmother would also say, "Don't become a teacher because teachers don't make any money." Sometimes, I really didn't understand the things that came out of her mouth. She wasn't even worth laughing out loud at, in my head.

Thoughts of my grandfather's illness made me sad. The one person—the one constant in my life—was about to change. My grandfather made me happy and I didn't want our relationship to change. It was the one thing that I wanted to stay the same. But the accident had changed our lives forever. It just goes to show you that life can change in an instant. I cried… Then, I closed my eyes and watched my life flash before me. I thought about all the things that I had gone through. I tried to focus on the good things. I tried to focus on things like dancing and modeling, but my grandmother was totally against those ideas too. *Yup, the vote was in.* Clearly, my grandmother didn't support any of my goals or *anything* that I liked! As a child growing up, I always thought that parents and grandparents were supposed to love, protect, and support you. It was no secret that there was no love lost between me, my mother, and my grandmother.

Over the years, I noticed that my grandmother became great at putting up a front to make the rest of the world think that she actually loved me. She pretended that she was protecting me. The truth is that the only thing my grandmother was good at protecting was her reputation, which meant more to her than anything else in the world. That is why my mother and I having a child out of wedlock was a death sentence to her. She would make sure that we both paid for our sins for the rest of our lives!

However, I could not (for the life of me) figure out why my grandmother did not approve of me becoming a fashion model or dancer. My eldest aunt was a model, but my love of music and dancing came from my mother. Memories of me dancing went back as far as I can remember (back to the good old days, when I was about five years old.)

My mother had every album that ever existed. She would lie in the bed, smoking cigarettes and drinking beer, while listening to *The Delfonics, Blue Magic, The Isley Brothers, The Stylistics, and The Temptations.* One of her favorite albums was "Lady Sings the Blues" by *Billie Holiday.* My mother was also obsessed with reggae and listened to Bob Marley every weekend. I grew to love all the same music that my mother listened to, and we would dance together (whenever she was around.)

I thought about how I would sit on the edge of the bed and smile, as I watched my mother shake her groove thing. She would sing and dance around our one-bedroom apartment while listening to *The Staple Singers* sing "I'll Take You There." My mother danced like she was auditioning for *Soul Train*, and she always reminded me of *Thelma* from "Good Times." When I was about eight years old, I joined the modern dance group at my school. I wanted to dance like my mother. The group met on Tuesdays, Wednesdays, and Thursdays each week. I became so interested in dancing that I dreamed of performing with the Alvin Ailey Dance Company.

When I was in high school, I actually auditioned for the well-known dance company in New York. After I graduated from college, I would travel back and forth from Jersey to take classes at the Alvin Ailey Dance Theater. I also took dance lessons at LY-BEN Dance Academy, a local dance company in Irvington. I remember my first performance so vividly. I danced to "Someday We'll All Be Free" from the *Malcolm X* movie soundtrack sang by *Aretha Franklin (1992)*. During my first dance and modeling auditions, I remember waiting anxiously for my name to be posted on the board. I always made it. I always got the call! That is, except for that one time when the lady at the Ford Agency told me that I was too short to model and that my legs were too hairy! Shenanigans!

I was as passionate about fashion as I was about dancing. While everyone else was playing with lifelike dolls, I would nurture my fashion interests by playing with cutout dolls. They were tiny pieces of cardboard that were shaped like little figurines. Each cutout came with outfits that I could mix and match. The dress-up closet was also a cardboard cutout that I could bend and fold into a miniature closet with little, tiny, plastic hangers. It was at this moment that I decided to become a fashion designer and model.

For a brief moment, I considered taking classes at the Fashion Institute of Technology in New York. I would daydream about all the designer outfits—different dresses, shoes, and pocketbooks that my cutout dolls would wear. I would use my black and white composition notebook to sketch out similar outfits that I had imagined myself wearing. When I thought that I had become too old to play with dolls, I imagined myself walking down a runway. I knew that I had the height to become a fashion model. Everyone was always telling me how tall I was.

But the woman at the Ford Agency insisted that I was too short. I was only 5'7", at the time. That's also when the woman sent me home and told me that I should shave my legs. My mother had told me never to shave my legs because the hair would grow back twice as thick. I remembered how she had also said that men would "love" my hairy legs, when I was older. My mother wasn't around often—but, when she was, she always took the time to teach me one of life's lessons.

Needless to say, I continued trying to focus on the good times. These were the times when life was filled with music, dancing, modeling, my grandfather, and our Dobermans! I went on go-sees and auditioned for as many fashion shows and dance roles as I possibly could. I will always be grateful for the opportunities that I've had, but I know that I would have achieved greater success as a model and dancer if I had the support of my mother or grandmother.

When things didn't quite work out with me becoming a famous model or professional dancer, I fell back on another thing that I knew how to do really well. I had always been good at working with children. I think deep down inside, I wanted to work with children because I didn't have a good childhood. Ever since I was a little girl, I loved taking care of other little children. I would babysit for my youngest aunt and my second cousins all the time. I thought back to the times when I helped take care of Egypt's little sister and two brothers.

I couldn't describe the feeling that I got when I was around young children. I felt so vibrant, so alive, so loved! It reminded me of the times when Egypt's little brother would run down the street and jump into my arms. I thought back to the relationship that I had with my grandfather (before he became ill.) I thought about the times when he would be gone for three or four days in a row, and I had waited for him to come home. I would run and leap into his arms, just like Egypt's little brother did when he saw me come down the street.

Sometimes, my grandfather would be gone for an entire week. I often wondered if he had another family. Any family would be better than *our* dysfunctional family. I wondered if he was cheating on my grandmother. It would serve her right! She never even gave him a hug, or acted like she missed him. I would always be the one to greet him with open arms.

Whenever he returned from one of his long "work trips," he would come home and slap a check down on the kitchen table. One day, I took a peek at the check lying on the middle of the table. It was over a thousand dollars! I really didn't have any concept of money back then (especially since my mother and I never had any.) Most of the money that I came in contact with was printed on funny paper and stapled together in a food stamp book, or came in the form of color-coded plastic coins.

One thousand dollars seemed like a lot of money for bringing home a truck full of fruits, vegetables, and pig's feet every week. I laughed out loud in my head! It didn't matter to me where he had been, or what he had done. My grandfather could do no wrong. We shared a love that no one else had. We had a connection that no one else knew about. We had his Lava soap, his truck, and "our" Dobermans!

My mother and youngest aunt were deathly afraid of the Dobermans. I heard that my youngest aunt had been bitten by one of the dogs, but I didn't believe it. My precious Dobies wouldn't hurt a fly! Well, there was that one time that they bit the mailman. He had no business sticking his hand all the way through the mail slot. *Really... Who does that? Drop the mail and back away from the door!*

All of my cousins—and most of my other relatives—were also afraid of the Dobermans. My eldest aunt (like me) was not afraid. I think she must have been an animal lover. She had a bird, a cat, and a dog, all at one time. She had trained each of them to answer the phone and poop in the toilet. It was crazy!

My grandfather taught me all about how to care for the dogs from the time they were puppies. We would have dozens of Dobermans at a time because he would breed and sell them. He always kept the mothers and fathers so that the bloodline would remain pure. He didn't believe in mixing breeds. Our Dobermans had to be thoroughbreds!

I fed, bathed, and watched over the dogs for my grandfather every day when he was away. He trusted me to do so, and I never let him down. The dogs had exotic names, such as Napoleon and Venus, which depicted them as great leaders. There was even a Rip and King! There was the first Napoleon, Napoleon the Second, and Napoleon the Third. They were three generations of fathers. Then, there was Lady and Kenya, who were the wives of the Napoleons. Each litter of Dobies gave birth to a new generation, and my grandfather let me choose which puppies we would keep and which puppies to sell.

By the time that my grandfather became ill, two of the Napoleons had passed away. One night, my grandmother said that she was taking "Napoleon the Third" to the vet for his normal checkup. She came back alone! I should have known that something was up because my grandmother never went out at night (especially not to the vet.) She knew how much the Dobies meant to me and my grandfather. She never even said a word… and just like that, "Napoleon the Third" was gone!

I remember how my grandfather always chose to clip the ears and the tails of the black Dobies, while the red Dobies pounced around like goofballs. Kenya was one of the first red Dobies that we decided to let keep her long, floppy ears and wagging tail. My eldest aunt became very fond of her. When the generation of Cocoas was born, I decided that they would each be as goofy as the litter of red Dobies that preceded it. The black Dobies watched over the house like true guard dogs, while the red Dobies pretended to be lapdogs.

My grandfather and our dogs were my constants. They were the only things loyal that I knew. My Dobermans have always been loyal and have never let me down (just like my grandfather.) My grandfather wasn't perfect, and neither were our dogs. But they were a very special part of my life. I will always remember the times, when I was a young child and my grandfather would walk the Dobies to pick me up from school. That was how we became known around the neighborhood as the "Doberman family."

I will always have fond memories of my grandfather raising the Dobermans and washing his hands with green Lava soap. I will never forget jumping into his arms, after he climbed down from his green truck (with his dirty army green shirt.) Every morning, I glance over to a black and white picture of my grandfather lying on the couch with a cigarette in his hand. He seemed to be in deep thought (staring in a daze, as I have often done.)

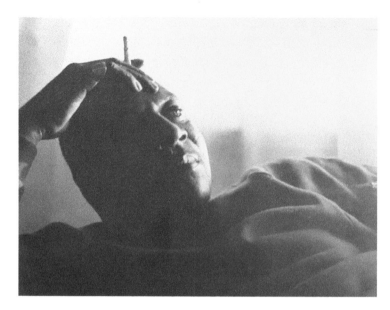

CHAPTER 9

The Birth Of A Son

After my grandfather's death, nothing else seemed to matter - at first. I no longer felt a need to focus on the good times. I had no time to reminisce about the past and all the things that I had gone through. My son was born right before my grandfather passed. Before my grandfather's death, I had only been to one funeral. It was the one where a man got cursed out for crashing into the back of my grandfather's Lincoln Continental. Then came so many emotions... There was a birth. There was a death. I didn't understand... No one had ever talked to me about life and death.

I had given birth to a beautiful baby boy! I was happy, but sad. His father was happy. My ex-boyfriend—my first love, was not so happy about my new news. Thinking about my grandfather and the love that we shared (the bond that we had) made me think of the type of man I wanted. I wanted a family of my own—a husband for me and a father for my baby. Unfortunately, my son's father was nothing like my grandfather... As always, he was accusing me of sneaking away to cheat with my ex. I admit that I still loved my ex-boyfriend, but I loved my unborn child even more and was trying to give my new relationship the "old college try."

Contrary to my grandmother's belief, I didn't want to "disgrace the family" by giving birth to a child out of wedlock or by shacking up with my "baby's daddy." I thought about the chain of events that happened before my son was born. When I first found out that I was pregnant, I wanted to keep it a secret. I didn't want anyone to know. This was my joy, my chance for happiness. It was a chance to have something of my own—my chance for someone to love ME! I didn't want to tell a sole. I didn't want to share my baby with anyone.

Then, reality snuck in. *Who was I to keep such a beautiful thing from the rest of the world? Didn't his father have a right to know? Shouldn't I make sure that my baby had people in his life who loved him? And people he could love back?* But I didn't trust anyone. I learned a long time ago that people couldn't be trusted. The first time that I learned adults couldn't be trusted was when I was ten.

It was the time right before my eleventh birthday. It was when my mother lied to me about the eviction notice. The next time that I learned adults couldn't be trusted was when I was fifteen. It was when my grandmother let my mother and the police take me. Then, there was the time with the nurse at Planned Parenthood. She lied to my face and said that she wouldn't tell my mother that I was having sex. Ten minutes later, she was standing right in my face telling my mother that I was no longer a virgin!

Then, the love of my life—"my first love"—cheated on me. It was right after he had promised that we would be together forever! No one in my life had ever done what they said they were going to do. My youngest aunt said that she would always be there for me. Now, she was in and out of my life - just like my mother. No one cared, and everybody lied! I knew since then that love hurts. Boyfriends cheat. Girlfriends are secretly jealous. And adults leave! *Why should I trust anyone now?*

On Mother's Day in 1986, I went into labor (or so I thought!) It was Sunday morning, and my grandmother was on her way to church. I walked slowly to the back door as she was heading down the stairs, toward the garage. I was holding my stomach and pleading with her to take me to the hospital. She told me that she couldn't miss church. I decided to call a cab, as I watched my grandmother pull out of the driveway. Tears rolled down my face. I was scared!

I walked slowly back to my bedroom to get my baby bag. Minutes later, I heard the cab blowing its horn. I walked to the front door and locked it from the outside. When I arrived to the hospital, they told me that my doctor was away on a fishing trip. I began to panic. *Who would deliver my baby? I couldn't do this without him! Was I going to have my baby alone?* The residing doctor came in with a nurse. They examined me and timed my contractions. They sent me home, saying that my uterus was not fully dilated.

Before I left the hospital, the residing doctor called my primary obstetrician-gynecologist (OB-GYN) and let me speak with him over the phone. I demanded that he return from his fishing trip immediately and told him that I was not going to have this baby without him! He laughed out loud and promised he would be home in time to deliver my baby. When I got home, I walked around the block three times and mopped the kitchen floor like my doctor told me to do. I didn't say a word to my grandmother, when she came in the door. She had no idea of what I had gone through.

Tuesday morning seemed to be a repeat of Sunday morning. This time, I called the cab right away, rather than pleading with my grandmother to take me to the hospital. I watched her pull out of the driveway, as she left for work. The cab pulled up immediately afterward. My grandfather's first cousin lived above us on the second floor of the two-family house. Her boyfriend saw me trying to make it to the cab and rushed down the stairs to help me. He grabbed the baby bag from my arm and told me to sit on the brick steps. I was afraid to sit down. I watched him walk to the curb and wave the cab away.

He came back to where I was standing and waiting for him. He asked if it was time. I said, "Yes!" He said that he had just seen my grandmother pull off and wanted to know where she was going. I said that she had to go to work. He shook his head and drove me to the hospital. He dropped me off and asked if I would be okay. I told him that I would call my boyfriend.

My "soon-to-be" son's father came to the hospital right away. It seemed like I was in labor all day. My water never broke, and they had to induce labor. My contractions were getting worse by the minute. I refused to get an epidural. Just as they were taking me into the delivery room, I heard my grandmother's voice. She was threatening that "I'd be sorry" because I chose my baby's father to be present at the birth instead of her! She never came back to the hospital to see me, or my baby. Shenanigans!

As I looked at my beautiful, new baby, I smiled and closed my eyes. I thought back to everything that happened before now, including my very first date with his father. We went to Weequahic Park. He had just picked me up for a summer concert in the park, and I was wearing a cute, white short set. *Iman* was a high-fashion model, at the time. And I wanted to be just like her. She had become my idol. But my son's father was constantly criticizing me. He told me that I needed to change my clothes. I had previously worn the outfit for a modeling shoot. I laughed out loud in my head. My outfit was good enough for the photo shoot, but wasn't good enough for my new boyfriend. He claimed that he could see through the shorts, even though I was wearing black underwear. He ridiculed me all that day.

I knew right then and there that I should have left him, but we continued to date. Once I was over the initial shock of becoming pregnant, I was determined to give my child a better life than I had. I didn't want my child to grow up without a father, like I did. My son would not be a motherless child, or fatherless child (like me.) My "soon-to-be" son's father, on the other hand, had other plans. He was determined to "make" me love and "obey" him, by any means necessary—and that included using me as a punching bag.

I continued to reminisce about the day I found out that I was pregnant. Two months passed, and I had not gotten my period. This reminded me of the time when I first became a "woman" (at the ripe, young age of twelve.) I was on my way to school one morning, and a car stopped short at the stop sign. Before speeding around the corner, the driver managed to take half of my knee with him. The car had actually knocked me right down on the street, and I was lying there with blood gushing out of my right knee cap. It was the same knee that I had to get stitches in when that brute (Andre) tripped me in the parking lot of our building on Wainwright Street.

I limped the rest of the way and finally made it to the school nurse. She confirmed that nothing was broken and gave me a bandage and a big hug! I felt like such a big girl (until she said that she was going to call my mother.) *What the hell?* I laughed out loud in my head, as I repeated the words, "my mother." *Who was that?* She had been long gone. She had disappeared and was missing in action again. I thought - *Good luck with that!* - As I looked back down at my knee. The school nurse had confirmed that most of the blood was from my period and not from the car accident.

Along with my period came the worst pain I'd ever felt in my life. At least that's what I thought, before I gave birth to my son! My period lasted for seven days, but my cramps lasted for two days. The pain was so bad that I had to be hospitalized for the first two days of my period, every month. Sometimes, my great-grandmother would mix a couple of drops of rum in a hot cup of tea to help ease the pain. I would later find out that the pain was caused by endometriosis. My OB-GYN told me that there was a fifty percent chance that I might not be able to get pregnant. He had said that, even if I did become pregnant, I might not carry full-term.

After I found out that I was pregnant, I immediately went into survival mode. I had to decide whether, or not, I wanted to tell the father. Summer was over and we were no longer dating. My period didn't come in September. I thought it was due to the stress of returning back to school. When it didn't come again in October, I got nervous. A thousand and one thoughts went through my head. I was scared to tell anyone. I couldn't even tell my roommate, or my best friend. I wasn't sure what to do. The only thing I knew for sure is that I wanted my child to have a mother and a father. I wanted his life to be better than mine.

I went to Student Services and made an appointment with my Educational Opportunity Fund (EOF) counselor. He seemed disappointed, but told me not to panic. He said that I was not the first and only student to become pregnant. He told me my options and said that there was still a good chance that I could graduate on time, if I stayed focus. We talked about my emancipation and what would be needed for me to get into an apartment. We filled out applications and I was put on a waiting list. I still hadn't told anyone.

This was something that I needed to do on my own. My roommate must have sensed that something was up. She claimed that she noticed the box of pads in my closet was still full. *What was she doing in my closet anyway?* I laughed out loud in my head. She came right out and asked me if I was pregnant. I swore her to secrecy. I then decided to tell the father. My best friend was upset that she wasn't the first to know. I could tell from then on that I would be making important decisions for the rest of my life.

The nurse confirmed my pregnancy. It was October and the campus nurse was telling me that I was seven weeks pregnant. She gave me some very large vitamins and a big hug, just like the elementary school nurse had done when I first got my period. I was happy about the baby, but sad about the father. I didn't want to be pregnant at that time and definitely didn't want to be pregnant by my new boyfriend.

I knew my family was going to be disappointed in me. I was disappointed in myself! I could already hear my mother and my grandmother telling me how bad my life was going to be, as if it wasn't already bad. I wasn't sure how my ex-boyfriend—"my first love"—would take the news of me being pregnant. My first thought was that my ex is going to kill me! I was in a brand-new relationship and was about to start a family. It had only been six months since we had broken up! I also wasn't sure how my new boyfriend would take the news of becoming a father. He was overjoyed! I laughed out loud in my head, as I thought about him and his friends buying cigars to celebrate.

My son's father wasn't *all* bad. In between the fighting and arguing, he could actually be quite funny and romantic. We often went to *Blue Magic* music concerts at the Peppermint Lounge in East Orange and Symphony Hall in Newark. On special occasions, he took me to see *Luther Vandross* at Jones Beach. We would laugh at the fact that I nicknamed him "Dookie." When I was pregnant, I would walk around his dorm room fully naked. He loved when I pranced around in his shoes and called them "Herb" shoes. He rubbed my belly, when our baby moved around inside me. He even drank my breast milk. And, ironically, he stood up for me when my grandmother and eldest aunt tormented me. Then, just when things appeared to be normal, he would resort back to humiliating me for no apparent reason.

The verbal abuse had already started. Now, he had begun to physically abuse me. I continued to reminisce about the months before I became pregnant—back when I first met my son's father. It was Memorial Day weekend, and I was leaving my youngest aunt's house. It was her birthday. My cousins and I (along with my aunt's new husband) had a small celebration. As I walked down Lyons Avenue, I remembered that the buses were running on a holiday schedule. I stopped at a light and, before I could cross the street, someone blew the horn and called out my name.

I didn't recognize the young man and had no idea that he would end up being my son's father. I laughed out loud, as he left his gray van in the middle of the street. The young man reminded me that we had originally met at a basketball game. He had seen me with my ex-boyfriend, when I was in high school. Now, the unfamiliar young man was also a student at Rutgers. However, he was a senior, and I had just finished my freshman year. We were both staying on campus for the summer, but were home for a visit during the holiday weekend.

That summer, we spent a lot of time together at the beach. He introduced me to his family, who lived near my grandparent's house in the Weequahic section of Newark. His parents owned a home in the neighborhood, but it was not as nice as my grandmother's and my eldest aunt's house. It certainly wasn't as nice as Elly and Maddie's house in Toms River. My new boyfriend had a large family like Amy, with six siblings. He had one sister and five brothers, two of whom were twins.

I didn't like him as much as I liked my previous boyfriend, "my first love." I gather that he sensed this because he became very jealous and started to hit me (the way my mother and youngest aunt had been hit by *their* boyfriends.) The very first time he hit me, we were waiting for the bus on Broad Street (downtown Newark.) We had just come back from Greenwich Village in New York. We spent most weekends in New York, just like me and my ex-boyfriend.

Wham! My new boyfriend slapped me right across the face because I was looking at a car that looked like my ex's car. It was just like the time that my mother slapped me in the bathtub (when

I was six years old.) One time, he hit me in the face at Dairy Queen in Irvington Center. I was pushing our son's baby carriage, and I let two Puerto Rican guys go ahead of us in line. We weren't "politically correct" back then and everyone was either *Black, White, Mixed, or Puerto Rican.* He claimed that I knew them and was flirting. Another time, he got mad at me because I laid his clothes on the top of my car. I had just picked them up from the dry cleaners for him. They were still in the plastic and my car was clean - But, somehow, this was worth fighting over. This seemed to make him as mad as the time that I kissed him on the cheek in front of his friends. He said that it was disrespectful and that I should kiss him on the lips to show that I loved him. Shenanigans!

Later in our relationship, he began to complain that I used the "same seasoning for everything." It didn't matter that the food tasted good and he had a home-cooked meal every night. It seemed like he was always looking for a fight!

I thought back to our first "real" fight—the one where he had nearly killed me and our unborn child. I had spent that weekend over at my youngest aunt's house to avoid having to be around my grandmother. Thinking back to the fight with my new boyfriend, I wish that I would have kept walking the first time I saw him (when I was walking down Lyons Avenue and he had left his gray van in the middle of the street to chase me down.) In reality, I think that the only reason I hooked up with him was because I was on the rebound and missed my ex, "my first love." I really had no intention of staying with him, and I definitely had no intention of getting pregnant.

There I was, a college student with a promising future. I was pregnant by a man who I despised and who seemed to despise me! The phone continued to ring. We didn't have cell phones back then, and the house phone kept ringing. I didn't answer it because it wasn't my house, or my telephone. I assumed it was my "soon-to-be" baby's daddy. He was my new boyfriend, the father of my unborn child, the one whom I had met on Memorial Day weekend.

My aunt finally answered the phone and came to my cousin's bedroom to find me. She told me that my "baby's daddy" was on his way. I instantly became scared because I had not asked him to come pick me up. When he arrived, he put on quite a show for my aunt and her new husband. Although my aunt's husband had beaten her in the past, it had been a long while since I had seen him hurt her. In fact, I hadn't recalled him ever hitting her again after they got married. Instead, he honored their vows and loved and protected her like he said he would.

My aunt's new husband even "manned up" and took care of her three children, like they were his own. I guess I was too old to be adopted. Nevertheless, I had grown fond of my new uncle, and he seemed to like me too. I knew this because when the doorbell rang, he looked at me with concern and asked if everything was okay. I knew that he was all too familiar with the signs and symptoms of domestic abuse.

He could tell that I was scared and, unlike anyone else had done, he stepped up to protect me. Stupidly, I lied and told him that everything was fine. In disbelief, he gave a quick stare at my boy-friend and led me to the front door by the hand. He told me to call him, if I needed anything. In the past, my new uncle had shunned me by acting like he didn't want me around. This time, he made it clear that I was welcome whenever I wanted or needed a place to stay.

In front of my uncle, my boyfriend pretended to show genuine concern about my well-being. When we got outside near his van, it was a different story. He immediately went around to the driver side of his gray van and didn't even bother helping me into the passen-ger's seat. We didn't speak until we reached my grandmother's house. I had left word with my grandmother that, if my boyfriend should call, she was to tell him to call me at my aunt and uncle's house in Irvington. I did not ask him to pick me up! I left with him silently because I didn't want there to be a scene. I hated being embarrassed by him.

Deep down, I knew that the message might not get delivered because my grandmother hated my new boyfriend the same way that she hated my ex. She also hated the fact that I was having a baby out of wedlock. In her mind, I was following in my mother's footsteps and "disgracing the family." When the van pulled up to my grand-mother's house, I sat in my seat and watched my boyfriend throw all of my bags out on the lawn. He was yelling and screaming that I had left him for days and he didn't know where I was.

I jumped out of the van and ran inside, ignoring the clothes that my boyfriend had scattered all over my grandmother's front lawn. I thought that I would be much safer inside. I tried to close the door, but my boyfriend stuck his foot in the door and pried it open. He chased me into the back bedroom, where my mother also slept. As usual, she wasn't home and I was all alone. My boyfriend punched me in the face. He hit me so hard that I caved and fell to the floor. He crouched down into a karate stance and kicked me in the stomach.

I blacked out. For a brief moment, I thought back to the number of times that I had seen my boyfriend stand in this same position as he prepared for a karate tournament. Now, he was using it with me! I wished that my new uncle was here. I wished that I had the knife that my grandfather gave me. Moments later, I heard the front door open again. I couldn't move. There I was, lying on the floor, waiting for whomever was coming back to finish the job. It was my mother! She had been "missing in action" again and was obviously coming in from one of her "disappearing acts."

My mother was stumbling and blurting out things that made no sense. She saw me lying on the floor and decided that it was the perfect time to "kick me when I was already down." She didn't kick me literally, but she said some of the most hurtful things I had ever heard her say. My mother told me that she was glad that I "got my ass beat" because now I knew what it felt like. She went on to say that I probably deserved it because of my smart mouth and because "I think I'm so much smarter than everybody else!" I was mad and confused.

All the times that I saw her lying on the floor, drunken and beaten, I never left her there. *Didn't she want me to be smart? Wasn't she the one telling me that education was power, my key to getting out of Newark?* It's so funny how the people who are supposed to care for you the most are the same people who will say the most hurtful things to you. It's like the people who have less are the ones who are mad that you have more than them.

For instance, people with a high school education will be the first to call someone who went to college, "Miss College Degree," like that's a bad thing. Or if you are attractive, people will say, "You think you're cute." Or if you have money and they don't, they would call you, "Miss Money Bags." Again, like that's a bad thing! I once heard a friend say, "There are only twelve months in a year… If people spent six months staying out of other folk's business and the other six months minding their own business, the year would go a lot faster."

With those thoughts in mind, I ignored my drunk mother and grabbed a hold of the nearest chair to prop myself up. I was near the doorway at the entrance of the kitchen, and I could reach the table and chairs that I had eaten at so many times during my childhood. The kitchen always made me think of my grandfather. Without any help from my mother, I managed to make it to the kitchen sink. I wanted a glass of water, but decided to sit in the chair to catch my breath instead. Holding my stomach, I walked slowly back to the bathroom so that I could get a good look at the damage my boyfriend had done to my face. There was a bruise below my right eye and my jaw was swollen. There was no blood coming from down below, so I assumed that the baby was okay.

I didn't want to go to the hospital. Just when I thought it couldn't get any worse, I heard the garage door go up and back down. Then, the back door opened. My grandmother was home and already in the kitchen arguing with my drunk mother. I tried to listen, but I was in so much pain. Besides, I wanted to get away from the both of them without another word said. I should have known that was an impossible task. I could hear bits and pieces of the conversation. My grandmother was scolding my mother for disappearing for days and leaving the front door unlocked.

My mother couldn't even remember where she lost her keys and didn't care whether, or not, someone robbed my grandmother's house. Suddenly, I remembered that my boyfriend had scattered all of my clothes on the front lawn when we returned from my aunt's house. I attempted to sneak pass the kitchen, in an effort to make it outside without being noticed. My mother made sure that my grandmother noticed me. Right in the middle of their argument, she told my grandmother that my boyfriend "whooped my ass!"

I thought for sure that my grandmother would be more concerned about the fact that my mother was using profanity. No one had ever heard my grandmother curse and knew that she wasn't a fan of it. Instead of addressing my mother, she turned toward me and shook her head. Neither one of them bothered to help me, or ask if I was okay. My mother continued with her usual name-calling. She called me a "bastard child" and said that my baby was going to be a "bastard child," just like me. *The nerve!*

The only time that I hated my mother more than this very moment was when we fought and nearly killed each other. It was the day that my youngest aunt called the police. It was when *she* too had abandoned me. I remember the police had come to the "family" house (the one that my grandmother bought in Irvington, back when I was in high school and was going through it.) That day, my youngest aunt heard us yelling and came upstairs to stop the fight. But I gave my mother one last punch and knocked her over the couch.

I thought back to the fight and how my youngest aunt had intervened. She had never done that before, and it made me feel like I couldn't trust her anymore. Through the years, and all the things I had gone through, we had managed to remain close. After all, she was the cute, sweet, and light-skinned one whom my mother accused me of loving more than her. Shenanigans! She would even be the one to throw a baby shower for me and my new baby.

After me and my mother fought, I remembered how my mother just laid there, looking stupid and lying to my aunt and the police about how I attacked her. She was very good at lying and manipulating people. I guess she got that from her mother, my "loving" grandmother. Remembering the look on my mother's face when I knocked her over the couch, I could understand why she was now taunting me and had left me lying on the floor nearly beaten to death.

However, the fight between me and my "soon-to-be" son's father had nothing to do with my mother. The thing I couldn't figure out is how she had forgotten about all the times that I knocked her boyfriends in the head and beat them off her, in order to save her life.

When my grandmother saw me, she decided to add her two cents. She was going on and on about the mess on her front lawn and how she told me that my "baby's daddy" was no good. I ignored both of them and went to retrieve my clothes from the front of the house.

When I got outside, I saw that my new boyfriend had obviously decided to make an even bigger mess by tearing up my clothes to shreds and throwing every personal item that I owned on the lawn for the neighbors to see. He was good at doing that—always making a scene. He would leave threatening notes taped to the door of my dorm room and his. I remembered the times that he wrote, "You will be penalized!" Everyone and anyone who came to visit would see the horrifying notes. I was always so embarrassed.

Strangely, my mind shifted from all the fights and I thought "happy thoughts." Summer was fast approaching. It was starting to get hot, and my belly was ready to pop! My baby was due and I was determined to push it out on, or near, Mother's Day! I thought it was a sign. My son was no "bastard child," and we were going to have a special bond. We were going to be closer than my mother and I had ever been!

Mother's Day passed, and my special day had finally come! It was the Tuesday after Mother's Day. I hadn't gone to church that Sunday. As a matter of fact, I hadn't gone in a while. I didn't go to church every Sunday, but I enjoyed going on the holidays. It reminded me of the holidays when the whole family got together at my grandmother's house to celebrate. I thought back to the Christmas when everyone spent the night because of the snowstorm. It was a magical time, a time when all was right with the world.

I hoped that giving birth to my son would also be a magical time. I remembered how my grandmother had gone to church (as if it was just a normal day.) I remembered how I grabbed the baby bag that had been packed for months and sitting on the floor, over in the corner of me and my mother's bedroom. I remembered how I called a cab and went to the hospital, alone. Now, all would be right with the world again. I was going to give birth to my very own child! On that Tuesday in May, forty-eight hours and thirty-seven stitches later, I would become a mother!

My mind continued to wander, as I laid on the hospital bed. As I slipped in and out of consciousness, I remembered one contraction coming after another. I remembered how I had balled my left hand into a fist and threw a punch at my "soon-to-be" baby's daddy's face. I wanted to laugh out loud, but it hurt. I squeezed his hand tight with my right hand (the way my mother had squeezed my hand at the bus stop when I was three.) The doctor had told me not to push again, but the pressure was telling me something else. I pushed, and my butt felt like it had exploded!

My son was twice the size that I was, when I was born. He was definitely a "firecracker," and he was also very long. When I was born, I barely weighed four pounds and had to stay in an incubator because I was so small. My son's baby balls were so big that his father and I decided to call him "Baby Nut." Of course, that nickname did not go over too well, and he eventually grew out of it. I'm not sure when we started calling each other "Pook," but my son and I would yell out our new nicknames for each other across the mall and down the aisle at the supermarket. I was "Medium Pook," and he was "Little Pook."

I passed out. When I awakened, the first person that I saw was my "baby's daddy's" sister. I was tired from giving birth and dozed in and out during her visit. She looked proud to become an aunt. She too was a college student, but she was younger than her brother. I was tired from her visit and went back to sleep. This time when I woke, I looked up into the faces of three "Bobbsey twins."

I couldn't believe my eyes. Standing in front of me were my mother and my two aunts. They were standing over me looking like triplets. They were all together, standing at my bedside and looking down at me. No one was drunk, or fighting! I looked around the room and tried to remember where I was.

The three of them staring down at me, with their different skin tones and individual styles, reminded me of the three sisters in the 1976 movie, "*Sparkle.*" I smiled, as I noticed that they were each beautiful in their own way. The only other time I recalled seeing them together and this happy was on Christmas Eve in 1976. There was a major snowstorm that year, and my entire family spent the night at my grandmother's house. The snow was too deep to drive in, and we all chose to stay warm and close together.

I remembered feeling overjoyed, as I watched my mother and her two sisters laughing with each other that night. They were dressed in black, with matching satin vests and bow ties. There wouldn't be a time after that when we would all be together. I closed my eyes and thought about my new baby. My mother and both of my aunts were here, now. And I had just given birth to my perfect son!

I remembered how my mother had described my birth as "fireworks!" She had said that I was a little "firecracker" because I was born at 11:40 p.m. on the night before July 4th! My son was a "firecracker" too! He came out with a bang (complete and perfect, with ten fingers and ten toes.) Strangely, he was light-skinned. I was considered "brown-skinned" or "cinnamon," and my baby's daddy was "blue-black." Eyebrows were raised when my son was born with a head full of long, curly hair and a "high-yellow" skin complexion.

His father said that our son looked like a "Puerto Rican." The only people who had this hair texture and skin color were my grandfather's side of the family and my ex-boyfriend's family. I admit that I still had feelings for my ex, but I'm pretty sure that we did not sleep together at the time in question. I laughed out loud in my head. As a matter of fact, my OB-GYN had been able to pinpoint the exact day that I became pregnant. Unfortunately, I remembered that day too.

My new boyfriend and I had gone to the beach. We rode down to Seaside Heights in his gray van—the same van that he left in the middle of the street when we first met. It was also the same gray van that he had thrown my clothes out of, when we left my youngest aunt's house on that other dreadful day. The old van looked like the bus on *The Partridge Family*, except that it was gray instead of multi-colored. It was embarrassing to be seen in, but it was no worse than my mother's "mysterious" orange car with the mismatch doors.

My new boyfriend and I got a motel room on the beach and spent the night. There was no boom box, or cassette player, playing my favorite slow songs. I undressed myself, and he did the same. We sat on the bed, with our backs turned toward each other. There certainly were no fireworks during or after, and I didn't see stars!

Afterward, I only remember feeling like I had done something terribly wrong. We continued to date through the rest of the summer and into the school year.

Summer was over, and we returned to Rutgers. It was my sophomore year, and I had a new roommate. April and I had been friends in high school, and I had no idea that we would be attending the same college. We were close, but we weren't "besties." We both had boyfriends and often spent nights away from our dorm room. We lived on Livingston Campus, which everyone referred to as the Rock.

The dorms were referred to as the Quads, and the basement that led from dorm to dorm was referred to as the Tunnel. As April and I became closer, she introduced me to some of her friends. One friend, Lisa, I remembered from high school. She was also cute and light-skinned, like my youngest aunt, but was very "thick." April was somewhat big-boned too. April and Lisa were tough, and though most people were scared of them, they were not bullies.

I had been the victim of bullying throughout elementary and junior high school, but my mother's life lessons taught me well. I was more afraid of my mother than I was of any child in my neighborhood. When we lived in our rat- and roach-infested, one-bedroom apartment building on the corner of Wainwright Street and Chancellor Avenue, a boy upstairs would constantly start fights with me. Andre was two years younger than I was, and we became "frenemies," while our mothers did drugs together.

Although I tried to stay focused on school, Andre and other bullies would taunt me every chance they got. Sometimes, they would follow me home from school and throw rocks at me. Other times, they would stick their feet out and trip me so that I fell down in the classroom. One day after school, Andre tripped me and I fell on a Coca-Cola bottle in the parking lot of our apartment building.

The bottle shattered, and glass flew everywhere, including my face. For once, my mother was home, and I was glad. This would be one of the few times that she was around to protect me. Elly and Maddie ran upstairs to tell my mother what had happened, and she called the ambulance. I remembered wondering where the mysterious orange car with the mismatched doors was. It was always parked in the same spot, and I had only seen my mother drive it once or twice.

Of course, my mother cursed the whole neighborhood out. The ambulance arrived and took me to Beth Israel Hospital on Lyons Avenue in Newark. My entire family, including me, and everyone else that I knew had been born in this same hospital. I looked down at the blood gushing from my knee. I had not noticed the white bone piercing through my boney right kneecap.

I cried because it burned, as the blood dripped from my top lip to my bottom lip. There was a huge piece of glass stuck in the corner of my top lip. The way that the doctor stitched my busted top lip reminded me of the way my grandmother crocheted my dresses. I looked just as hideous as the dresses. There I was, with black thread hanging from my top lip and matching stitches through my right kneecap. The Coca-Cola bottle left a permanent mark over my left eye. Shenanigans!

When I came home from the hospital that night, my mother told me that the next time I saw Andre, I better "knock him in the back of his head." My mother often talked like she was crazy because of her addictions - But this time, she was serious. Although they did drugs together, my mother cursed Andre's mother out the same way she had cursed my preschool teacher out.

I took heed to my mother's words. The next time I saw Andre, I busted him in the back of his head with a loose brick from our apartment building. I had watched Andre as he came down the stairwell and headed toward the door to go outside. I followed him outside, picked up a loose brick, and used all my might to knock Andre's head off his shoulders!

Blood gushed from his head, just as it did from my right kneecap and top lip one week earlier. It was the same lip that I had busted falling off the sliding board, when I was three. After the day that I bust Andre in his head, no one else from school bullied me ever again. As a matter of fact, other kids started following me around like lost puppies. Our teachers thought we had formed a gang!

I guess this was why I wasn't scared of April and Lisa, or anyone else for that matter. April and Lisa were best friends like me, Elly, and Maddie, like me and Karen, like me and Egypt, and like me and Amy had been throughout elementary and junior high school. Lisa came to visit the college campus every weekend. She and April drank, smoked, and partied all weekend long. Sometimes, I partied with them. But I never drank or smoked (not like my mother.) I had given birth to a son—and I was going to be a good mother.

CHAPTER 10

Are You My Father?

I didn't have a mother, or a father—but I had a son and good friends (who I considered family.) One Friday night—April, Lisa, and I went to a party off campus. I saw them "snorting a line" in the bathroom. I had seen people get high, take pills, and drink themselves into oblivion. I had even seen people shoot drugs into their veins, and in between their fingers and toes. But I had never seen anyone actually snort cocaine before. Not my mother—Not my aunt—Not anyone. I didn't say anything because I liked April and she always had my back. She had stood up to my "baby's daddy", when he tried to bust our dorm room door down.

That morning, his jealousy and paranoia had taken over, and he thought I was cheating on him (again.) I came out of the shower and was waddling down the hall toward our room when I saw him and April arguing. April was telling him that I was in the shower and that he could not come into our room. He was determined to get in because he thought I was in the room, hiding someone. Shenanigans!

Over the years, April and I continued to grow closer. Originally, we attempted to pledge a sorority together. April quit after two weeks. Six weeks in, with only one more week to go, I decided that I did not fit into anyone's "mold." I wasn't going to stand for anymore abuse.

Although the three of us never really discussed our families (our mothers and our fathers) in detail, we knew that we shared a secret bond. After everything—April, Lisa, the *Sorors*, and I remained close.

They all took turns watching my son, while I attended classes. They even made up a daily schedule and gave me a copy. They also took turns standing guard to make sure that my baby's daddy didn't "sneak attack" me, as he often tried to do. We were young dynamic women who had each other's back and were determined to be successful.

After April lost her mother, she eventually dropped out of college. And I lost a line sister, a roommate, and a good friend. I got a job and moved into my new apartment off campus. Although my mother rarely worked, keeping a full-time job was a priority for me. I remained in school, but my college classes had taken a seat on the back burner. I was just trying to make it through, and I was no longer afraid of my "baby's daddy."

Our last physical encounter occurred when he caused me to be burned by a steaming hot iron. After following me home from work one night, he hid in a tree and kicked in the door to my new apartment. Afterwards, I asked my neighbor to watch my son while I went to the hospital and police station. I filed a claim for harassment and domestic abuse and was granted a restraining order against my son's father.

My downstairs neighbor and I were not close, but she was also a single woman. She too was raising a very young son and had been abused. She and her son both seemed a little slow, and I kept my distance, but this was an emergency! While waiting for the doctor, I recalled the last "emergency" that I had experienced with my "baby's daddy." My next-door neighbors died in a fire over Thanksgiving weekend. I had planned to spend the holiday alone with my son in our new apartment. My "baby's daddy" showed up unexpectedly, banging on the door and pleading for me to let him spend the holiday with his son.

I didn't drink, smoke, or do drugs (as Muslims were not supposed to.) But I celebrated the Christian holidays because they reminded me of good times spent with my "family" as a child. My "baby's daddy," on the other hand, was supposed to be a devout Muslim who did not believe in celebrating holidays. Somehow, he always managed to come around on Valentine's Day, Thanksgiving, and his birthday, which was New Year's Eve.

He would always say, "We still have to eat!" Of course, we argued and I ended up leaving the apartment. It was a good thing that I did because the fire spread from across the hall. When I returned to my apartment, the firemen told me the sad news and explained how my next-door neighbors had died in a fire caused by a kerosene lamp.

My new apartment was filled with smoke, and I couldn't breathe. The firemen told me to go inside quickly to gather any important documents and personal belongings. I held my breath and covered my baby's face with his hooded jacket. I went inside the apartment to gather a few things.

It reminded me of the time I had to pack my backpack full of stuff because my mother and I were getting evicted. Once again, I was homeless and had nowhere to go. Oddly enough, I found myself knocking on the door of my "baby's daddy's" dorm room. After all, he was a senior with no roommate and was staying on campus because he didn't celebrate holidays. He welcomed us with open arms! I knew this was asking for trouble.

The only other problem was that babies were not allowed in the dorm rooms overnight. My "baby's daddy" called a friend who he had talked into letting us stay with him for the weekend. I wasn't sure whether, or not, my new apartment would be ready for me to move back into by the end of the weekend - But, at least, my son and I had somewhere to lay our heads for a few days. My perfect baby was healthy and safe, and all was right with the world again!

After the fire incident, things went back to normal. It was me and my son against the world. The birth of my son caused me to give birth to new ideas. My goals in life changed. When I was alone and it was just me, my only goal was to stay alive. I knew that I had to earn money, in order to keep a roof over my head and food on the table. Now, I had two mouths to feed. I knew that, no matter what, I had to keep a roof over both our heads. I also knew that I needed a car to make sure that we had the means to get from point A to point B. I bought a new car and was able to provide safe transportation for my son.

I soon realized that college was not as fun as high school. I was an adult and was responsible for my own well-being, as well as my son's. There wasn't much time for partying and having fun because I was always working, attending class, and taking care of my son. He was getting older, and we needed new things, such as furniture.

Once again, I was arguing with my "baby's daddy" over money. He agreed to pay for only half of a new crib for my son. He also said that he would "splurge" and give me $50 toward a small kitchen table. It was the least he could do after the whole "welfare" situation with me being found guilty of fraud because of his lies and him not wanting to pay child support.

Finally, I would be graduating soon and had to start thinking about life after college. I wondered where I would work and where I would live. I was still determined not to be like my mother. As much as I didn't want to admit it, I envisioned a life similar to that of my grandmother's. I wanted a nice house, with a family, and a good husband who would adopt my son. My son's father had become so abusive, and I no longer wanted him to be a part of our lives.

It had been four horrific years, and I had started thinking about ways to get away from him for good. It went against my original hopes of raising my son with a mother and a father, but I had to keep my son safe. I hated myself for becoming a victim of domestic abuse, like my mother and youngest aunt. I remembered the things that my EOF counselor and I talked about, such as weighing my financial options and becoming an independent adult.

For the first time in my life, I felt like I was in control. Before graduating, I applied for a tech position with New Jersey Bell. I didn't pass the computer tests at NJ Bell, but I did manage to pass the series of tests at AT&T. There were three different positions available. I was offered a customer service representative job from 8:00 a.m. to 5:00 p.m. There was a sales clerk position, which I knew I didn't want.

Lastly, there was a tech support position with good pay and good benefits. The sales position was from 9:00 a.m. to 5:00 p.m. and paid the lowest salary. The tech position was from 11:00 p.m. to 7:00 a.m. and offered the highest salary. I thought about how much money I could earn and how I could stay home with my son all day long.

I would no longer have to struggle to pay for day care. This idea seemed like a no-brainer. Although I was a night owl and could really use the money, I accepted the customer service rep position. I was twenty-two years old and would be earning an annual salary of almost $35,000, which wasn't bad for a college grad in 1988. After working as a customer service rep for seven years, I decided to apply for the tech position. All of my education and training in computer technology was finally starting to pay off.

Being a full-time mother, while working full-time, was not easy. I loved the money that I was making and was glad that I was able to pay my bills. Although I found a way for us to live comfortably, I never forgot about my dream of working with young children. Early childhood education had become a passion of mine, and I needed to find a way to earn the salary that I desired in the field that I was most passionate about. I put my plan into motion.

I decided to put my graduation on hold just so that I could stay in my new on-campus apartment and keep a roof over my and my son's head for another year. A close friend from high school, Tammy, "hipped" me to a job opening for another tech position at AT&T. She gave me the contact information for the HR department where she worked. It was for the same company, but in a different department. I called and applied for the job. I passed the tech test and got the job! I was on my way up! I called my friend and thanked her. Throughout high school, Tammy and I had been good friends like April and Lisa were. Even though she had a boyfriend, my boyfriend taught her how to drive and often treated her to dinner when the three of us were out together. Tammy and I bought the same dresses for our junior prom and took our boyfriends as double dates.

I ended up going all out for senior prom and asked my grandfather's younger sister, who was a seamstress like my eldest aunt, to help me make a one-of-a-kind gown. I sketched my prom dress like I did back when I was nine, or ten, years old and had sketched outfits for me and my dolls. "My first love" rented a navy blue Rose Royce for the special occasion. Unfortunately, the driver hit a huge deer on the way to the prom. We were stranded until the next couple happened to come by.

We ended up arriving at the senior prom in a classic and corny, black stretch limo—like everybody else. My boyfriend made it up to me by taking me to the Poconos for the weekend. He rented a hotel suite with a champagne hot tub and heart-shaped bed. We were able to salvage the weekend after all.

By this time, my youngest aunt and her new husband were living in their house—near Irvington Park. My mother had since found her way back to my grandmother's house in Newark. I heard that my grandmother paid for my aunt's new house (along with a new car) and gave her money for new furniture. She was always doing things like that (buying things and buying people.) She would never admit it, but my grandmother's love came with a price. It didn't matter who you were. She was incapable of showing true love; so she bought people's love, affection, and loyalty by "helping" them get the things that they needed.

I didn't want my grandmother's help. I just wanted the "perfect" father for my perfect son (especially since I had never known my own father.) But my son's father was less than perfect. Throughout my life, I often felt all alone and wished I had the love of both a mother and a father. My son needed a father since I wouldn't be able to teach him how to be a man. That would be his father's job - but, based on his actions so far, my son's father was not cut out to be a father.

My grandfather had been the only father I had ever really known. He had been the one person who truly loved me. Although she had a mother and a father, my mother was a motherless child (like me.) She had not been loved and didn't know what "true" love felt like. Therefore, she didn't' know how to really love me! Now, my grandfather was gone. It happened soon after the accident. His truck had hit a small, white car. There was a head-on collision, (and just like that), they said his memory was gone. My grandfather died not long after my son was born.

When my grandfather died, I think a piece of each of us died with him. By the time of his funeral, we had become completely undone. My family was totally dysfunctional. I remember my eldest aunt blocking the doorway of my grandmother's house so that I couldn't come in. She was threatening that I "better not hurt my grandmother!" I thought—*What a thing to say!* I was hurting just like everybody else (probably even more so.) Surprisingly, my grandmother came to my defense and told my aunt to move her arm and let me in! After all, it was 11:00 p.m. and I had just driven (with my son crying in his car seat) all the way from the college campus in New Brunswick. I didn't know what was happening, but I remember my grandmother acting very strange. She had called and said that she was in pain. She said that her arm hurt and that I needed to come "home" right away!

I knew she wasn't telling the truth. I ran to my grandparents' bedroom. I knew he wasn't there, but I ran to his closet and looked for him anyway. I couldn't believe what was happening. I didn't understand. He couldn't be gone. All kinds of thoughts ran through my head. *Who would love me? Who would take care of me? Who would protect me? Who would help me raise my son, as a man?* I looked through my grandfather's closet in disbelief! I saw his clothes, his army green work shirts and his sweaters. I saw the gun that he always kept hidden on the shelf. I began to smell his shirts. I wanted to remember his scent. Tears rolled down my face. Just then, my grandmother walked over and handed me his watch.

I stood frozen, while everyone else began acting strangely. Even my youngest aunt began to act strange at my grandfather's funeral. I remember noticing my cousin crying and went to console her. My youngest aunt yelled at me and said, "I'm *her* mother!" (as if I didn't know that.) It was if my grandfather's death was causing the whole family to crumble right then and there. Instead of coming closer together, we became distant (and we haven't been right since.) We were already on a slippery slope of becoming a dysfunctional family, but his death seemed to take us over the edge.

My grandfather's death made me think about my father and what my life might have been like if he had been a part of it. I wondered if my mother would have ever gotten on drugs, or beat me the way she did. Maybe, I would not have gone through any of the things that I went through. I recalled the day that I saw my "father" on South Clinton Street. I had been playing hide-and-seek outside with Karen, Egypt, and my other friends. A strange, tall man wearing a black leather jacket approached me. He asked me my name and told me that I looked exactly like my mother. He called her by name.

I stared at him with confusion. I was never really good at hiding my emotions. As I got older, my stare down became a "screw face"—you know that look where your eyes and nose are squinted, and you look like something stinks. I wondered who this man was and how he knew my mother. I immediately guessed from his height and the questions he asked that he must have been my father. I remembered the pictures that my mother had shown me. I wished that I had the courage to come straight out and ask him, "Are you my father?"

I thought about all the other questions that I wanted to ask. I wanted to know where he had been all my life and why he had disappeared. I wondered if he had ever loved my mother and, if he did, why he had left her (left us.) I remembered the picture of my father that my mother showed me when I was five years old. He had a twin sister. She was light-skinned like my youngest aunt, and he had brown skin like me and my mother.

My mother said that my father was the football quarterback at the high school they attended. They went to her junior prom together, but she went with someone else to her senior prom. I wondered which of the two men my father was. My mother said that she was already pregnant with me by the time she went to her senior prom. She said—on the night of the senior prom—that my father's mother came to my grandmother's house and warned her to keep her "whore daughter" away from her son. Soon afterward, my father and his parents packed up and moved to Detroit.

I was told that my father came to see me when I was six months old. So many things had happened since then. Ten years had passed. My mother had long since given birth to me, and we had gone through some things. We lived a very challenging life. We had moved from my grandparents' house behind Weequahic high school, and I had suffered greatly at the hands of my mother for many years. By this time, I had run away from South Clinton Street more than once. Now, I was ten years old and would be abandoned (again.) If only I had met my father sooner, things might have been different. I might have lived and loved differently!

Other than my grandfather, I never really saw a man actually "love" and stay with a woman. I wondered what made men leave their women and children. In my mind, a man should not lie down with a woman if he didn't love her and want to be with her. I know that I was only a child, but this philosophy made sense to me. I was one to talk because (as it would turn out) I didn't love my son's father and did not want to stay with him.

My mother had no one to stay with her. My grandfather had tried to be a father to her, but something had gone wrong. Something had gone terribly wrong in my life too! Unfortunately, my "baby's daddy" turned out to be not such a nice person and a bad influence on my son. Although I tried my best to provide a stable life for my son, he became angry at the fact that his father was in and out of his life. The older he got, the angrier he became.

When our son was born, eyebrows were raised! He was light-skinned and had the curliest hair I had ever seen. Even I had to take a double look and laughed out loud in my head. Although he did not look anything like "my first love," he closely resembled my ex's mother because she too was light-skinned with curly hair. My son's father had the audacity to ask for a paternity test, which proved (99.999%) that he was the father. Regardless of the fact that our son did not look like him, there was no doubt in my mind who the father was.

Sometimes, I laugh out loud at the thought of him questioning me (because I would have chosen the option behind door number two, if I actually had a choice.) I had not seen "my first love" since April when he and I broke up in 1985. I talked on the phone with my son's father every night from the time we ran into each other on Memorial Day, until our first date on my birthday in July of that same year. He worked every night during the week, and we only spent the weekends together. I became pregnant in August, which was the very first time we had been together physically. Our son was born the following year, in May.

Still, this did not excuse the fact that my son's father acted like an asshole from day one. The physical and verbal abuse—and the constant insecurity... Besides, he is one to talk because it would come to light that he fathered another child outside of our relationship (who happens to be close in age with our son.) Shenanigans!

I knew that I had to step up to be a mother and a father to my son. I thought about how hard it had been being a single mother and a full-time student. I had given up all hopes of finding a high-quality daycare program that I could afford. I had lessened my school hours by decreasing my credits from 15 to 12, and I had increased my work hours. After classes, I worked on campus in the Student Dining Hall, making sub sandwiches and selling ice cream. On the weekends, I continued to work as a salesgirl at Joyce Leslie clothing store. This all happened before I began my career with AT&T.

My stupid and oh-so-cheap "baby's daddy" had talked me into the bright idea of getting on welfare so that he wouldn't have to pay child support. I hated the idea of getting on welfare because it reminded me of all the times that I waited on those long lines with my mother at the welfare office. We would get up at the crack of dawn and catch the bus downtown Newark (just to get government cheese, milk, cereal, and a few dollars.) Every month, I hated it more and more. Now, I would be doing the same thing!

The state caught up with me and was charging me with "conspiracy to commit fraud" because I received welfare while I was working. I was trying my best to raise my son… *But how else did they expect me to take care of my child with the little bit of money they were giving me?* I didn't serve time, but was found guilty of "theft/deception by fraud" and was placed on probation for one year. I was released on my own recognizance (ROR), which basically meant that I accepted responsibility for my own actions and would be required to pay the state back the money they had given me.

I also had to do two hundred hours of community service, which put a damper on my college life. My life was in turmoil and I wondered if I was being punished for my sins. My careless actions still didn't make his actions right. No matter how much you think you love a woman, there is no call to abuse her, emotionally or physically. After all I had gone through and everything that I had done for my son's father, he continued to mistreat me. He even went so far as to kidnap our son!

I thought back to when my son's father told me that his niece had been "kidnapped" by her father. It all sounded crazy to me and I wondered if that's when my son's father got the bright idea to kidnap *our* son. I reflected back to the time when my son's father didn't even believe that our son was his. Although I did not appreciate the accusation that I cheated on him, I couldn't blame him for asking the question because my son (with his caramel skin color and thick, curly hair) didn't have the same complexion, or blood type, as me or his father.

Thinking back to the day that my son went "missing," I remembered that his father got the brilliant idea to take my son from his childcare center in Irvington (without my knowledge and consent.) He was not on the pickup list, and the center director called me just in time! I left work immediately to go to the school, and my son's father was not there when I arrived. I was so glad that my son was still there! Unfortunately, this was not the first or the last time that his father attempted to kidnap him.

The first time was when I had just graduated from college and was working part-time, on the weekends. I had taken my son out of that dreadful daycare center, off campus on Davidson Road, where he caught a really bad diaper rash. I found a family from Pakistan to babysit for me while I worked. One day, my new babysitter's husband called me in hysterics. He was screaming and shouting, and I could barely make out what he was saying. I could hear his wife crying in the background.

Apparently, my son's father found out where my son was and decided to take him out of his care. We weren't together as a couple then, and I don't know how he could have known where the babysitter lived. He must have followed me there before. The family was in an uproar and extremely apologetic because they cared for me and my son very much. I drove around the school campus, frantically, trying to think where my son and his father might be. He was not at his job and didn't appear to be anywhere on campus.

Then, I remembered that my son's father had come to my job to pay me a little visit that same afternoon. He had never come to my job before. He seemed nicer and was in a much better mood than usual. At the time, I didn't pay much attention to the fact that he had actually offered to buy me an outfit. He was extremely cheap and had never bought me anything! My friend and coworker, Angie, was also surprised because I had told her how awful he was. She said, "He doesn't seem that bad buying you clothes and stuff." I laughed out loud in my head. My son's father left the store smiling, and I didn't hear from him at all that night.

I stopped home after work. I thought about everything that had transpired that day. I wondered why my son's father had come to the store. He had never done that before. I wondered why he hadn't called me from work, like he said he would. I had forgotten that his job was closed due to the holiday and decided to call him. There was no answer, so I rode out to his job. The parking lot was empty. Suddenly, it dawned on me that this was all part of his plan.

My son's father had taken our child! When I couldn't find him at work, or at his apartment, I realized that he must have taken our son to his parents' house in Newark. It was late and I was tired, but I was determined to find my son! I made the forty-five-minute drive to see if my hunch was right. My son's grandmother opened the door. She and I were not as close as me and my ex's mother, but she was nice and I liked her. Her husband was a different story.

My son's grandfather and I didn't seem to have much in common, except for the fact that we both thought we were chefs. Sometimes, we would have a debate about how long it took to cook a "perfect" pot of rice. We finally agreed that it takes exactly sixteen minutes to cook perfect rice. That was the "alouicious technique." That's what we called it when someone mastered a particular skill, such as cooking.

When I was a little girl, I would cook with my Betty Crocker Easy-Bake Oven. I would make little cakes and brownies - and you couldn't tell me a thing! I was born to be a chef! I laughed out loud in my head. I would later find out that we had more than the joy of cooking in common. I learned that we actually shared the same birthday, which was surprising to me because we were so different.

Then, something changed. He seemed softer... Nicer... I saw a sparkle in his eye. I stood still—remembering the smile he had on his face, as he sat in a chair on the porch of his house. He was holding his new grandson—my son—his son's son—for the very first time. He said, "I shouldn't hold the baby. I might break him!" I laughed out loud.

But here we were—now—and my son's grandmother didn't seem surprised to see me. In fact, she told me very calmly that she did not want to be in the middle of whatever was going on between me and her son. She left the door open slightly and walked away quietly, while I waited on the front porch. When she returned, she handed my son over to me with his blue diaper bag and closed the door just as quietly as she had walked away a few minutes before. Thus began the war between me and my son's father!

Sitting at my kitchen table, I stared at my son as he played—safe and sound. I had worked so hard to finish school, keep a job, maintain my car, and pay my rent. I was not going to sit by and let my son's father, or anyone else, take it all away from me. Still, I wondered about these so-called men and fathers.

I couldn't understand how they could claim to love us so much, but always ended up hurting us so badly. We were the women in their lives. We are the mothers of their children. I had been a mother and a father to my son. I thought about my own father (the strange man who I met on South Clinton Street, when I was ten years old.) There was still one burning question I wished that I had asked him—
Are you my father?

CHAPTER 11

Being Muslim

Growing up without a mother and father made me wish that I belonged to someone, or something. Over the years, I had plenty of time to think about my past and future life. I thought about who and what I wanted to become. I had made up my mind that I was never going to see my mother again—no matter what. She would never be the cause of me going through anything else! I tried to remember that life with my mother wasn't always bad. I recalled the times when we danced around the apartment (even when there was no light.) I remember the times when we watched old black-and-white movies, like *Mommie Dearest, Hush... Hush, Sweet Charlotte*, and *What Ever Happened to Baby Jane?*

My mother was a true fan of classic movies. I can't count the number of times that we watched Robert Redford and Barbara Streisand in *The Way We Were*! I became a fan of classic movies and actresses, such as Betty Davis and Joan Crawford so much so that I would later take classes in film and cinematography at Rutgers in Newark, over the summer. As much as I hated to admit it, my mother had a definite impact on my life. As I continued to think about my life and its turn of events, I continued to feel like I didn't belong—I didn't belong to anything, or anyone.

I thought about how Egypt and her family had taken me in and made me a part of their family. Egypt's family life was much like mine, except that her mother loved her. Her mother was often abused in the same way that my mother and youngest aunt were. Her father would talk to her mother like a dog and beat her so severely that she walked around with black eyes all the time. Egypt spent most of her time taking care of her mother, while I took care of the other children.

Egypt's mother and father seemed to live a very interesting life. They were "Five Percenters," which I thought meant that they followed the rules of Islam about five percent of the time. Although I had not seen Egypt and her family in a long time, I never stopped thinking of her little brother. I had thought of naming my son after her little brother because he too was so cute and perfect that I could just eat him up! I thought about all the times that he would try to pronounce my name. He would get so excited when he saw me coming down the street, as I walked home from school.

He and my son had the same hair texture, same skin tone, and same personality. They were both perfect! I decided not to name my son after Egypt's younger brother, but I chose a name that began with the same first initial as his. I figured that the same letter was close enough. Of course, I chose an Arabic name that meant "perfect and complete." My son's middle name was also Arabic and meant "gentle and kind." My first name means "merciful" and "compassionate." My middle name is also Arabic and means "pleasant and loved." I decided that my son and I would lead a Muslim life.

Growing up, I didn't make my son go to church. My mother never made me go to church either. As a matter of fact, she didn't go much herself. My grandmother was the churchgoer. She was the one who made everyone go to church, when we were all younger. Thinking back, I wish that I had made my son go. Maybe, things would have been different. Maybe, if I had given him the spiritual foundation that he needed as a child, he would have been more like me. But he wanted to be Muslim. He wanted to be more like his father.

Although his father was born Muslim, he didn't have the qualities that I had read about. He smoked. He drank. He was not a provider. And he was not a protector. Most of all, he was abusive! I had made the decision not to drink or smoke, when I was seven years old. The only thing that we both did religiously was not eat pork. I may not have given my son the spiritual foundation that he needed, but

I certainly provided him with a strong foundation at home. He had everything he needed as a child, except a good father.

In his heart, I'm sure my son's father wanted to be a good father. But his need to try and control me outweighed his need to be a good father to our son. Back then, everything he said and did was about control. He wanted to control how I dressed, what I did, and who my friends were. When I didn't do what he wanted, there was hell to pay. He always became so violent. He would rant and rave, tear up stuff, and curse at me. When that didn't work, things got physical!

The worse was when he would write nasty things on my door at college. Once again, I was reminded of how he would write, "You will be penalized!" He would tape that and other threats to the door. When I got my apartment, he would go through my clothes and things and leave them all over the place. Then, he would leave me nasty notes about my dirty laundry. One time, I didn't want to have sex with him… So, he pleasured himself and left it all over my bedroom wall. I didn't see it until I woke up the next morning. He was already gone.

Sometimes, I was so scared of him that I wondered if he would actually kill me. I didn't recall reading about any of these things in the Quran. The more I read, the more I learned that there was not much difference between the Ten Commandments in the Holy Bible and the Five Pillars of Islam. In addition to "Thou shall not lie, cheat, steal, kill, or covert thy neighbor's wife"—the things that seemed most important were believing in God, praying daily, and showing kindness and humbleness.

I thought back to my childhood. I thought about how my grandmother dragged me to church whenever she got the chance. I had seen pictures of me getting christened as a baby. I sang in the church choir. I was a Christian, but I had always been curious about Islam. I recalled my first introduction to Islam… I must have been about eight years old. My mother had broken up with her boyfriend, Will, for the first time.

It was just long enough for her to date the owner of the small grocery store beneath our apartment building. I can't recall the store owner's name or his son's name, but I remember that they were Muslim and both very cute. They were also very light-skinned (like my youngest aunt.) The son barely spoke, other than to say, "As-Salaam-Alaikum." Although he acted like he hated me, he was actually saying, "Peace be unto you." Maybe he hated the thought of having a new "cute little sister." I laughed out loud in my head.

Unlike most of my friends, he had a father and no mother. My mother's new boyfriend and his son lived in our apartment building on the corner of Wainwright Street and Chancellor Avenue, in Newark. I had never actually been inside their apartment—but, of course, I was sent downstairs to the store as often as possible. There I was, buying groceries with my colored food stamp coins. Actually, I preferred to buy food from the Muslim Steak-n-Take truck on the corner by the liquor store—but they didn't accept food stamps, or matching plastic coins.

As I continued to reminisce about my journey of being Muslim, I remembered how it was always challenging because my grandmother continued to take me and my cousins to church on Sundays. Sometimes, my cousins didn't go to church and I had to go alone (with my grandmother.) After my grandfather's accident, he lost his memory and my grandmother made him start going to church. That's how conniving she was! I never saw or heard my grandmother praying for my grandfather, but the next thing I knew—he was joining the Usher Board. Shenanigans!

It's not that church was a bad thing. It's just that my grandfather hated going to church and would never have gone, if he had full use of all his faculties. Nevertheless, church was interesting and I learned a lot from listening to the preachers. My cousins and I served on the Junior Usher Board, which meant that we wore all white while we stood in the back of the church and waited to take fans to the people who raised one finger.

Every now and then, it got exciting when a church member would "catch the Holy Ghost" and start screaming. The church nurse would come running down the aisle with a fan and a glass of water. My cousins and I would give the church nurse the "screw face" because passing out fans was *our* job! I was told that my family belonged to the church for many years and the same reverend pastored at the church since it was built. The pastor always dressed in the nicest suits, shirt, and tie. The pastor, at that time, was also light-skinned. He had "good" hair (curly like my son's), and he wore really nice shoes.

One of the deacons and his wife happened to live right next door to my grandmother's house, on Goldsmith Avenue, in Newark. Except for the large houses that were provided for pastors and graced Elizabeth Avenue with a scenic view of Weequahic Park, most of the houses in the Weequahic section looked alike. They were all two-family homes, with bricks that went around the bottom of the house and aluminum siding on the top half of the house. Newark was called *Brick City* partially because of its cobblestone and red brick streets, but mainly because of all the brick housing apartments (otherwise known as "the projects".) My mother and her two sisters grew up in the projects.

I was told that my great grandparents were originally from Philadelphia before moving to Newark. Saying the word "Philly" always made me think about Philly cheesesteaks. Although they were good, Philly cheesesteaks tasted nothing like the infamous "Steak-n-Takes" from the Muslim trucks on the corners of Newark. The one by our apartment sat right in front of the liquor store that my mother and I stole from on the way to the park most Saturdays.

One minute, I was stealing for my mother. The next minute, I was in church. Although I continued to go to church, Sunday visits to my grandmother's house became less and less frequent as I got older. I was still Christian, but I continued to learn about being Muslim. I began to compare the similarities and differences between Christianity and Islam. My grandmother owned a huge Bible, which she kept on a large wooden stand in the dining room. Her dining room window overlooked Untermann Field. Instead of watching the football games and the high school students run track on the field, I would sit in a huge chair in the corner of the dining room and read scriptures from the Bible.

I was also no stranger to the Islamic way of life, but I wanted to learn more. I asked Egypt's mother about the Arabic names and their meanings. I had completely stopped eating pork, by the time I was ten years old. At first, I laughed out loud at the thought of giving up bacon. And there was no way I could tell my grandfather that I was not going to eat his pickled pigs' feet. He brought them home from his truck-driving trips every week and stored them in glass mason jars in the basement. They actually tasted and smelled good, but were the most disgusting-looking things that I had ever seen. I was surprised to learn that the Bible also supports the ideology that eating swine is unhealthy. (Leviticus 11:7–8); (Isaiah 65:4)

On my twenty-fifth birthday, I took my Shahada at the Masjid in Newark. I remember it like it was yesterday. I learned how to make Salat. I longed to go to Mecca. It was the Holy Land where Muslims took their pilgrimage. I was told that only men could make that journey. I became familiar with the seven conditions for making Salat the correct way. I thought back to the first time that I prayed in Arabic. Before making Salat, I made Wudu (which is a special way that Muslims wash their hands before eating and praying.) I purchased a prayer rug, rolled it up, and put it away after each prayer to keep it clean.

The Sheik gave me a Quran, and I was guided by an Imam, as I started the next chapter of my life. I had long gotten past the challenges of not eating pork. I replaced pork bacon with beef bacon and started using ground turkey to make chili. The challenge had now become wearing my hijab to cover my hair. I never really wore makeup, so that wasn't a big problem. I began purchasing different-colored hijabs and learned how to wear them properly. I finally felt like I belonged to something. I was going to be a good Muslim—a proud Muslim.

I learned that one of the main beliefs in being Muslim is that there is no Trinity. Muslims do not believe in the Father, the Son, and the Holy Ghost. The Quran teaches that Allah is God, and Jesus is a prophet - a messenger. Soon after taking my Shahada, I dated the brother of a close friend. He bought me a huge picture of Malcolm X. It was our very first date, and we saw the picture being finished by a young man on the corner of Broad and Market, in Newark. It was a black-and-white chalk drawing, which I still have hanging on the wall to this day.

The first time that I fasted for Ramadan, I was surprised that I made it through the entire month. I only ate before sunrise and at sundown, and drank water only when I felt like I was about to pass out. Before eating, I asked Allah to bless me and the food that I was about to eat by saying "Bismillah." Being Muslim meant more than making Salat and not eating pork. Back then, Muslims were known as the Black guys who stood on the corners with their black suits and bow ties (selling bean pies and newspapers.) But I learned a very important fact. All Muslims were not Black! Muslims of all skin colors, and of all races, could pray and work together.

I had a full-time job and had begun to leave work early on Friday afternoons so that I wouldn't miss Jumu'ah at the Masjid at one o'clock. Muslim prayer was held at different times for the men and women. After Jumu'ah, I would often go and meet with the Sheik to discuss my future. The Sheik always made it a point to let me know which men were interested in becoming my husband.

I always laughed out loud in my head at this thought because I was not interested in any of the Muslim men I saw there. I knew that there was an expectation of Muslim women to marry Muslim men. But, somehow, my son's father had painted a horrible image of life with a Muslim husband. It made me think back to when I struggled to become independent of my mother and grandmother. I had also remained independent of men.

I had long since left the nest, so to speak. As a young woman, I had a new apartment and lived alone with my beautiful and "not-so-perfect" son. I remember how I applied for Section 8 and was denied. They said that I made too much money. I was disappointed, but proud—no Section 8, no welfare, and no more food stamps. I was doing things on my own!

Along with education and religion, I had been taught the importance of being independent. I was determined to make a good life for me and my son, even if it meant doing it all by myself. I liked being Muslim, but I was not ready to be a wife. By the time I was in my thirties, my curiosity had grown even more, and I continued to learn from the Quran while reading the Bible from front to back. The first two scriptures that I learned in the Bible were the Lord's Prayer and Psalm 23. I was particularly moved by verse 4, which reads, "Yea, though I walk through the valley of the shadow of death, I will fear no evil for thou art with me."

The custody battles between me, my grandmother, and my son's father began when I was in my early thirties. Around that time, I started to watch Joel Osteen on TV and began to post scriptures around the mirror on my bedroom dresser. To this day, I still have Post-it notes of Psalm 4:1, "Give me relief from my distress, be merciful to me and hear my prayer"; Psalm 37:8, "Refrain from anger and turn from wrath"; and Psalm 139:23–24, "Search me and know my heart, test me and know my anxious thoughts, see if there is any offensive way in me and lead me in the way everlasting."

At times when I am beyond hope, I find solace in the words from Isaiah 54:17, "No weapon formed against me shall prosper," and Romans 8:31, "If God be for me, who dare be against me." I have continued to learn from Philippians 4:13, "I can do all things through Christ who strengthens me!" Being Muslim taught me to be a better Christian.

Islam gave me a whole new perspective on life because it was more than a religion. It was a way of life! I learned about excellence, integrity, and perseverance. I was taught to be humble, to be merciful, and to have compassion. I learned the true meaning of my Islamic name, and I learned that patience is a virtue. More importantly, I learned that things may not happen when we want them to, but they happen in God's time. We may not like it, but everything happens for a reason.

The times that we question God because something in our lives didn't happen the way that we wanted it to are the times that we should trust in Him the most! In education—and in life, we've learned that an "A" usually stands for amazing, awesome, and above average; whereas an "F" means failure. But in life, an "F" can be a good thing. During one of his Sunday sermons, Joel Osteen preached about the hurt and pain that "the three Fs"—flood, fire, and famine—can bring. He then went on to say that such trauma prepares you for transition and "the good F" (Favor) would bring you into a "new level of your destiny."—(October 9, 2017)

Throughout my life, I have always felt like I was going through a storm. Each storm seemed worse and different than the one before. The one thing that stayed the same was my trust in God! My faith has always brought me through the storm! My loss may not have been as tragic as some of the people who lost love ones and homes in an actual storm. Nonetheless, I have suffered! I've felt so broken down and so tired. But no matter what we lose and how we suffer, God always brings us through the storm. Sometimes, it's a short rain - And other times, it's a hurricane.

No matter who you are and what God you believe in, know that there is a God watching over you. I continue to have faith and start each day with a positive thought, by taking the time to think about all the good things that have happened in my life. In the past, I was torn between living my life in Christianity as a Baptist and living my life in Islam as a Muslim. I've always been spiritual and intrigued by both Islam and Christianity—and, as I strive to be closer to God, I'm learning to be more disciplined. Each time I pray, my prayers are answered. In His time… I pray daily. *I trust in Him! I believe in Him! I thank Him!* No matter where I am or what I do, I try to remember that I am one of God's children—and *He* is my father!

CHAPTER 12

A Brush With Death

I have always had faith in God. I had tried to be a good person, a good mother, a good Christian, *and* a good Muslim. In Islam, Muslims say, "Inshallah"—which means "If it is the will of God." I wondered if this was God's will. My son had been diagnosed with Lymphoma, a cancer of the abdomen. A malignant tumor had grown and was taking him away from me! He was only twelve years old! *How could God let this happen?* I drew from my inner strength, as I listened to the doctors telling me that my son only had three days to live!

I had to make a decision very quickly because my son was dying. I couldn't breathe! I couldn't think! I didn't know who to call first! I thought about calling my grandmother because I knew how much she had grown to love my son. However, her love for my son was not always evident (just as her love for me was not always evident.) I remembered how she had tried to sell me on the idea of getting an abortion. She told me to think about how a baby would ruin her life and my future. I wondered how *my* baby would ruin *her* life. He had nothing to do with her, and he was not her child! *Besides, how could my perfect son ruin anyone's life?*

My son was dying, and I couldn't fathom the thought of losing the one thing—the only person—who really mattered in my life! My grandfather was already gone. My mother was gone (missing in action), and I still wasn't quite over all the hurt that she and my grandmother had caused me. My grandmother and my eldest aunt were in cahoots (again.) Trying to control my life. I thought about how they suddenly became interested in my future as a model. Before I got pregnant, all they ever talked about was getting a good education. Then, there was a sudden turn of events and a sudden interest in my modeling "career". Before, they had always said that modeling was only a hobby.

My grandmother and my eldest aunt were so conniving. They actually pretended to care about my dream of becoming a high-fashion model in New York City. My eldest aunt married a photographer and modeled occasionally for him. After school, I remembered how I would watch her practice her poses. Her husband would often take pictures of me in Weequahic Park. He also set up a photography studio in the attic of their house to take pictures of us. One day, he took black-and-white pictures of me for my portfolio.

As I drifted down memory lane, the doctor's voice startled me. I heard him calling my name, as I was sitting in a waiting-room chair. He was telling me that he needed both parents' signatures before they could operate on my son. I thought that was odd since I had been the only one raising him up until that point. It had been hours since I left the voice message for his father. I decided to call his father immediately after I called my grandmother. I was trying to figure out what "malignant" meant. I was sure that it meant something bad, but I had no idea that it meant my son—my one and only child—was going to die from cancer!

We needed to sign the release forms that would allow the doctors to perform surgery on our son. Then, the doors to the waiting room flew open, and his father came running through them. He grabbed me, and we hugged each other with deep compassion. For the first time since our son was born, his father and I were crying together. Tears ran down his face, as I told him what the doctor had said. The initial shock of hearing that our son might only have three days to live would last for quite a while.

My son's father signed his name below mine, and I dropped to my knees and prayed. I wasn't sure which God would answer my prayers. I knew the Bible backward and forward and could recite any verse of any scripture. I still knew how to pray in Arabic, but had not been to the Masjid in a while. After what seemed like an eternity, the doors to the operating room flew open, and the doctor announced that our son had survived surgery. They were rolling him down the hall to the recovery room.

I closed my eyes and thanked God! I kept my eyes closed, as I reminisced about the events that took place prior to us coming to the hospital. It was a Saturday, and I had taken my son and a few of his friends to Seaside Heights. We loved going to the beach on the weekends. It was the one thing that I loved doing since I was a child. My son and his friends were on a Ferris wheel, and I could hear my son screaming.

I sat on the bench close to the rides and carried all the bags. It was getting late, and I was tired. I watched my son run toward me with his hand on his stomach. He told me that he was tired too. I told him to sit and rest for a while. A few minutes later, my son told me that his stomach hurt really badly. I gathered his friends and drove them home. When we got to our house, I gave my son a spoonful of Pepto-Bismol and told him to lie down on his bed. Instead, my son laid in my bed, which he often did when he was watching TV or didn't feel well.

I was awakened by a scream. I realized that it was coming from my son, who was still lying next to me. I grabbed my pocketbook and rushed my son to the emergency room at Irvington General Hospital. We had never gone to that hospital before because everyone said that it was worse than Beth Israel. In this case, I thought it would be okay because it was the closest to our house. My son and I sat in the emergency room of Irvington General Hospital for over three hours.

We had been checked in, but no doctor had been to see us and my son was in pain. I yelled at every person who walked by us. Finally, a lab technician came and escorted us to a room where we sat for another three hours. My son, his friends, and I had left Seaside Park at 6:30 p.m. My son and I had been at the hospital since 10:30 p.m. The tech had brought us into the room three hours later, at 1:30 a.m. It was now going on 5:00 a.m., and we had not been seen by a doctor yet!

I yelled at the tech as he walked by the room where my son and I were waiting. He was surprised that no one had been to see us. The tech asked me what was wrong with my son. I explained that we had gone to Seaside Heights and left in a hurry because my son was complaining of a stomachache. The tech hooked up a monitor and listened to my son's heartbeat and took his temperature. He took notes of other vital signs and told me to wait while he went to get a doctor. The tech came back immediately and asked me if my son had ever been sick before. I was scared.

My son had never been ill, and I couldn't understand what was going on. I wondered why the lab technician was acting so peculiar. When the doctor finally arrived to the room, he and the tech talked privately and spoke in codes. The next thing I knew, we were being rushed off to Beth Israel Medical Center in Newark, which is where I would have normally taken my son if I had not been in a rush. I was screaming at the doctors that I could not leave my car at Irvington General Hospital for fear that it would get towed or stolen, as it had been so many times before.

I followed the ambulance from Irvington to Newark and parked on Lyons Avenue across from the hospital, which was not much safer than where I was parked in Irvington. The doctor explained that he would need to work with another specialist from the hospital and would be flying in a top surgeon from the Sloan Kettering Cancer Center in New York. I walked around in a daze. My head was clouded with thoughts that I couldn't understand and questions that weren't answered. I wondered why this was happening to me—to *my* son. The nurse suggested that I go home to get enough clothes to stay at the hospital for a few days.

A few days turned into several months, during which time of course my car was broken into. But I would have to deal with that another time. I wasn't exactly sure why, but my son's father had disappeared... I was pretty sure that it had something to do with the fact that my "first love" and my ex-fiancé both came to the hospital to see about me and my son. I remember actually standing outside my son's hospital room, trying to explain to his father that he was not the only one who cared about me and our son. *God forbid!* When he finally showed up, the nurse wouldn't let him into my son's room because she didn't know who he was and visiting hours were over. I thank God every day that the "three-day death sentence" never came to fruition and, two years later, my son's cancer was in remission. The first year, most of our time was spent at the hospital with my son receiving chemotherapy, radiation, bone marrow tests, spinal taps, and blood transfusions. I felt so proud that many of my friends and coworkers were willing to donate.

Most of the second year was spent taking my son back and forth to the hospital to receive outpatient treatment. Every time he got a fever, we had to go back to the hospital. It seemed like his temperature was 103, or 104, every day. We spent four out of seven days in the hospital. Three days were to make sure he was not at risk for infection due to the fever. The fourth day was spent receiving chemo through his portacath, which had been inserted in his upper chest. We were always closer than we had ever been during those four days. I wanted to make sure my son was okay, and I never left his side.

I arranged for a nurse to come to the house weekly to give my son the injection that would increase his white blood cells. I stayed on top of his schoolwork. I was doing all that I could to take care of my son. I wanted to help him. I wanted him to be okay. I was so tired. I wondered who would help me. I prayed to God for something, or someone, to take away our pain and to get us through this thing.

Sometimes, while my son slept, I thought about volunteering at the hospital and working with the boarder babies. Strangely, this soothed me and took my mind off things for a little while. As if it were a sign from God, my inspiration came through a little girl who had been admitted to the hospital and was also fighting cancer. The little girl was only six years old, but she was strong and brave. Some nights, she slept in the room with me and my son, in the Pediatric Intensive Care Unit (PICU).

One night, as she began to fall asleep in my arms (in the recliner next to my son's bed) Shakira told me that her last wish was to eat spinach and to own a Barbie Townhouse. Later that night, after she and my son had fallen asleep, I went home to cook some sautéed spinach. Then, I went to Toys R Us on Route 22 to buy the Barbie Townhouse. When I returned to the hospital, my son was awake. I went to Shakira's room to leave the spinach on her food tray and to set up the dollhouse. She was sleeping. Her family was there. They came to my son's room to thank me and to tell me that Shakira woke up with a smile on her face. Her father laughed at the fact that his daughter preferred my sautéed spinach to his collard greens. I smiled. Shakira died three days later.

After she passed, I thought about her smile. I thought about all of the times that she had fallen asleep in my arms, while I rocked her in the large recliner that sat in the corner of my son's room. She was so sweet and innocent, just like a baby. I usually ate lunch with my son and fell asleep in the chair next to his bed. I would often sneak out of my son's room, after he fell asleep. Every night, I would help the nurses care for the babies. It made me feel good to feed the babies, to change their diapers, and to rock them to sleep.

The nurses told me that the babies had been abandoned by their mothers. They were left in blankets, or cardboard boxes, in front of the hospital. The hospital was their safe place too. It was a place where drug addicts, unwed mothers, and other women who couldn't take care of their babies could leave them without recourse. I felt for the babies. I felt connected to them. I wanted to help them, even if it only meant changing a diaper and feeding them.

Lying in the hospital bed next to my son, I thought about how much he had grown over the years. I remembered his first ten years and how close we were. I thought about the year when we met my "ex-fiancé." I had stayed at work that day until 5:15 p.m., which was later than I intended. I knew that I needed to leave work no later than 5:00 p.m., in order to get to the school to pick up my son on time. Aftercare for my son was becoming a huge problem.

Because of my son's behavior in school, I had been late to work every day for the past two weeks (which meant that I had to stay late every night to make up my time.) I couldn't afford to have my paycheck docked. I also couldn't afford the late fees at the school. Traffic was crazy, and I was sweating bullets. I was trying to rack my brain and figure a way out of this mess. I wondered how I could keep my job and keep my son in the afterschool program.

I really liked the private school, and I particularly liked the director because she reminded me of who I wanted to become. I thought about my vision, as I sat in traffic. I cut down a side street and noticed a crazy—but very cute—guy waving his arms, frantically, in the air. My first thought was - *Here we go again!* Another man had stopped dead in the middle of the street to get my attention, just like my "baby's daddy."

The man was tall, bald, and had very dark skin. He was extremely bowlegged and had the most gorgeous smile I had ever seen. I pressed my foot on the brake and slowed the car down. Although the street-light was still a few cars ahead, it was green, and I really had no excuse to be sitting in the middle of the street. As the "cutie" approached my car, I checked my face in the mirror. I still didn't wear makeup at the time, and I wanted to make sure that I looked cute. I hoped that my hair, nails, and outfit were in check. I rolled my window only halfway down, just in case the cutie was a deranged killer. I laughed out loud!

The cute guy smiled and asked why I was laughing. I lied and said that I was laughing at the way he ran to my car, which was half-way true. As this tall, well-built, bowlegged man, with a smile to die for approached my car, images of our future wedding passed through my mind. I was amazed at my own thoughts. I had thought about it briefly with my "first love" and my son's father, but I never really had this vision before! I sat in the middle of the street—in my car—dreaming of walking down the aisle.

Until that very moment, I had been opposed to marriage (for most of my life) because I had never really seen a good one. The only marriage that was even worth thinking about was my grandparents' marriage, which—thanks to my grandfather—seemed pretty solid. "Mr. Cutie" walked up to the car and introduced himself by telling me his first name. He asked me my name and then asked if I had a pen. I was happy that he didn't have his number already written down on a piece of paper. That would have made it feel like he picked up girls on a regular basis.

After he gave me his number, I folded the small piece of paper up like it was gold and put it in my pocketbook. I smiled as I watched my new friend walk back down the street. As he walked away, I noticed that there were at least five other cute guys waiting for him. As he got closer to his friends, "Mr. Cutie" ran the rest of the way and slapped them "high five!" I was thirty minutes late picking my son up. The school was about ten minutes from where I met my new "cutie" in the middle of the street. I had to pay a ten-dollar late fee (five dollars for every fifteen minutes.)

I picked up my gorgeous, but "not-so-perfect" son from the after-school program. Although he was only eight years old, he understood me better than anyone else in the world. I had finally made the decision to leave his father for good a few years earlier. My son and I were joined at the hip, and he had become my confidant. I smiled as I told him all about the cute, bowlegged, dark-skinned guy with the pretty smile. My son knew me all too well and asked all the right questions, such as "What does he look like?" "Where does he live?" "What does he do?"

I thought back to the time when my son was two years old, and he heard me and my mother yelling at one another. She was in another one of her drunken stupors and was belting out obscenities. I will never forget the words that I heard next - "Leave my mommy alone, Grammy!" That's what my baby told her and that's what he called her, before she disappeared from our lives (again.) I felt so proud!

I continued to reminisce. I thought about how my son and I were like bookends, until shortly after his brush with death. We would spend all of our time, sharing every detail of every day. I knew all about his schoolboy crushes, and he knew about all of my "school-girl" crushes. I had kept my struggles with his father a secret. I also kept the relationship that I had with my mother and grandmother a secret. That had been my way of protecting him. I wish that I had a way of protecting him from getting cancer.

CHAPTER 13

The Pregnant Stripper

I wish that my son had not heard us. He lie across his bed crying because he overheard me arguing with my *soon-to-be* ex-fiancé. I tried to explain the whole story to him but, somehow, he thought that he was to blame for the breakup. I explained that this couldn't be further from the truth and that his misbehavior in school had nothing to do with my decision to call off the wedding. I never told my son about his father's infidelities because I knew how much he loved him. However, I decided that I was going to tell him the whole truth about my ex-fiancé.

We cried together and hugged each other, as I told him the story about the pregnant stripper. By the time my son was eight, he seemed to accept the fact that his father was no longer in the picture. But he made it abundantly clear that he preferred his father over any other man in my life. Growing up, my son preferred to spend most of his time watching *Thank God It's Friday* or TGIF (as it was often referred to.) Our "special" night included a choice of pizza from Big Joe's, or shrimp and broccoli from the Chinese Halal restaurant on Chancellor Avenue in Newark.

Eating extra cheese pizza with beef pepperoni from Big Joe's and watching *Family Matters* were part of our Friday night ritual. Every Friday, I gave my son a choice of watching TGIF or going on a "date night." Our home life seemed so perfect, and I couldn't figure out where I had gone wrong. My son was no longer a little boy, and everything had changed. I thought back to when he was two years old when my great-grandmother (my grandfather's mother) and I had worked together to potty-train him.

Unbeknownst to me, this was another one of my grandmother's ploys to control us. Against my wishes, she had arranged for my great-grandmother to keep my son on nights and weekends so that I could work and finish school. She said that this was also a chance for my great-grandmother to earn some extra money. I would drive for forty-five minutes to Maplewood and back to the campus two nights each week. I only had two more months before graduation, and I needed to continue working. So I agreed, even though I already had a babysitter right on campus.

I received financial aid for my college tuition, but I still needed money for rent, my car payment, and to take care of my son. After graduation, we moved back to Irvington. By the second grade, he had already been kicked out of two schools. He attended the after-school program at the daycare center and later went to the Boys and Girls Club in Union. I remember trying to figure out how to tape episodes of *Melrose Place* on Wednesday nights so that I wouldn't miss my son's basketball games each week.

I continued to think about our lives and how things had begun to change. I remembered all of my son's favorite shows, including *Full House* and *Boy Meets World*. He and I would play a card game of "Five Hundred", if he didn't fall asleep after his shows went off. This particular night, my son seemed to have a vested interest in staying awake.

It was 10:15 p.m., and I was determined to call "Mr. Cutie" before 10:30 p.m. I thought that calling too close to 11:00 p.m. (or after) would appear disrespectful of a lady, such as myself. I laughed out loud in my head. I reached for the phone and dialed the telephone number that was written on a small piece of crumbled paper. I had taken the piece of paper out of my pocketbook, soon after my son and I arrived at our apartment.

All evening, I had been contemplating the moment when I would call. I wondered what I would say and what questions I would ask. I kept thinking about the events of the day and how I came to meet "Mr. Cutie." A deep, husky voice answered the phone. I almost didn't recognize the voice because of the accent. I asked for my new friend by name.

He responded by repeating his name and I could tell that he was smiling, with that gorgeous smile. "Mr. Cutie" must have overheard my son in the background and asked what we were playing. I explained that my mother taught me how to play "Five Hundred" as a young child, and I had recently taught my son. I told him that growing up, I had learned to play Spades, Monopoly, and Pokeno. Playing these games were part of our family tradition, before my life changed.

We finished playing cards, while I tried to listen to what "Mr. Cutie" was saying on the phone. My son won the game. His favorite shows were over. Most of the pizza was gone. He was off to bed, and I was ready to devote my undivided attention to "my new man."

We talked until midnight. This went on every night and every weekend for several months. "Mr. Cutie" took me and my son to the lake off Route 80, every Saturday. He introduced us to his family and friends—the five guys who waited for him on the street the day we met. He had two younger sisters and one younger brother. His mother and father seemed happily married and owned a house in Irvington. It was the same house where he approached me in the middle of the street.

I thought that his parents would judge me for giving birth to a son at such a young age because they seemed very traditional, but they never said anything (at least not to my face.) After several months of dating, we still spent every night talking on the phone until midnight. He had become a part of our TGIF routine and was learning how to play "Five Hundred", even though he couldn't beat us.

"Date night" previously meant eating dinner at Red Lobster and catching a movie at Menlo Mall, or on Route 22, with my son. Things had changed, and we would be eating dinner with "Mr. Cutie." It had been about six months, and one night in particular was different than the others. I lie across my bed, as I often did, and giggled on the phone like a schoolgirl. I stopped laughing, and my face became very serious, as I tried to make sure that I heard what I thought I heard.

It sounded like "Mr. Cutie" said the three words that I longed to hear. I wanted to be sure, so I sat up straight in my bed and asked him to repeat himself. I put my ear as close to the phone as I could and waited with bated breath. I heard the three words, "I love you!" I took a deep breath and repeated the words back. I said, *"I love you too!"*

"Mr. Cutie" acted surprised, as if he didn't already know that. We sat on the phone in silence for the next few minutes, waiting for the other person to say something. He told me that he had loved me for a while, but he had just gotten up the nerve to tell me so. I knew better than to press the issue by asking him why he felt that way. Instead, I reaffirmed my love for him and changed the subject by asking if he was going to call me the next day.

When we hung up the phone, I ran into my son's room (like a schoolgirl) and screamed the good news. My son was excited for me. Secretly, I knew that he still hoped for me and his father to get back together. My son told me that he was happy for me and that he liked "Mr. Cutie." We smiled at each other, hugged, and fell asleep.

The next night, "Mr. Cutie" did not call at his usual time, and I became worried. I wasn't really sure why I was worried. The phone rang, and I ran to my bedroom to answer it. We fell into our normal routine of talking on the phone all night, until midnight. My "baby's daddy" had long established a routine of not showing up to pick up our son for the weekend. This resulted in me and my son spending weekends together with "Mr. Cutie." He didn't seem to mind because he really liked my son.

One year later, he moved into my apartment and the three of us continued to be inseparable. Two years later, I bought a house. I had read about a first-time homeowners program whereby a person with a good credit score and at least $5,000 could qualify for a mortgage loan. I had a little over $10,000 in the bank and a credit score of 805. My grandmother had taught me a long time ago to always save my money. She would say, "Save every penny and every dime." - "Save all your change and put at least ten dollars away from each paycheck." When I told my grandmother my plans, she said that she was proud of me because I was the only one in the family who had never asked her for money. That's when she told me that my grandfather had left me $15,000 in his will. Besides that, she told me the house in Newark - the one in the Weequahic section - the one that I grew up in - "belonged" to me!" Apparently, my grandfather had also left *that* to me in his will. I was shocked and confused... My grandfather had been dead for ten years! *Why was she telling me this now?*

My first thought was to take all of the money - the $5,000 and the rest from my savings - the $15,000 from my grandfather - the $8,000 from my tax refund - and open my own business! I had always wanted to have my own childcare center. This would be a dream come true! Then, after a little research, I found out that $30,000 would only be a drop in the bucket. It was hardly enough to start a successful business. I came back to my senses. I would pay off my car so that I could use that money toward paying my monthly mortgage. I would purchase some new furniture and put the remainder of the money back into my savings. I would buy my first house! It would be a great investment. More importantly, it would be the start of a new future - a future with me, my son, and my "Mr. Cutie".

"Mr. Cutie" moved into the new house, and the three of us became the perfect family. Our new house was a one-family home. I had decided a long time ago that I did not want to live in a two-family house (like my grandparents' house in Newark), or a three-family house (like the one in Irvington where my mother and I had gone through it.)

As usual, my grandmother tried her best to control me and the entire situation. She wanted to help me choose the house that my son and I would live in. This reminded me of the time when she tried to convince me to let her "buy" me a car. It was the time when I was to pay her the monthly note rather than the car dealership because this would save me money! I laughed out loud in my head.

She also tried to convince me that going to the laundromat would also save me money. There she was, trying to "help" again! My grandmother said that I would never be able to afford my own washing machine and clothes dryer after purchasing a new home. I told her that I saw a great deal for a washer/dryer set at Sears for $450! Shenanigans!

I would pay my mortgage without her help and continue to raise my son all by myself. It was my decision, not hers. Of course, my "Mr. Cutie" was a major part of that plan, or so I thought. Although he was part of the plan, I kept enough money stored away for a rainy day. One of my mother's life lessons was that a woman should never count on a man for anything. My grandmother—though she often counted on my grandfather—had instilled those same values in me.

My mother and grandmother always said that a woman should be able to take care of herself. My grandmother believed that a woman should never leave home without enough money to get her back home on a bus or in a taxicab, if necessary. It was because of their beliefs about a woman's worth that I became so independent. One of the most important things that I learned from my mother and grandmother was that education was power, power was money, and a woman should always have her own money.

I chose a reasonable mortgage that I could afford to pay on my own. I paid all the bills and never asked "Mr. Cutie" to contribute. That was my first mistake. I cooked, cleaned, and "serviced" my new man every night. Those were my second, third, and fourth mistakes.

We decided to talk to "Mr. Cutie's" parents about our future. We wanted to get their opinion about our relationship, seeing how their relationship was so perfect. Although his father and I rarely spoke, his mother and I had become very close. I had begun to eat Sunday dinners at their house on a regular basis. Everything was going great. Things were going well at home and at work.

Out of nowhere, my supervisor offered me a promotion, with a higher salary and a chance to travel. I traveled around the country (from state to state) over the next couple of months. When school was out and whenever possible, I made arrangements for my son to fly out to visit me wherever I was staying. "Mr. Cutie" also visited, whenever he could. Most of my trips were for days at a time, and it began to take a toll on our relationship.

The feelings that I started to have reminded me of the feelings that I had when I first left for college. I felt unsettled and unsure, like I was about to lose something very important—just as I did when I lost "my first love." I tried to remember that I was doing a good thing. I knew that it would take a village to help me with my son during that year. But, after the cancer scare, I was sure that we could get through anything! This was for our future—for me and my son, and for me and my future husband. I was a good person, a good mother, a good worker, and a good woman! I couldn't figure out why I felt so worried. I felt insecure. We began to argue every day.

"Mr. Cutie" wasn't answering my phone calls and had become distant. Before I left for my California trip, he told me that we belonged together. He assured me that I was his "right arm," and he was mine. I believed him, or at least I wanted to believe him. We tried our best to make things work. I was home for a long weekend, and he and one of my closest friends from work (along with her husband) had taken a day trip to New York. They had been gone all day, and I knew why.

I was pretty sure that they had gone shopping to buy my engagement ring, although no one ever said anything. I was right! Two weeks after the mysterious day that "Mr. Cutie" and my best friend went missing in action, he proposed to me! I was home for a three-week stay. Most of my trips out of state were from Monday to Thursday with the weekend home. Sometimes, I stayed out of town for weeks at a time and would get to spend the next week home (with my new family.)

This was one of those weeks where I had combined my one week off with a two-week vacation to get the three weeks off from work. I was happy to spend the time off with my new family—my son and my new man. Mr. Cutie grabbed me by the arm and pulled me into the dining room. He dropped to the floor and got on one knee. He pulled out a small, cheap-looking gold box with a red ribbon tied around it. I thought he was kidding because I knew that my best friend would have warned him against using *that* box! When I opened the box, tears ran down my face. I was so caught up in the moment that I forgot all about the cheap, ugly box. The ring was beautiful!

It was a gold band with a huge round diamond in the center. I was mesmerized more by the fact that I was becoming engaged than about the ring itself, even though I had been learning all about engagement rings. I had become an "expert" on diamonds because I suspected that I would be getting married to "Mr. Cutie" in the very near future. My best friend called, and I told her about every detail of the engagement (step by step.) In return, she told me about the day that she, her husband, and my new "fiancé" went missing in action. We laughed together over the phone, as we swapped stories.

I thought things were going well, but my son had begun to act out immensely. He had gotten thrown out of school for the fourth time. I wanted everything to work out perfectly, but my "perfect" life had begun to unravel (again.) I wondered if my son wished for me to remain single and unhappy for the rest of my life! I wondered why he couldn't be as happy for me as he was for his father. I decided to ignore all the signs and proceed with my wedding plans.

The first thing that I needed to do was to exchange my ring and that cheap, ugly box. The box looked like something that came out of the bubble gum machine! However, I was surprised beyond belief when I went to get the ring appraised. I found out that I wasn't the only jewelry "expert." My grandmother had taught me all about the quality of gold (10k, 14k, 18k, and 24k), but my best friend had clearly taught "Mr. Cutie" all about the quality of diamonds. I learned that my engagement ring was close to top-notch!

The band was 18-carat yellow gold, centered with a 2-carat round diamond (I-color, VS1 clarity.) The jeweler on Canal Street in downtown Manhattan told me that the lower the alphabet (meaning letters D through I), the clearer the color of the diamond. On the other hand, the higher the alphabet (meaning letter S, T, U, V), the clearer the quality of the diamond. My engagement ring wasn't flawless, but valued at almost $7,000. *That's a lot of Cracker Jacks!* I laughed out loud in my head.

I exchanged the ring for a solitaire Marquise diamond setting with the same color and quality. The ring cost a little less money than the one my new fiancée had purchased, and I decided to buy us 14-carat gold matching wedding bands. I presented the new wedding bands to "Mr. Cutie", one day after church. Things started to fall back into place and everything was going along as planned, or so it seemed.

Then, out of nowhere, I got the call. A strange woman called me one day after work to tell me that she had been sleeping with my man. I thought there was no way that this could be true. It had to be a lie! My man was no cheater. He was part of my new family—the part that made us whole. He was not just my man. He was my fiancé.

The young woman explained how she had met my fiancé at work four months earlier, while I was working in California. They had dated off and on, and had slept together twice. He tried to break up with her and had stopped returning her calls. She was pissed. I was pissed too and wanted to find out the truth.

I waited patiently for my fiancé to come home from work. I had taken a bubble bath and soaked in my favorite body wash from Pier 1. I lie across my bed in his favorite position and greeted my fiancé with a smile, as he walked through the bedroom door. I asked my fiancé about his day at work and asked if he had anything he wanted to share with me.

"Mr. Cutie" told me that he had a good day at work and assured me that everything was fine. He had a puzzled look on his face. As I began to tell my fiancé about the strange phone call that I received from the strange woman, the look on his face became more and more perplexed. I had seen this look before and knew that it meant my fiancé was lying.

I thought about the time when I caught my "first love" cheating and asked him about the gift boxes under the bed. He had lied about the shirts and the phone calls from Goldie (the oh-so fabulous cheerleader.) The look on "Mr. Cutie's" face told me that he was lying to me the same way that my "first love" did. It was happening all over again!

My fiancé was sticking to his story that he had not cheated on me, and I had no "real" proof or reason to believe otherwise. I knew that I was treading on thin ice, but decided to ask his best friend. My fiancé's best friend had become a third wheel in our relationship. He was one of the five guys hanging around, when "Mr. Cutie" and I first met. The other guys were still around too, but his best friend "Mr. Third Wheel" was *always* around.

I knew that he must have known the whole truth and nothing but the truth. He refused to tell me anything and suggested that I talk to my fiancé about the situation. I didn't realize there was a "situation." I asked my best friend from work if she knew anything and, of course, she didn't. She seemed as upset as I was that a wedding might not take place. I had stopped traveling out of state for work and had been home for a while. Things were very different now.

My grandfather was dead, my eldest aunt was dead, and my mother was still gone (but not dead.) I felt all alone, with no one to turn to and nowhere to turn. "Mr. Third Wheel" had become a permanent fixture at our house (and my new confidant.) I cried in his arms many nights, as me and my fiancé became more distant.

I was sure that "Mr. Cutie" was cheating, and I was determined to find out the truth. Then, something strange came over me. I decided to see a fortune-teller. I had seen the sign many times, while driving on Main Street. I pulled up to the corner store with the blinking sign. Red letters that spelled out "FORTUNE TELLER" blinked off and on.

I parked my car on the corner and went inside. I stayed near the door because I felt unsure. I watched two women in the back of the store talking to each other quietly. One of the women looked up at me, as she continued to talk. I opened the door to head out, and the woman motioned for me to stay. I wanted to run, but my feet wouldn't move.

The woman who looked up at me earlier walked toward me and asked me why I came to see her. I explained that I was unsure because I didn't really believe in fortune-telling. The woman asked me to have a seat while she finished with her other customer. I sat in a large red leather chair and waited patiently for the woman to finish.

I tried to listen to their conversation, but I couldn't hear anything. A few minutes later, one woman walked passed me and out the door, while the other reached for my hand. I pulled my hand back and explained that I did not want the woman to touch me. She seemed surprised by my request. I explained that I had heard how certain facts could be determined from card readings, which did not involve touching or reading my hands. The woman agreed.

We sat across from each other, as the mysterious woman reached for a deck of cards and spread them out across a small table. She touched five cards and turned them over. The card reader told me stories about my grandfather and his undying love for me. She talked about the estranged relationship that I had with my mother.

The fortune-teller even described the bathroom at my grandparents' house, behind Weequahic High School, down to the little pink and black square tiles on the wall. This was the same bathroom where I had heard a young girl screaming, while being raped (when I was a young girl.) The most alarming story was the one about an older woman whom I was closely related to, but who I shouldn't trust because she would hurt me very badly later in life.

The fortune-teller also described my college dorm room in detail to me, without any previous information. She went on to say that I shouldn't trust my darling fiancé, "Mr. Cutie," because he was definitely cheating. She said that I should expect a call from a strange woman that would reveal everything about my fiancé. I wondered why the mysterious woman wasn't aware that I had already received a phone call from the strange woman, if indeed she was a "real" fortune-teller. After all, that's why I was there!

I proceeded to tell her about my uncomfortable phone conversation with the strange woman. I paid the fortune-teller $50 and she gave me two white candles in long, clear jars. She told me to keep them lit under my bed. She also told me to get a personal item that belonged to my fiancé and place it under the bed with the two candles. I didn't want to use a weird item like a piece of hair from his head. *That would be really weird!* I laughed out loud in my head. Instead, I decided to hide a pair of my fiancé's shoes under the bed.

I waited and waited, but nothing happened. My fiancé continued to stick with his story that he had not cheated on me. I couldn't stand the torture any longer and called the wedding off. I began cancelling appointments with the florist and the dee-jay. I made the dreaded call to my fiancé's parents and, last - but not least, members of my bridal party. Ironically, no one seemed surprised. In fact, everyone—except my girlfriend and her husband—seemed relieved that the wedding was called off.

"Mr. Cutie" walked around in all his arrogance, with a big attitude (sticking to his story.) Then, the one person who I had come to trust most in the world finally came forward with the truth. Our mutual friend, "Mr. Third Wheel," came to see me. We hugged, and he cried with me. He told me the story of how my man bragged about meeting this woman at his job. Later, they had gone to Liberty State Park in Jersey City to meet. The events of their day seemed very much like my first date with "Mr. Cutie", up at the lake on Route 80.

I became impatient. I wanted to hear more about this story and how this "fantastic first date" led to this strange woman sleeping with my man. "Mr. Third Wheel" told me that their first meeting took place while I was away. "Mr. Cutie" continued to date the woman, until I returned from California. As the story unfolded, I learned that the strange woman was the stripper who danced at my fiancé's bachelor party.

I remembered how I had begged and pleaded for him not to have a bachelor party because I knew it would cause trouble. He had "forbidden" me to have a bachelorette party, and I had honored his wishes (as usual.) Apparently, the stripper met my fiancé near his job and had offered him her number. He proceeded to call the stripper and continued to date and sleep with her, during the entire time that I traveled back and forth to California.

Originally, my boss asked me to work in California for three months only. I would work for four days at a time (Monday through Thursday) and catch the red-eye home to Jersey on Thursday nights to spend the weekend with my "family." Then, I would catch the red-eye back to Cali on Sunday nights or early Monday mornings (so that I could spend every moment with my son and fiancé) - and still make it to work on time on Monday.

Three months had turned into nine months and, before long, I had been working in California for almost one year. I tried to remember the exact words that the mysterious fortune-teller had used to describe the relationship between "Mr. Cutie" and the stripper. She told me that my fiancé and the stripper had sex "only" the two times—like that made a difference.

The word that she used to describe the sex act was "fellatio." I became sick to my stomach! The mysterious fortune-teller tried to soften the blow by actually defending my fiancé. She continued to explain that he did not love the stripper and that he had learned his deceitful behavior as a result of his relationship with his father.

I gave the mysterious fortune-teller woman my all-too-familiar stare down (the screw face.) I couldn't believe my ears. I almost laughed out loud in my head to keep myself from crying. I tried to figure out why she was talking about my ex-fiancé and his father. I could care less about their stupid meaningless relationship. Thinking back, I probably should have cared more about the relationship between "Mr. Cutie" and his father (especially since I didn't have a relationship with my own father.)

However, at that very moment, all I wanted to do was knock "Mr. Cutie" and his stripper in the back of their heads - like I had become accustomed to doing with anyone who hurt me, or mine. My son had grown to love my fiancé over the years. *What was I going to tell him?*

I packed the remainder of "Mr. Cutie's" clothes in brown paper bags and placed them in front of the garage door. I had already thrown him out of the house and he had moved back to the two-family house in Irvington (on the street where we first met.) Although I called Verizon and had his phone number blocked, my ex-fiancé continued to call me every day after work.

The phone calls from several different pay phones continued, consistently. After three months, I finally decided to answer the phone and speak with my ex-fiancé. He finally confirmed the story that the mysterious fortune-teller told me. He was a liar and a cheater! I never told him that our mutual best friend, "Mr. Third Wheel", had already confirmed the story. I also never told him that I had overheard him on the phone one day. I know God works in mysterious ways, but this was the strangest thing.

My fiancé was on his way to work one morning and the phone must have rung, as he was leaving out the door. Apparently, he grabbed the phone on the kitchen wall near the back door (just as the answering machine picked up.) The conversation was hard to understand because of their accents. He was Haitian and she was Jamaican.

When I called from work to check my voice mail, their entire conversation had been accidentally recorded. I asked his sister to translate the message for me. I couldn't believe my ears. My fiancé, who would soon become my ex-fiancé, had definitely cheated on me! The affair had gone on for months, and the truth would be known by everyone. My "Mr. Cutie" had gotten the stripper from his bachelor party pregnant!

CHAPTER 14

Married To A Married Man

The engagement, the lying, the cheating, and the hope of being married by the time I was thirty were all over! The thought of even considering marriage made me laugh out loud in my head, especially since I had never really believed in marriage in the first place. I just wanted another chance at happiness, someone to love and someone to love me. Instead, I decided to mope around the house and avoid all contact with other human beings.

It had been four months since I received that dreadful phone call from a strange woman, only to find out that my fiancé had gotten the stripper from his bachelor party pregnant. I laid around for months, angry and depressed. I didn't feel much like talking to anyone, other than my son. I put on my happy face and went to work every day. My weekends were spent lying on the couch watching reruns of *Columbo*. I laughed out loud in my head, as Columbo got on everybody's nerves by acting clueless when he knew exactly who the killer was. It reminded me of when I was trying to catch my ex-fiancé cheating.

I continued to watch Columbo walk the killer out (without handcuffs and in such a dignified manner.) I flipped back and forth from *Columbo* to *Lifetime*. Lifetime movies had a way of helping me escape from my own life. I would get so wrapped up in the characters and what was going on in the movie that I would forget about whatever was bothering me. Every now and then, I glanced away from the TV. I would listen through the bay window of our living room, as my son played outside with his friends. The phone rang again. I didn't answer it (again.) After the high school reunion, one of my old classmates had gotten in touch with me and invited me to a party. I was in no mood to go.

Dana called the house again and threatened that she would ring my doorbell until I answered it. She, I, and another high school friend had become inseparable since the recent fifteen-year reunion. I managed to drag myself to a few cookouts over the summer, but most of my time was spent alone at home. My son was outside riding his bike with his friends. The deep dark cloud that seemed to live above our heads was gone, and our relationship had gotten much better.

My son's cancer was in remission, and he had a tutor that helped us with his homeschooling. He seemed happy, and I liked seeing him happy. The phone rang again. I jumped up and ran to answer it. I told my friend that I would meet her at the party in forty-five minutes. I found a cute tank top to wear and a jean "skort", which looked like shorts from the back and a skirt from the front. I didn't like my strappy sandals, but they would have to do.

I still didn't wear makeup. But my hair, nails, and outfit were cute enough. I arrived at the party, which was really a fish fry, later than I expected. I felt depressed and didn't want to be there. My high school friend promised that I would have fun. She was determined to get me out of my funk. I parked around the corner and walked up to the gate. I spotted my friend sitting at a picnic table with some other friends of ours from high school. I was making my way over to the table where they were sitting, when my eye caught the attention of the cutest guy I had ever seen in my life.

He was staring at me and obviously trying to get my attention. He was not the usual suspect—tall, dark-skinned, and bald. Instead, he had a caramel complexion, with a medium build and average height. Although he wasn't my usual cup of tea, he had legs to die for and we couldn't stop staring at each other. I knew that this was the beginning of a very "special" relationship. I pretended to walk toward the picnic table where my girlfriends were sitting, but I couldn't stop staring at the cute stranger. It was as if my head couldn't turn, and my feet wouldn't move. I stood there mesmerized, trying to act and look normal. My body followed my legs, and I made my way over to the long table where the cute stranger was serving food.

He wore plastic serving gloves over both his hands and threw a bunch of fried Whiting on my plate. I wanted to ask for macaroni and cheese (my favorite dish in the whole wide world), but I decided to take my fish and go. The cute stranger asked me if I wanted anything else and I paused before saying, *"Not right now!"* Little did he know that he was the only "anything else" that I wanted at that moment.

By the time I made my way over to the table where my girlfriends were sitting, they already had me and the cute stranger married. Dana asked if I knew the man previously, while my other girlfriends commented on how nice we looked together. Of course, Dana couldn't wait to gloat and remind me that she was the one who got me out of the house. I hated to admit it, but she was right! I was dancing to one of my favorite "House Music" songs and eating two of my favorite foods (a fried Whiting fish sandwich, with a side of macaroni and cheese.) I was actually having fun (the time of my life), and I owed it all to Dana and the cute stranger.

Twelve hours had passed. My girlfriends and I, along with the cute stranger and his friends, were still eating and dancing up a storm. I arrived to the fish fry at 1:30 p.m., and it was now 1:30 a.m. Two of our other friends decided that it was time to leave the party. The cute stranger was now manning the bar and asked me not to leave. Dana told me that she would stay with me for as long as I wanted her there.

Although the stranger was cute, he was still a stranger, and I felt better with my girlfriend by my side. We continued to eat and dance until 3:00 a.m. I didn't drink alcohol, but Dana drank plenty, and she was plenty drunk. As the cute stranger walked me to my car, we noticed one of his friends attempting to help Dana into her car. She was stumbling drunk, and I was reminded why I never wanted to drink. Then, she did something that changed my world forever. She lifted her skirt up and pulled her panties down. Then, she squatted like she was on the toilet and peed on the ground. I couldn't believe my eyes. Dana was squatting near a tree and peeing, like a dog!

I wasn't sure what to do and decided to drive my girlfriend to the nearest diner. After helping us into my car, the cute stranger gave me a folded up piece of paper and a long hug. He also gave me twenty dollars and told me it was for my breakfast. He made a point of letting me know that the money was "not for my drunk friend." I laughed out loud, as I got into the car.

When we arrived at the diner, our other girlfriends were already there. We joined them for breakfast, and I told my other friends all about my night with the cute stranger. When our friend sobered up, she joined the conversation and started telling me to remember the things she told me about my "new" man. I was curious and wanted to know what else Dana could possibly know about the cute stranger. I wasn't aware that she knew him previously because she hadn't mentioned it all night. I knew that this was not the time, or the place, to talk about it and decided that I would wait until the next day to call her.

We finished our breakfast around 5:00 a.m., and I drove Dana back to get her car. Later that day, I told my son all about the fish fry and the after-party. He told me that he had fun spending the night with his friend and he was happy that I decided to get out of the house. I didn't tell him about the cute stranger. I figured it was way too soon and wasn't sure if he was ready to hear about another guy after the whole "pregnant stripper and engagement fiasco." I unfolded the piece of paper that the cute stranger had given me.

To my surprise, there were three phone numbers written on it. The first number had "home" written next to it. The second number had "work" written next to it. The third number had "cell" written next to it. I felt like the luckiest woman in the world. I sat back in my favorite black leather recliner and wondered what I had done to deserve such a man. Then, I remembered the awful year I had thus far and decided that God "owed" me a favor. I laughed out loud, as I walked toward the bay window in my living room. My son was riding his bike outside, as he often did. I decided that it would be the perfect time to call the cute stranger.

I dialed the number that had "home" written next to it. An automated voice message came on, and I decided not to leave a message. Instead, I dialed the number that had "cell" written next to it.

It was Sunday afternoon, and I figured the cute stranger would not be at work. A husky, sexy voice answered the phone and asked, "Is this my new wife?" I blushed and answered, *"Yes. It is!"* I hadn't given the cute stranger my telephone number and was surprised that he recognized my voice. He told me that he wanted to see me and asked for my address. Fifteen minutes later, I noticed a black truck pulling up outside my house.

I tried to see if my son was still nearby riding his bike. I couldn't see him from the window, but I had a feeling he was nearby. The doorbell rang, and the cute stranger was in my sight again! I opened the door and leaped into his arms, like we had been together forever. For the first time, the cute stranger and I were alone. I thought back to the things that he whispered in my ear, the first night that we met.

After twelve hours of dancing and flirting with one another, we sat on the front stoop. Eventually, the cute stranger came clean. Of course, this admission of guilt only came to light after my girlfriend put him on "Front Street" and told me that she knew he was married, with a family and a dog! Against my better judgment and every-thing that I believed in, I proceeded to date this cute man because he "promised" to love and cherish me. He said that he would take care of me and never hurt me. I "vowed" to love and be faithful to him forever.

It sounded crazy, but this was the kind of love that I had been waiting for all of my life. At the time, it felt like it was what I needed to stay alive. My son was doing well. I had gone back to work. I was finally over my ex-fiancé's shenanigans. I felt alive - again! And I needed this man, like I needed the air we breathe - to keep on living!

The cute stranger meant what he said and did his best to keep me happy. There was another promise that he would not break, and that was he would "never" leave his wife. I knew it was wrong, but I couldn't help myself! I couldn't stop loving him. I wondered how a woman of God could do such a thing. These thoughts made me question my faith and, thus, began my seven years of celibacy. I had decided to become committed to a married man, in a way that I had never been with a man before.

Our love was a different kind of love—not different in a bad way, but different in a strange way—a special way. It was not his caramel complexion that aroused me (because everyone knows that I prefer dark-skinned men.) Although he had the body of a Greek god, it was not his physique that aroused me. It was the fact that we would go for endless walks down the pier in Hoboken. We would sit in the car and talk for hours, as we looked out at the dirty lake in Weequahic Park. He would bring me a croissant toasted with a little butter, just the way I liked it, from Dunkin' Donuts every morning before work. He made it his business to be at my house every day after work by five o'clock and left every night by midnight.

He wasn't a movie buff, like me, and didn't watch a whole lot of television. One night, me and my new man laid in bed and watched "Titanic." It felt like an eight-hour movie and I know my cutie just wanted to die. I laughed out loud in my head. My new man fixed my furnace, when it was broken. He paid for the plumber, when the water pipes burst. He had been there for me, after my son's brush with death. He made me feel valued. He made me feel like he cared - for me - and my son. It had been thirteen years since we met and one year since we last stared into each other's eyes across the dinner table. I had gone home to Jersey during the summer, and we met for dinner and one of our usual long walks on the pier. Now, I was back in Phoenix.

The phone rang at 12:30 a.m., which meant that it was 3:30 a.m. on the East Coast. Much like the 973 area code of Newark, I recognized the 908 area code of Union. It was late, and I ignored the call. Later that morning, I checked my voice mail and heard an unfamiliar voice. The voice on the other end of the phone sounded sad and was saying that she needed to speak with me about an urgent matter. My first thought was - *Here we go again!* It was like déjá vu.

I began wondering if someone was pregnant. I knew that I wasn't. The woman proceeded to say that her husband was ill and that I should contact her right away. I was confused and didn't know what to do. I sat on the floor of the walk-in closet, in my Arizona home, and thought about my next steps. I decided to brush my teeth and get ready for work. But I felt compelled to call the woman back.

Reggie came into the bathroom to greet me "good morning" and sensed that something was wrong. I told him about the mysterious voice message that the woman left on my cell phone at 12:30 a.m. He was already aware of my previous relationship and asked me what I wanted to do. I told him that I felt compelled to call the woman back.

Later that day, I returned the mysterious woman's phone call and she confirmed that she was the wife of the cute stranger that I met (more than thirteen years earlier.) As we spoke, her story changed from her husband being ill to *her* being ill. I became suspicious and decided to end our conversation. I thought it would be best if I heard it directly from the horse's mouth and decided to contact my old friend, the cute stranger.

I rang his phone three times before he answered. He was at work and couldn't speak. I waited for my "cute stranger" to call me back at a more convenient time (when he thought we could speak in private.) I told him about the voice message that I received from his wife at 12:30 that morning, and the strange conversation that we had. I had become sick and tired of women questioning me about "their" man. I began to wonder why women blame "the other woman" when their man cheats.

We don't always get to choose who we love and who loves us back. I had been a victim, just like her…loved and betrayed…hurt and thrown away. This was not the first time, and it probably would not be the last time. I thought about the number of times that I had been a victim of insecure women staring me up and down while giving me the "screw face", whenever I entered a room. I laughed out loud in my head at the women, who held onto their men (for dear life), when they saw another attractive woman in the vicinity. Some of those women were my supposed friends.

It reminded me of the old White women, who clinched their pocketbooks on the subway (when they saw a Black guy with a hoodie get on the train.) *Yes—It happens!* But not all young Black men with hoodies are thieves, or thugs. And not all single women want someone else's husband! When a man cheats, check your man—not the other woman. When men cheat, they need to be held accountable for their actions.

The conversation I had with his wife played over and over in my head. So many thoughts and questions ran through my mind. *Would he have told me the truth, if Dana hadn't? Would I be the cause of their breakup?* As women, we all wonder why men cheat; especially married men. *Why do they lie?* More importantly—*Why do we stay with them?* The answer is because most women think that they can't do any better. We also want to protect what we think is ours. Women shouldn't have to beg and grovel for a man to tell the truth. We shouldn't have to check a man's ring finger for a wedding band, or do a background check, to see if he's married.

When I finally spoke with my cute stranger—"my married man" on the phone, he told me that he was not ill and had no knowledge of his wife being ill. He told me that he and his wife had gotten into an argument over a check that he had given me. She wanted to know who I was and whether, or not, we were sleeping together. I vowed to love this man! I had taken a vow of celibacy! *Was it all for nothing? Would God ever forgive me?* If only he had gotten the money from the ATM, like he had always done.

CHAPTER 15

Love, Lies, And Shenanigans

I had been living a lie. My entire life had become a vicious cycle of lies. It was if I had fallen into an abyss of untruth and couldn't climb out. Growing up, there were so many lies and so many shenanigans. When I was younger, I remembered hearing about one cousin who went to jail because she was caught smuggling drugs into the country. Another cousin and her husband did drugs right in front of me, at a party, and asked me if I knew where they could get more. I was only thirteen! I remember one time when my youngest aunt, who had never been to my house, was suddenly at my door.

She was ringing my bell, frantically, with her new boyfriend—10:30 at night. I had work the next day and my son had school! She wanted to "borrow" ten dollars. Her daughter was my favorite cousin. She was the one who licked my grandmother's cake bowl with me during the holidays and who fought with me over my grandmother's front seat every weekend on the way to the beach. She was the one who I loved like a sister. When we were older, and our children were younger, we had slumber parties at my apartment. We would wake up early to cook a big breakfast together, every weekend.

Now, she allows her children to believe a lie about something that happened way before they were barely a thought in their mother's belly. *How can you dislike someone you don't even know, or have never had a conversation with? More importantly, why stick your nose in where it doesn't belong—worrying about "grown-folk business"—catch-*

ing feelings about something that has absolutely nothing to do with you? Besides, I thought we had already made up several different times and several years ago. I guess some people just like to keep the fuel going. Shenanigans!"

It always seemed like my mother and I were to blame for everyone else's troubles. We've all done our share of dirt. But no one else was ever at fault, or had to take responsibility for their actions. First, there was my mother's addiction to men. *Did I have this same addiction?* Then, her addiction grew to drugs and alcohol. *Would I manage to get through life without becoming an addict?* I thought back to my childhood, back when life seemed good. Before I knew it, our lives had become one big mess—and one big lie.

I am ashamed to admit that I did nothing to help my mother until it was too late. I had abandoned my mother, when she needed me most. *But as a child, was it my responsibility to take care of her?* It was supposed to be the other way around. She had robbed me of the chance to have a normal childhood. She had robbed me of the chance to be loved. She had abandoned *me*! Maybe, subconsciously—as an adult—I was paying her back for abandoning me.

Sometimes, I try to think back to when my mother's addiction began. I thought about the first time that I saw her get high. *Was that her first time ever? Was that the beginning of her demise? Or had that been a lie too?* I remembered hearing stories about my mother when she was a teenager. As a child, I often thought about the lifestyle that she had subjected me to—the lies, the hurt, and the pain. I had been subjected to a life of alcohol, drugs, and crime. A little white lie seemed like nothing compared to these things.

I often felt unbearable shame and was the brunt of cruel jokes, as my so-called friends and family members alluded to my mother's addictions and wayward life. I thought about all the unsavory characters who passed in and out of our lives. I thought back to the number of times that I saw our flamboyant neighborhood pimp exit our building on South Clinton Street, followed by a string of prostitutes. He reminded me of "Huggy Bear" from *Starsky and Hutch*, with his long colorful coat and big floppy hat. I wondered if my mother knew then that she would sell her soul for money. *How would she lie her way out of this one?*

One day, Stephanie and I waited for the police to leave the building after they busted "our friendly neighborhood pimp" for selling drugs and soliciting. Unlike the padlocked apartment where my mother and I lived, the pimp's door was unlocked. Stephanie and I would sneak inside to see what we could see. His apartment looked like a scene from *The Partridge Family*. There was a shag rug with oversized chairs and psychedelic pictures all over the place. There was a really cool sunken living room with stairs that led up to an ugly round waterbed. As we looked around the pimp's apartment, thoughts of Stephanie's alcoholic mother and her abusive father— who happened to be our building superintendent—consumed my mind. I remembered that I had seen them fighting and vomiting in the hallway of our building. Her father would often beat her mother and leave her all bloody and bruised on the elevator floor. She would try to pick herself up and make it back to their basement apartment, bleeding and stumbling on many occasions. This is not something that Stephanie and I discussed.

There was not much Stephanie, or I, felt that we could do to help our mothers. As I grew older, I became painfully and consciously aware that my guilt outweighed my shame. I imagine that the same holds true for my grandmother. After all, she was my mother's mother. I recalled the time when my mother was hospitalized at Beth Israel in Newark, after being brutally raped and beaten. A local drug dealer and three of his brutes from our neighborhood beat my mother savagely in the face with a metal pipe, and then sodomized her in the garage of my grandmother's house on Goldsmith Avenue. When I arrived to the hospital, she was bent over on a bed and kneeling on her knees. I could see the large hole in her butt. I figured that this must have been when my mother contracted HIV.

I learned about HIV and AIDS when I was in junior high school. We had a "Sex Ed" class and learned all about sexually transmitted diseases. Other than that, the subjects of sex and STDs were taboo in my grandmother's house. No one talked about them, and we dare not ask about them! My grandmother and I never spoke a word about my mother's condition. She never took the time to explain to me that my mother was dying. I was left to figure that out all on my own. Sometimes, I would hear them arguing, and I suspected—from the number of men and the number of rapes—that she had contracted some type of disease. That night at the hospital, my grandmother just stood there shaking her head in disgust and making her usual *loving* comments. "This is quite the mess you've gotten yourself into." "You look terrible!" "Your feet stink!" "You disgust me." I couldn't believe that my grandmother could be so cruel to her own daughter. I hated her! I hated both of them! I hated my grandmother because she was a worse mother than my own mother. I hated my mother because she cared about her drugs more than she cared about me, or anyone else. I closed my eyes and pretended to be somewhere else, anywhere but there.

As much as I hated my mother at that very moment, it hurt me to see her lying there in so much pain. And my grandmother was getting on my last nerve. I walked over to the hospital bed and pulled the blanket up over my mother. I wanted to protect her from the bad men who had hurt her. I wanted to protect her from my grandmother. I wanted to yell out, *"Leave my mommy alone!"* The same way my son did, when he was a little boy and wanted to protect me from my mother. My grandmother acted like my mother was the "black sheep" of the family." But many of my relatives had grown up in Newark. There were cousins, aunts, and uncles—all of who had also succumbed to the pressures of street life. The grandfather, who I had known all my life, was not my grandfather. My "real" grandfather (my grandmother's first husband and the father of two of her children) was also an alcoholic. It would seem that alcoholism and drug addiction had become a family trait. One might say that it was a "family lie."

There were so many lies, I didn't know what to believe. I had never met my grandmother's parents and was told that they died in a car accident. I would later find out that they both died from cancer. My grandmother harbored many hurtful lies and secrets, and seemed to take them all out on my mother for some reason. Looking back, I can't say that I didn't understand the shame my grandmother must have felt. The thing that I truly did not understand was the discontentment that my grandmother felt toward *me*. She would pretend to love me, while hating me the whole time, when she too was a product of the same environment. Unfortunately, much love was lost and the lies did not end there.

The vicious cycle continued, as I struggled to get past the hurt and pain in my life. My mother's life was passing right before my eyes. She continued to live her life and do what she had always done. She lived without a care in the world. I watched the decline of my other family members, my close friends, and their parents. It seemed like each one of my friends had a mother, father, sister, brother, aunt, uncle, or other relative who became an addict. Secretly, I prayed for each and every one of them, just as I continued to pray for my mother and my own family.

As my son grew older, I began to think about his life. I wondered what kind of parent he would become. I thought about the decisions that I made with his father and wondered what I could have done differently. I had hoped that the lies would end, when my son became an adult. When he was born, I made a decision not to subject him to the lifestyle to which I had become accustomed. My son's upbringing was very different from mine. I showed him undying love and tried to raise him the best way I knew how, even though I never knew what that really looked like. The only way that I knew how to keep him safe was to keep him away from my mother. On the contrary, no one took the time to protect me. No one cared about me and my mother.

Instead, everyone stood around snickering and sneering. They didn't have enough nerve to stand up to my grandmother, the matriarch of the family. She was beyond reproach. When I look at my son's life, I mostly think about how different our lives would have been (if I had kept him away from his father and my grandmother, instead of my mother.) My heart skips a beat, whenever I see my son smoke and drink. He says that he doesn't want to be like me. He wants to be so much like his father. I often think about the pain and suffering that my son and I endured, while he overcame his brush with death.

I cannot figure out for the life of me why he would choose to drink and smoke after a near-death experience, such as surviving cancer.

I often wonder if my son remembers that I was the only one who slept by his bedside each and every night. I was the one who took a leave of absence from work so that I could stay home with him. I was always there for him. My son and I had been inseparable from the time he was born. I still have memories of him jumping up and down on our first couch. He would yell, "Outside! Outside! Outside!" We lived in an apartment on the Rutgers campus. The rent was $850 each month (with utilities included.) The university paid half of the rent because the apartment was part of the graduate and family housing program. The extra money that I saved was used to pay for my son's child care. The rent for my first campus apartment was $795 and did not include utilities. It was a one-bedroom, unlike the second apartment (which was a two-story townhouse.) The first one was not as nice as the second, but I liked it just because it was my very first apartment. It was the first place that my son and I could call "our own." By the time my son turned two years old, we had moved into our second apartment. He seemed to really enjoy living there. Jumping up and down on the couch was his way of letting me know that he wanted to go outside to play.

There was a swing set. I had never seen a real swing set before. I laughed out loud in my head. We stayed in the graduate and family housing development for an extra year, just so I could keep a roof over our heads. Soon after graduation, we moved to the Vailsburg section of Newark. When he was four, we moved to Irvington and he would later start school at Florence Avenue Elementary. Our garden apartment complex appeared nice on the outside, but there was no garden. Instead, there were mice and roaches (just like the apartment buildings where I grew up.) We lived on the bottom floor and had to get bars on the window to keep people from breaking in. Although I could see my new car from the window, it was broken into three times, stolen twice, and stripped once. We lived there for four years. When my son turned eight years old, we moved to Stuyvesant Avenue in Irvington. We lived there for almost four years also. We had come a long way, and I was proud.

Unlike my life, my son's life was good until he became a teenager. I had done everything I could to make sure that he had a good life. But my son seemed to be doing everything he could to mess it up. He had a mother who loved and cared for him, and who was always there when he needed her. His teen years were hard. We dealt with the cancer and his brush with death from age twelve to fourteen. By age thirteen, he had already begun to act out.

Things began to change and life took a turn for the worse. My son and I weren't perfect, but we had a normal mother-son relationship. After his brush with death, I thought that he was just going through a rebellious phase. Then, I thought that he was just experiencing the horrible phase that all teens go through. I guess I didn't realize that my son was mad at the world—mad at me! I had been trying to overcompensate, by giving him things and allowing him to behave in a manner that I wouldn't have under normal circumstances. But, at some point, enough was enough!

What came next? More lies… More deception…from my own grandmother—(the mother of my mother)—from my ex-boyfriend—(the father of my son)—*against me!* A single Black woman, motherless and fatherless—struggling to beat the odds. Struggling to raise a son from a boy to a man. It's sad that it had to come to this with the two people who I should have been able to trust the most. The two people who should have had my back. They should have praised me instead of berated me.

I thought about how, after college, I rented the one-bedroom apartment in a two-family house in Vailsburg. It was a nice two-family house on a quiet street. It was small, but it would have to do until I found something better for him (for us.) It was during this time that he went to the childcare center in Irvington, the one his father tried to *take* him from.

I thought back to his first day of preschool and how I had watched him through the small classroom window, as he took off his jacket. He hung his backpack on the hook of his new cubby. Then, he walked right over to the other children and started playing. I laughed out loud in my head at the thought that he didn't even cry, or look up, to see if I was there. My son was so independent! It reminded me of my first day of school, back when my mother watched me from her bedroom window.

My son and I were happy. But, once again, his father was on a "warpath" and had secretly moved to 38th Street. He was actually living right around the corner from the apartment where my son and I lived. He never told me that he had moved there, but I learned this fact as I was coming home from work one day and saw him. *Of all the streets in the world...* Shenanigans!

Now, after all the hard work was done, my son's father and my grandmother wanted to swoop down to take him from me. I felt like I was being robbed. There were no high school proms—No high school graduation—No college applications. Instead, there were back-and-forth court proceedings and family counseling (of which no one seemed to be a part of except me.) Then, there was juvenile detention. All of my hard work went down the drain. The son who I carried for nine months around the college campus, rushed through a final exam so that I could still graduate and give birth to in Newark, was not the son I had raised. *How dare him! How dare them!* They had not been the ones who sacrificed for him.

I remembered how my grandmother didn't even want me to keep my baby. She had said that we couldn't stay in her home. We would have been confined to the basement with my mother, if we had no place else to go. I didn't want my son around my mother. He would not be subjected to drugs. I wasn't a statistic and I was determined to do anything to make sure that my son wasn't a statistic either. We were going to be a drug-free family, by any means necessary. But things weren't turning out as I planned.

This was not how I envisioned my life! I didn't know exactly when it started, but I remembered how I found out. The police called me. They asked whom they were speaking with, as if I called them. They had my son. He had been drinking and getting high in the park, near the school. They said that he was throwing up. I went to pick him up. I couldn't even look him in the eyes. I was hurt and disappointed. I had flashbacks of my mother. This is how it starts! After everything... *How could he do this?*

The next time, he was bagging it up on his bed. He was selling it at school. It wasn't the first time, and it wouldn't be the last time, that I was called down to the Union police station. I cried for days. Now, he was stealing in Walgreen's across from his school. I went through this with my mother! I wasn't about to go through it again. He failed drug tests at his pediatrician's office. I was so embarrassed! I couldn't believe that *my* son was selling marijuana from the backpack that I bought him for school! Now, he had been suspended. I tried family counseling, alternative day programs, "Scared Straight", and boot camp.

He had been given so many chances. He jeopardized everything I had worked for—His freedom, my career, and our home! *When was it all going to stop?* I asked for help… His father's response was "Give him to me, if you can't handle him!" My grandmother saw this as a perfect opportunity to weasel her way into our lives and try to take my son away from me. She was determined to prove that I was an "unfit mother." *Who was she to question my parenting skills, or my love for my son?* I fought for my son. She gave up on her daughters. My grandmother and my son's father would have a fight on their hands, if they tried to take my son. *It would be okay…* I had been fighting all my life. I was used to it. *Buckle up!*

The war between my son's father and I started way back when he first decided to "kidnap" him! Many people ask, *"How can a parent kidnap his or her own child?"* The answer is this… If one parent has full or sole custody of the child, while the other parent may or may not have visitation rights, the parent with full custody has the right to know where that child is at all times because he or she is the primary caretaker of that child. Therefore, the other parent cannot take the child out of child care, another person's care, or move to another location with the child without the knowledge and/or consent of the parent who has full, sole, or primary custody.

When I received the letter in the mail, I froze! I started having panic attacks… I was anxious… I remembered that I would have panic attacks before every "away" track meet. I'm not sure why. They just happened. Maybe, I was just nervous even though I enjoyed running and could run fast. I hadn't had a panic attack since high school.

Here it was, fifteen years later, and I was clinching my chest. I couldn't breathe. Then, I remembered that my son's father had taken me to court before to lower his child support payments—twice. Shenanigans!

I thought back to the first time my son's father had taken me to court. He and his lawyer had arrived before me. My son's father nudged his lawyer and pointed me out. I proceeded to walk toward the courtroom and overheard his lawyer say, "Man, you didn't tell me she was *Miss Thing!*" I wore my usual business attire—a tailored pantsuit (grey with a white tuxedo blouse and three-inch black pumps.) His lawyer was dressed in a five-piece "Steve Harvey suit." Shenanigans!

It had been five years since then. I was now standing in my garage, staring at another white envelope. I opened the envelope and read the letter. My son's father wanted custody of my son—the son who I carried for nine months. The son to whom I gave birth. The son who I loved and cared for since he was born. We went back and forth to court for two whole years. The judge decided that I would remain the primary custodial parent, and I was granted full custody of my son (whom I had raised since he was born.) Shenanigans!

By this time, my grandfather and eldest aunt were gone—gone from my grandmother's life and mine. Thus began the war between me and my grandmother. After my grandfather passed, my grandmother was all alone and went to live with my eldest aunt. My eldest aunt had been divorced from her second husband, and was also all alone. After my eldest aunt passed away, my grandmother's sister went to live with her in my aunt's home. She too soon found out that living with my grandmother was unbearable. My great aunt moved out and my grandmother assumed that I would take her place. She had already chosen the bedrooms where my son and I would sleep.

My grandmother had no one else to control and no one to give in to her. Since she no longer had anyone in her own life, it was like she wanted *my* life! When my best friend died, my grandmother showed up at the hospital and the funeral, even though I asked her not to. Kyle and I had been best friends since freshman year in high school. I knew that he had been suffering from migraines. One night, his girlfriend called and told me that he fell onto the floor in his apartment and went into a coma. I shared the news with my grandmother because he had come over to her house with me a few times. I'm sure that my grandmother thought she was being supportive... But Kyle was *my* best friend. When I wasn't with my boyfriend, I would spend many days after school at Kyle's house with him and his mother.

When he went into a coma, I just wanted to spend time with our other high school friends—reminiscing about old school days. I couldn't believe that my grandmother just showed up at the hospital and the funeral, even though this had absolutely nothing to do with her. Kyle was *my* friend, not hers! When he passed away, I grew closer to his mother and older brother. Although he was a few years older, Eric and I became almost as close as Kyle and I were. On the day that my son went to stay with my grandmother "temporarily," Eric showed up at my house in Union. I was torn up inside that day and didn't know how I would go on. I will never forget the relief that I felt, when I looked up and saw a familiar face. Someone actually cared about me and what I was going through. Like Kyle, Eric was always supportive. He even helped my grandmother with things around the house, when I asked him to. But my grandmother never seemed to realize that these were *my* friends and they were only helping her because of *me*!

Another time, while I was working at AT&T, we were celebrating Black History Month. My manager asked me to make a presentation about someone who I admired and who had an impact on my life. I decided to talk about my grandmother because she was a strong Black woman who had an obvious impact on my life. On the day of the presentation, I was out sick with the flu. I called my grandmother to let her know that I wasn't going to work. Much to my surprise, my boss later informed me that my grandmother showed up to my workplace without me to receive her award! He was stunned because there was no one to present an award to her and he wanted to know if she knew that I was out sick. So rather than check on me, I guess my grandmother just showed up at my work and pretended that she had no idea I was sick. Shenanigans!

CHAPTER 16

A Vicious Cycle

I was in my thirties and my grandmother was still trying to run my life. It was another vicious cycle. I thought back to the time when my college professor invited me to study abroad in France. My instructor had selected a few honor students and told us to let her know if we were interested. I had been studying French for years and wanted to go to Paris. When I told my grandmother and eldest aunt, they laughed out loud in my face and said that they should be the ones going to Paris.

After my aunt's death, I thought about all the times that I had heard her and my grandmother ridicule my mother. I thought about all the times that they had ridiculed me. Now, my grandmother had no one to laugh with her. She already had her chance to laugh. She had her chance to be a mother. She had her chance to be a grandmother. She had made her bed and, now, she had to lie in it. Every day, I would ask myself, *"Why couldn't she just leave me alone?"* *"Why couldn't she just let me have my chance to be a mother?"* *"Why couldn't she just let me live my life?"* Instead, she insinuated herself into my life (repeatedly)—and I just couldn't seem to live my life without her interfering.

When I told my grandmother that I had no intention of selling the house that I had just bought, just to move in with her, all hell broke loose. She threatened me and things went downhill from there. I tried to remember that grief-stricken moment when my life would change forever. I was sitting in my cubicle at work, when my cell phone rang. I was talking with a coworker. I was familiar with the main numbers from the Irvington and Elizabeth local police stations. But I didn't recognize this telephone number. My coworker must have sensed that I needed some privacy and walked back to her cubicle, which was directly across from mine. I tried to roll my chair as close to my desk as possible so that I could speak without her hearing me. My cell phone continued to ring. The call was coming from a 908 area code, which I knew was Union County.

The voice on the phone was husky and deep, like that of a man's voice. This sounded like a Black man. I responded to his question by confirming my first and last name. I asked him to do the same. The voice was unfamiliar to me, and I had no idea who the person on the other end of the phone was. The strange man proceeded to tell me that he worked for the Division of Youth and Family Services. I wondered why someone from DYFS would be calling *me*. I was more curious as to how he got my cell phone number. That could only mean one thing… I decided to ask him why he was calling. He told me that he was following up on a "situation" that he was made aware of by an anonymous caller. The situation was undoubtedly no laughing matter, but I laughed out loud in my head at the story I was hearing.

I was surprised that the man was calling me on my cell phone. I was surprised that he was calling me period. DYFS was mainly known for child abuse cases. So many questions ran through my mind. *How did he get my cell number? Who was the anonymous caller?* Imagine my surprise when I arrived to court and saw my own grandmother sitting with my son's father. I remembered how my grandmother had shown up at my house earlier that morning. I had taken the day off from work and she said that she was there to check on me. As I pulled out of my garage, she leaned into my car and hugged me. Her exact words were, "Everything will work out. You just gotta fight fire with fire!" Just two weeks earlier, she was begging and pleading for me and my son to move in with her. Now, here she was - sitting in court with my son's father! I was convinced that my grandmother and my son's father were two of the most sneaky, conniving, and vindictive people I had ever met in my entire life.

My son had continued to act out ever since his brush with death. The fact that he had been in and out of juvenile detention a number of times ran through my mind. I thought back to when he was ten years old and had gotten kicked out of Catholic school. That was when he ran away. My son left a note on the dining room table that read, "I hate you!" It hurt me to my heart! I stared at the note and cried, as I shook my head in disbelief. I couldn't believe it, after all the things I had done for him. After all the things we had gone through... We had "gone through it" the same way that I had done with my mother.

I recalled the number of times my boss had threatened to fire me because I was late to work. I was always late because I always had to speak with my son's teacher, or the school principal, first thing in the morning. Sometimes, I would just make it in to work and the little red light on my phone would be blinking. They were already calling me to pick him up from school! I remembered the number of incentives and the number of times that I begged my son to "just behave." And the number of times I prayed... I recalled the number of times that I lied to my son because his father didn't pay the child support, or pick him up for the weekend, when he was supposed to.

After I read my son's note, I went to the police department and asked a friend to help me. Half of the police force had graduated with me from Irvington High School. Ironically, I had also programmed the new 911 phone system at the police station. My friend put out an All-Points Bulletin (APB) and my son was found in Orange trying to make his way to my grandmother's house.

He had gotten lost and ended up at a stranger's house. He could have been kidnapped, or killed! When my cousin (who had been riding around with me) and I heard that the cops found him, we went straight back to the police department. My son and I ran into each other's arms and cried. After that, he still continued to get into trouble and was often suspended from school. Eventually, he got kicked out. I didn't know what else to do. That was when I decided to put him in the "Day Program", until school was out. Then, he would go to a military program. It was a ten-week summer camp that would teach him discipline. I visited my son every weekend and he wrote me a letter every week. We didn't get to speak on the phone too often, but he wrote all about how much fun he was having. Other than driving the go-karts and playing paintball, the school was similar to the junior ROTC program that he participated in when he was younger.

My son seemed to enjoy the summer camp. He even had personalized dog tags made, which read "K-Dogg Loves His Pookie." Although the letters indicated that my son liked the summer camp and was having fun, my grandmother and my son's father continued to try and prove that I was neglectful because my son had been getting high, drinking, and skipping school on a regular basis.

I refocused my attention back to the strange man on the phone. I tried to explain how, at first, I thought that my son's poor choices were coping mechanisms to help him deal with his brush with death. His behavior was also a consequence of the instability of his father popping in and out of his life, whenever he felt like it. I had tried everything to get and keep my son on track. I wondered whether, or not, the man on the phone had children - And, if so, had he ever gone through what I was going through.

A counselor told me about a "Scared Straight" program that my son could participate in. It was a one-day program in which wayward teens could visit a prison and observe inmates. The visit consisted of a guided tour and a presentation about the things that could happen, if the teens didn't straighten up. One of the counselors of the program called to tell me that my son's uncle, one of his father's older brothers, intercepted the tour by pulling my son out of the presentation. My son did not straighten up. And I threatened to throw him out of the house, if his bad behavior continued. After talking on the phone with the strange man for nearly forty-five minutes, I decided that I didn't want to answer any more of his ridiculous questions. I politely told him that I had to get back to work. I knew that I was a good mother (not like my mother) and that was that!

After the strange conversation with the strange man, I decided to call my son's probation officer. She and I had become close over the past two years, and I trusted her. She had been a big help to me and genuinely seemed to care about me and my son. I told her about my conversation with the strange man from DYFS and the wild accusations that he had made. She gasped and told me that she would make some calls. I also made some calls…

It was suggested that I contact a pastor of a church in Elizabeth. My son had been ordered by the judge to participate in a program there. Ironically, I had started volunteering at this same church as a youth counselor to help wayward teens. That summer, I worked at the church two nights per week and on weekends. I helped students with their homework and set up recreational activities to keep children off the streets. On Friday nights, two teen girls in particular would spend the night with me. They were runaways (motherless children.) It made me feel good to know that I was helping them.

The girls seemed very appreciative and couldn't understand why my son didn't feel the same way. Whenever they spent the night, we would order pizza from Big Joe's and watch their favorite DVDs. I shook my head and laughed out loud because this was something that my son and I did, before *he* became a wayward teen. Now, I couldn't get my own child in the house and off the streets. When my son's probation officer called me back, she told me that she knew who the strange man from DYFS was. She didn't know him personally, but she knew someone who had worked with him on a couple of cases. It had been confirmed that the "anonymous" call came from my grandmother. My son's probation officer was appalled and didn't understand why my own grandmother was making such accusations.

Apparently, my grandmother also told the DYFS worker that I refused to let her see my son. Shenanigans! I was in shock because I had called and checked on her, almost every night. I remembered how I had taken care of my grandfather so that she wouldn't have to put him in a nursing home. I had been there for her from the time he and my eldest aunt passed away. And, against my better judgment, I had always let my son visit her whenever he wanted. As a matter of fact, he had begun to spend most of his weekends with her. I had never allowed him to be around my mother, but I was attempting to repair the relationship between me and my grandmother while helping to build a strong relationship between her and my son. There would be no relationship, if it were not for me fostering it! My son was too young to nurture it on his own and she couldn't have done it without me.

My grandmother was lonely and decided to fill a void with me and my son. She had become a permanent fixture in my life. She had become a pest, a nuisance, a stalker. It was like a real-life "fatal attraction." Every day, when I came home from work, she would be sitting on my porch. Sometimes, I could barely get in the door before she was ringing the front or side bell. It had gotten so bad that my son and I would peek through the blinds before answering the door—to see whether, or not, it was her. I should have taken my "perfect" son and ran for the hills, when he was born. That's what my gut told me to do. Instead, I didn't follow my instincts and allowed her to become a part of our lives—me and my son's lives. I would live to regret this decision for the rest of my life.

My grandmother began to undermine my authority by doing things like buying my son a computer and cell phone, without my knowledge or consent. She even bought him his first car, which he managed to crash into a tree while driving drunk! I didn't want my son to have a computer in his bedroom because of all the perversion on the Internet. I also thought it might interfere with his schoolwork. If I wanted him to have a computer, I was perfectly capable of buying him one myself!

It seemed funny how my grandmother was never around when my son got into trouble, but she always managed to butt in my life during all the other times. One time, I had to shell out a hundred bucks because he had gotten into a fight. The other boy's mother called right after the school principal to let me know that my son had ripped her son's jacket. Of course, she made it seem worse than it probably was. But I paid the hundred dollars just to shut her up. I fixed that situation with the jacket, the same way that I fixed the situation with the two girls who were cyberbullying my son (on the same computer that I told my grandmother not to buy him.) Shenanigans!

My son was always finding ways to get into trouble. Some of it was understandable—regular teen stuff (like sneaking girls into the house.) But he always went too far. Like the time when he knew I would be home by six o'clock, and he hid this White girl under the bed in our guest room while he went to the store. I was in the living room and heard someone moving around upstairs. I went to check out the noise. After I found her hiding under the bed in our guestroom, she started crying. She said that she was scared and had never done anything like that before. When my son returned from the store, his only concern was how I knew she was there. Then, there were the times when he would deliberately come in the house late. He knew that he had a curfew. There was also a city curfew, which stipulated a certain time for children to be off the street unless an adult was present.

And there was that time that I found the brown paper bag full of marijuana in his bedroom. It was one thing to experiment with drugs, but it was another thing to *sell* drugs! He could have jeopardized everything that I worked so hard for. The last draw was when he thought he could call me by my first name, like he did his father, and put his hands on me (like his father did.) I was horrified! That night, I cooked dinner and we ate together like we always did. I asked him to wash the dishes, which he rarely did. He said "No!" and called me by my first name very sarcastically. Then, he brushed by me—knocking me into the kitchen wall. He had become so disrespectful! He had to go! I had to get him help. We both needed help, and I was willing to do anything to help my son.

After talking with my son's probation officer and the man from DYFS, I left work and went home. I was emotionally drained. I went into my bedroom and closed the door. I lie across my king-sized bed and cried like a baby. I couldn't believe that my own grandmother had called DYFS on me. I couldn't even confront her. I was advised to get a lawyer, which I did immediately. I limited my contact with my grandmother, at that point, and decided to put a phone in my son's bedroom. We needed an extra phone in the house anyway because my son had been placed on house arrest. This meant that he couldn't go far from the house and needed to be there whenever the phone rang.

I wondered why my grandmother had remained anonymous, if she was truly concerned about my son's well-being. I glanced over and laughed out loud in my head, as I thought about how my son's new phone reminded me of the beige trimline phone that my boyfriend bought me in high school. Nevertheless, I wanted to make sure that my grandmother had no reason to say that I was "keeping" my son from her. Just then, the doorbell rang. Another strange man introduced himself to me. *Now what?* This man was short and White, unlike the strange man who called me at work. I laughed out loud in my head because I had surmised that the strange man on the phone was tall and Black.

I opened the front door and unlocked the screen door to let him in. The strange man had a manila folder with him. He sat beside me on my black leather couch and looked around. My son was upstairs in his bedroom. Strangely, he had been on his best behavior over the past couple of days. The strange man pulled out papers from his folder and started taking notes. He asked the same questions that the strange man on the phone asked. Annoyed, I gave him the same answers. I wondered if the two of them had spoken and whether, or not, this was just a tactic to see if I was lying before. The man asked if he could speak with my son.

Just as I was about to lead him upstairs, my son came down from his bedroom. I wondered if he had been listening. I noticed the man admiring our home. Our house was immaculate, as always. The furniture was new and nice. The three of us sat on the couch, as I listened to the strange man ask my son a bunch of questions about school. The subject of my grandmother was not brought up, until my son left the room. Before leaving, the strange man handed me his business card and explained that he was an advocate for my son. He also asked me if I was aware that my grandmother had "grandparent rights," which gave her the right to see my son. I laughed out loud in my head. Shenanigans!

I had done a little digging myself and had spoken with a lawyer. I sarcastically asked the strange man if he was aware of the term "custodial interference." I went on to explain how I had nurtured the relationship between my grandmother and my son, but that I was under no obligation to fill the empty void in her life. This meant that I had every right to love and protect my son, and she had no right to interfere in *my* life. I never heard from the strange White man, or the stranger on the phone, ever again. My grandmother must have felt defeated and turned to the one person who I trusted less and hated more than her. The vicious cycle and the wrath of my grandmother would continue.

CHAPTER 17

What Lies Beneath: The Lies That Tore Us Apart

Desperate people do desperate things! Now, here I was in court—listening to all the horrible things that my son's father and my grandmother were saying. They had tried to fill the judge's head with lies about how I was such a bad parent. The judge wanted to know all about the summer camp and all the ways that I had been providing for my son. I testified that I had been gainfully employed by the same company since I graduated college. I owned my own home, had bought a new and reliable car every four years, and had provided a stable home for my son (since he was born.)

I added that I most definitely was not a drug addict, like my grandmother was painting me out to be. She actually stood up and blurted out that I was "on drugs" and my son was "in a gang!" I would have actually laughed out loud, if it wasn't so painful. I was heartbroken - torn apart! I told the judge that anyone and everyone who knew me, knew these five things… I don't smoke, drink, do drugs, or gamble. And I love my son! I showed the judge the letters that my son had written to me while he was away. The judge read the letters and told the court that it appeared that my son and I loved each other very much!

I felt proud when the judge said that it seemed like my son loved me. Ironically, it was my son's own testimony that helped the judge to decide that blatant lies were being told. This must have been at least the second or third go-around of custody battles between me, my grandmother, and my son's father. The judge made it clear that, based on my son's interview, I was a good mother who clearly loved her son. My son was fifteen at the time and testified in the judge's chambers, with only the judge and court clerk present. I was later given a copy of the tape.

However, the judge (in his infinite wisdom) decided that it might be a good idea to "give me a break." He granted my grandmother "temporary" custody of my son. I thought, "*He must be experiencing temporary insanity.*" I didn't want a break! I wanted my son! But the truth was that I was tired and did need a break—a break from life! Several months passed, and I got another call at work—on my same cell phone. *Who was it now?* A nurse from East Orange General Hospital was calling to ask if I was my son's mother! *What an odd question!* She proceeded to tell me that my son had been left there after a car accident and that my grandmother had refused to pick him up from the hospital. She went on to say that my son had stolen a car and crashed it, but was in stable condition. *That's* why he was in the hospital. The stolen car belonged to my grandmother. That's why the nurse was calling *me*. Shenanigans!

My grandmother had relinquished her "parental rights" and left the custody papers with the nurse. The nurse explained that, if I did not come for my son, she would call DYFS and he would become a ward of the state. *The irony of it all…* I left work immediately and caught the train from New York to Jersey. When I arrived at the hospital, my son sat up in the bed and smiled. He said, "I knew you would come!" I ran over and hugged him. After a long embrace, the lies would start again. My son tried to convince me that my grandmother "had gone crazy and should be locked up in a mental institution." I silently agreed with him and hated my grandmother, but I knew that he was lying about what happened. The nurse came in with the release forms and a piece of paper that relinquished all parental rights back to me.

My grandmother no longer wanted custody of my son. My son, like my grandmother, had a knack for manipulating people and situations. I knew that the only reason he had the nurse call me was because my grandmother didn't want him in her home anymore. I went back to the court, immediately, and told the judge what happened. My grandmother's "temporary guardianship" was terminated and, once again, I was granted full custody. But my son continued to act out. As much as it hurt my heart to do so, I made one of the hardest decisions I ever had to make. I knew someday that I might regret it, but I did what I thought was right at the time.

I made a decision that I thought would help my son. I agreed to let him stay with his father, temporarily. Then, something went wrong. My son had been the one to call me - again! My son was living with his father and things had gone too far. They were supposed to be living in New Brunswick with his father's then current wife, but he took him to live with another woman in East Orange. I had no idea who this other woman was and where my son was living.

For once, my son actually believed that his father was doing something wrong and called me for help (like he always did.) Once again, my son's behavior had taken a turn for the worse and his grades fell behind. The principal called me because my son had not been to school and he couldn't reach his father. I had spoken with my son several times since he left the house. I had previously spoken with his father about the calls that I was getting from the school principal. His father claimed that my son needed time to adjust to the new school and to living with him.

I contacted the school principal to see if my son's attendance and grades had improved. He informed me that my son had missed several days and would be expelled. I tried calling his father's cell phone number and continued to get his voice mail. I tried calling his home number and his wife told me that she didn't know where her own husband was. She said that he and my son had left in the middle of the night. *What the hell was going on?* I hired another lawyer, just like I did during the custody battles. I had the original custody papers that proved that I was my son's mother and had full custody, before all of the "temporary custody" shenanigans. I tried to be patient with my new lawyer, but it seemed like another court hearing would take forever.

I had to find my son, and there was no time to wait! His father had already taken him! Then, I remembered the caller ID. My son had called me from an unfamiliar number at least three different times. I didn't think of it at the time. I scrolled through and found the number. I called, but his father hung up when he heard my voice. I dialed 411 and asked for the address to the phone number. I got it! I called my lawyer to let him know that I was going to get my son. He told me to wait until the court hearing. *No way!* I called a friend to let him know where I was going. I jumped into the car and went to the address that I had written down on a piece of paper. I arrived at a huge white building in East Orange. There were so many names and I didn't have an apartment number.

I had already called the police (just in case things got ugly.) While I waited for them, I began to ring every bell. I was determined to get my son! Then, I noticed a bell with a Muslim last name. I rang the bell and heard the voice of my son's father through the intercom. I yelled at him to give me my son! Just as he came downstairs, the police arrived. My son's father walked up to me, as if he was about to hit me. One of the police officers grabbed him by the arm and said, "Wait a minute!" I showed him my custody papers, and he demanded that my son be turned over to me. My son's father claimed that my son wasn't there. He said that he was in school.

I knew that there was a Masjid around the corner and I asked the police officers to come with me. They followed me to the school, but didn't come inside. Once again, I was determined to get my son. I walked up to the counter and asked for my son by name. To my surprise, my son was in the front of the building. He had been acting out in class and was being punished. I called out to him and he looked surprised to see me. He had the same look on his face that he had when I entered his hospital room, after he had stolen my grandmother's car and crashed it. There was a woman at the front desk of the Masjid, who looked confused because she didn't know what was going on. I told her who I was and why I was there. She called a man to the front desk to assist. The man said that he couldn't let my son go with me.

I was already fuming about this whole "kidnapping" situation and was in no mood for more shenanigans! I demanded that my son be handed over to me. I knew this tactic wouldn't work because I was speaking to a Muslim man. So, I informed him that the police were waiting outside. Without looking at my custody papers, the man grabbed my son from the corner he was sitting in and told him to go. When we got home, my son ran up to his room crying. I wondered why he was so upset since he had been the one to call me. He's the one who called me crying—saying that he was scared and that I should come and get him. Not only had *he* called me, but the principal had called too because my son was no longer going to school. Now, he had been kicked out of so many schools that I wondered if he would ever have a chance at a successful life. I will never understand how, or why, my grandmother and my son's father thought that they would be better parents than I was to my own son!

I thought back to when my grandmother just left my son at East Orange General Hospital. Once again, my son continued to act out and make poor choices. And, now, here we were—back in court… After showing the judge my son's report cards and copies of letters from the schools he attended while he was away from me, he said that my grandmother and my son's father obviously had not done any better. The judge said that he was tired of seeing my son in his courtroom. He asked me what I thought should happen to my son, but I couldn't speak. I was speechless! The judge said that he wouldn't put the burden of making such a decision on me. He sympathized with me and said that it was shameful—the number of times I had been in his courtroom with my son. He said that he would not put any added pressure on me and "would relieve me from the burden" of having to decide what should be done with my son.

The judge decided that juvenile detention was not the answer. He decided that one year in jail might help my son to make better choices. That's when I knew the relationship between me and my son was over. I didn't realize it then, but that's when my plan to move to Arizona came to fruition. The next time that I saw my son, he was wearing an orange jumpsuit. Over that year, I had tried to visit him in jail. I didn't want to, but I felt that I had to. To my surprise, he didn't want to see me. As usual, I was to blame for everything that had gone wrong. All the lies… As usual, everything was my fault. My son took no responsibility, whatsoever, and he definitely did not blame his father or my grandmother.

I even got blamed for the time when my son's younger uncle wasn't allowed to visit him in jail. A woman from the jail and one of the correction officers called to ask me of the relationship between the young man and my son. I explained that the man was my son's uncle (his father's younger brother.) Apparently, a decision had been made that only immediate family could visit. When my son's uncle arrived and found that he was not on the list, everyone automatically assumed that I had something to do with it. I told them that they give me too much credit. I wasn't a conniving, hateful person, and I wasn't a liar. That was my grandmother's and his father's thing.

I thought back to the court shenanigans and how my grandmother had tried to convince me that she was trying to do a "good" thing. She claimed that she was only *mediating* between me, my son, and his father. She actually stood on the steps of the courthouse and had the audacity to tell me that "she was doing what was best for my son!" My first thought was to knock her down the steps. Then, I remembered that we had just left a court of law and I did not want to go to jail. So, I laughed out loud in my head instead. *The nerve! How could being away from me be best for him? What kind of mother did she think I was?*

All the times that my mother drank and used drugs; all the times that she beat me; all the times that I watched her get beaten and raped; all the times she had left me all alone—never once had anyone tried to protect me, or do what they thought was best for me! Never once had my grandmother taken my mother to court! Never once had she called DYFS on my mother! *Where had my grandmother been then? Where had my mother—my grandmother—and my son's father been when my son had cancer?*

I was in debt up to my ears in hospital bills and neither of them offered to help me. There was no financial support and definitely no emotional support. One of the few times, in my entire life, that I remember someone else attempting to stand up for me and lend some type of emotional support was when my grandmother's sister told my grandmother that she should let me go outside and play sometimes (instead of staying in the house cleaning.) I was a child then. Now, here she was telling me that she wouldn't let my grandmother take my son from me. Yet, another lie.

My ex-boyfriend's mother, the mother of my "first love", was also determined to support me by finding out the truth. She had taken off work for the first time in thirty years. After we left the courtroom, she told me that she would not have believed the lies my grandmother was telling had she not heard them with her own ears. Through all her lies and family secrets, I found out one of the biggest lies of all. I found out that my youngest aunt had a different father than my mother and my eldest aunt. *Could it be true? Had my very own grandmother (Miss Holier-Than-Thou) actually had a child out of wedlock?* I thought back to the time when I found out that my grandfather wasn't even my "real" grandfather. That was when I learned that my mother was not the only addict in the family.

None of this seemed to matter, as my life continued to unravel. I kept trying to recall where I went wrong. I had worked hard all of my life! I was trying to be a parent; not my son's friend. Now, after all was said and done, my grandmother wanted to take credit for "raising" my son. Like I was some kind of deadbeat mother… I wanted to forgive them, but I blamed my grandmother for ruining the relationship between me and my son. And I blamed his father for subjecting my son to a life that I would have never exposed him to. My grandmother preferred to keep the ongoing battle between me and her a secret because she wanted to protect her reputation. She didn't want anyone to know the truth. She did the same thing to me that she did to my mother. She had tormented us until we couldn't take it anymore. Ironically, she wanted to punish us for having a child out of wedlock. She wanted to punish us for her *own* sins!

She wanted to make up for her life's mistakes by claiming my son. But you can't live on a lie. I am the one who sat up with him all night, when he was colicky. I am the one who tucked him in at night. I am the one who taught my son life's lessons, just as my mother taught me. I am the one who took him to Little League practice, and to all of his basketball and softball games. I am the one who slept at the hospital day and night, when he had cancer. I am the one who hugged away the pain, when his father didn't show up on the weekends. I am the one who held him by the hand, when he was scared and wiped his tears away, whenever he was hurt.

At the end of the day, no matter how much she lied and how hard she tried, my grandmother would never be my son's mother. I was his mother, but the days when I was my son's "Pook" and he was mine were over. This had become our life now. I didn't understand all the pain and hatred that lie beneath… This was another one of those situations that would be a test of my faith. I would have to trust that God would get me through. My family was torn apart. But I wasn't going to let them distract me from my purpose in life. I kept moving forward with my vision.

CHAPTER 18

My Vision; My Dream:
Not Like My Mother

N ow that my son was gone, I wasn't sure what I wanted to do
with my life. I had worked with computers since I was in elementary school and enjoyed working with children (whenever I got
the chance.) A coworker told me that I should get away and clear my
head. He and his fiancée had visited Arizona and told me how beautiful the state was. I decided that I had no longer wanted to visit the
jail because I didn't want to see my son locked up behind bars, like my
mother. Seeing him in that orange jumpsuit, with handcuffs around
his wrists, brought tears to my eyes. I decided to visit Arizona instead.
I thought about how my grandmother and I never talked about all
the times my mother spent in jail. She kept this little tidbit to herself,
along with all the other lies and family secrets. As I grew older, more
lies and family secrets began to unfold.

I was not going to let my confidence be shattered. I was not going
to be defeated. I was not going to be an addict. I was not going to be
like my mother. The first time I knew that I didn't want to be like my
mother was when I was six years old. It was right after kindergarten,
and I had just started the first grade. My mother and her boyfriend
drank all the time. Those were the days that we spent stealing from the
corner liquor store, before going to Weequahic Park. For some strange
reason, we always had a baby carriage with us (but there was no baby.)

I knew right then and there that my life was going to be a hot mess. By the time I was seven, I had started cooking and taking care of my mother. She was always drunk, or high. When she wasn't drinking or smoking, she was a good mother. But I always knew that I didn't want to be like her. Years passed, and by the time I was ten years old, I knew that I needed to come up with a plan. I needed a plan, a vision, a dream.

I spent each day thinking of ways to survive. The first promise that I made to myself was to *not* drink, or smoke. The only time that I drank and smoked was when my mother offered me sips of her wine coolers and let me puff off her cigarette. As much as I hated cigarettes, I loved to watch my mother smoke and make those rings come off the end. Other than my eighth-grade graduation, I never took another drink. That day, Amy and I stood in her back yard exchanging sips from a 40 oz bottle of Colt 45. Staying clean and sober was something that I would not compromise on, and it was more than a decision. It was a conviction!

I learned in church that a conviction determines a sense of purpose. Convictions require character and courage. My convictions define who I am and the choices I make in life. It took courage to stand up to the challenges of my life and the people who didn't believe in my convictions. I have always believed that "if you don't stand for something, you'll fall for anything!"

I hated the taste and smell of cigarettes. In high school, I let someone give me a "shotgun." That's when someone blows smoke from a joint directly into your face so that you get an immediate "contact high." I couldn't breathe and almost choked. After that, high school was a breeze. I was never tempted again and never got the urge to smoke, or drink.

I had other convictions. I was convinced that if you'll lie, you'll cheat. If you'll cheat, you'll steal. If you steal, you'll kill. I would live by these rules for the rest of my life and have tried to instill the same in my son. It was important for me to make good choices, if I did not want to be like my mother. Now, I was an adult. I had tried so hard to do the right thing. I wanted to make good choices, but things weren't working out as I had planned.

My plan was to give my son a better life than I had. My plan was to "not" be like my mother. Then, *she* came back into my life. It was ironic... But throughout my life, I found myself making choices based upon things that I learned from my mother and grandmother. For instance, I chose my first home in Union because it was near Stuyvesant Avenue. My grandmother owned a house off Stuyvesant Avenue in Irvington. It was the house where my mother lived on the third floor and my youngest aunt lived on the second floor; the house where we had our first fight.

I didn't like my grandmother, but I respected her. I would watch and listen as she handled her business transactions on Stuyvesant Avenue in Union. Every weekend, she would run errands, such as going to the bank and paying bills. I would pay special attention, whenever she paid her bills and talked about balancing her checkbook. I would always admire how big, pretty, and clean Stuyvesant Avenue was. I swore that, when I became an adult, I would work on that same street and buy a house in that area. Well, I did just that.

When I was fifteen, I walked up and down Stuyvesant Avenue looking for a job. When I was sixteen and a junior at Irvington High, I worked at a bank on Stuyvesant Avenue in Union. It was my second "real" job, and I worked the Automatic Teller Machine (ATM.) I liked my job at the bank. However, I sometimes hated going to work because one of my coworkers was sexist and racist. He was a White man, who looked to be in his early thirties. He would always make sexist remarks about women and tell stupid jokes about Black people.

Later, as a young adult, I would also be sexually harassed by an HR rep at AT&T. The irony is that he was Black and had also made a pass at me. It all started, when I went to talk to him because one of my White coworkers slapped me on the ass, when I walked passed his desk. *Was he crazy? Was the HR manager also crazy? Had the whole world gone mad?* Another manager at AT&T said that my hairstyle was "too ethnic." She was a Black woman! *Was my mother right all along? Was I being treated differently because of the color of my skin?*

I couldn't afford to quit my job. I needed the money for me and my son. I had always worked. Although I worked at KFC as a summer job when I was only fourteen, my first "real" job had been as a file clerk in Haynes Department store on Halsey Street, downtown Newark. I had many jobs, including a fast-food cashier, an unpaid internship, and a childcare provider—all by the time I turned twenty. When I was about thirty years old, I bought my first house off Stuyvesant Avenue in Union.

Several months later, I saw my mother begging in the parking lot of the Pathmark on Bergen Street in Newark. After panhandling at several other cars, she came right up to my car and asked me for money. I was hurt, disgusted, and embarrassed all at the same time. She didn't even recognize me! That's when she entered my life (again.)

When I asked if she knew who I was, she said, "No. Should I?" When I told her that I was her daughter, she immediately called out my name. I felt better. I told her that I wouldn't give her money, but that I would buy her something to eat. I decided to go shopping and get her some clean underwear and new clothes. My mother ended up staying with me at the new house for about three weeks, before she pulled one of her disappearing acts and went missing in action again.

For three whole weeks, she lived like a normal person in a nice house, with her own bedroom and clean sheets. My mother didn't have a key to the house, but she was free to eat and roam about as she pleased. I cooked every night when I got home from work and asked her not to leave the house. Sometimes, I would come home to find her smoking on the front porch. I didn't mind because it was better than her smoking inside the house. She seemed to like the swing bench as much as I did.

My mother started talking to my neighbors, which I didn't like. I didn't want them in my business. They knew I had a son and an ex-fiancé, and that was all they needed to know. I came home from work one day to find the upstairs guest bedroom empty. The bed was unmade, and my mother's things were gone. I immediately checked the rest of the house to see if anything else was missing. I was relieved that everything seemed to be in its rightful place, but sad that my mother was missing. For a short moment, we were a family. And just like that, she was gone!

I thought back to the time when my mother and my two aunts were at the hospital with me—when I gave birth to my son. I had wondered why the three of them were there, since I had not spoken to my mother in years other than the time at my grandmother's house when she commented on my "ass-whooping" and called me and my unborn child "bastards." My eldest aunt and I were not close at all, and I really thought that she didn't like me. At that time, the only one of them that seemed to care about me was my youngest aunt. But, now, I no longer trusted her.

As it turned out, I was right about my youngest aunt. She had been the one who called the police, after me and my mother's fight. *How could she have abandoned me, when she was supposed to be my favorite?* After all, she was the cute, sweet, light-skinned one who always had my back, except for that one time. We had always been more like sisters than aunt and niece. When I found out that I was pregnant, she was the first person in my family who I told.

I remembered how I had gone to her house to spend the weekend with my cousins and how we had all sat and talked for hours. Back then, I spent most of my time watching Bruce Lee karate movies on TV my uncle. I had grown fond of my youngest aunt's new husband because he made me laugh, when he wasn't drinking. I hated when my uncle got drunk. He would yell and scream. Then, my aunt would have a black eye. He'd always say that he wasn't hurting her. But he was!

Still, it was hard to stay mad at him. Even when my new uncle threatened my youngest aunt, he made me laugh. He would say things like, "If you don't get your monkey-ass in that bedroom…" He was laugh out loud funny! He would always talk about my aunt's toe jam and "stinky feet." After she came out of the bathroom, he would say, "Something must have crawled up in you and died!"

My new uncle would cook breakfast and dinner. And we would watch the *Five Fingers of Death*, *Drunken Monkey*, and other classic kung fu flicks all day long on Sundays. I loved him like I had known him forever, especially after he saved me from drowning at the beach (when I was nine.) We had gone to Asbury Park and I thought that I would try out my new swimming lessons in the ocean. That didn't work out so well!

I had become a part of my aunt's new family, and we were a happy family. At some point, I decided to tell them that I was pregnant. Back then, I knew that I could trust my aunt and that she would understand. Her only daughter, who was four years younger than me and who was my closest cousin, had given birth to a son the year before.

My cousin was very young and had just begun high school. I had just begun my sophomore year of college. Our sons would be ten months apart. Like our mothers, my cousin and I had gone through everything together and we would also share this special time in our lives together. After breaking the news to my aunt, I waited for my cousin to come downstairs with the number for her OB-GYN. She was very poised and mature for such a young girl.

My aunt suggested that I tell my grandmother the news right away. I told her that I did not want to do that and asked if she would do it for me. My aunt told me that it was my news and I should be the one to tell people. She picked up the receiver of the telephone mounted to the kitchen wall, dialed my grandmother's number, and handed me the phone. My aunt stood next to me as I told my grandmother that I was pregnant.

My grandmother demanded that I come to her house immediately to talk about the situation. I explained that I would come, but that I was not getting an abortion and I didn't need or want her help with anything. I headed to my grandmother's house and made a pit stop at my new boyfriend's house to pick him up for backup.

When we arrived, my grandmother was sitting on the couch with my grandfather's mother and it was obvious that she had already shared the news. That's when I knew that I would find my own apartment for me and my child and would no longer be staying at my grandmother's house over summer break. I returned back to Rutgers and finished my classes, until it was time for me to have my baby.

Much to my chagrin, my eldest aunt arrived to pick me and my beautiful new baby up from the hospital. The original plan was that we would stay at my grandmother's house for the summer, until I went back to school. Then, my grandmother decided that she would renovate the basement so that we could live with her forever. Of course, this was done without any input from me! There she was, doing it again… My grandmother was making decisions about other people's lives.

When we left the hospital, my eldest aunt and her husband took me out for breakfast. We ate, and I pretended to enjoy myself. I disliked my eldest aunt because, unlike my youngest aunt, she sided with my grandmother on every occasion and had never really been there for me. During my childhood, and all the times when my mother was missing in action, I never remember my eldest aunt coming to my rescue. I wondered why she was here now.

Once she realized that I intended to keep my baby, my eldest aunt bought me a used book from the library on "How to be a Mother." I laughed out loud in my head. She had never been a mother. Motherhood is something that I had hoped to learn from my own mother, or my grandmother. Motherhood comes from the heart. It wasn't something that I wanted to learn from a used library book.

After breakfast that day, I was in a hurry to get home and spend some alone time with my new perfect baby boy. I wondered if my mother felt the same way that I did the first time that I laid my eyes on my new baby. I remember laying my new son on his back in his new crib. His father "went all out" and paid for half of the crib. I played with my son's fingers and toes, and turned the mobile on so that it would play music while he slept.

Thinking back, he must have loved music as much as my mother and I did. When he was beginning to walk, he would hold on to the edge of the coffee table in the living room, bend his knees, and bounce up and down to the music playing on the radio. It was the cutest thing I had ever seen, and it made me proud to know that he appreciated music and dancing the way my mother and I did.

When my son was older, he would dance on my feet to "Ooh Child" by *The Five Stairsteps*. My new perfect son was my new inspiration. He made all the wrongs right, and all was right with the world again! Every time that I looked at him, I smiled. Each night before we went to bed, I stood over his crib and watched him sleep. He was so perfect—his curly hair, his caramel complexion, and his baby-soft skin. I wanted to eat him up!

Watching my son, I remembered that I never danced on my mother's feet. But I loved to watch her dance to her favorite songs. My grandmother wasn't a music buff like me and my mother, but she loved *Kool & The Gang*. Whenever "Ladies' Night" came on the radio, she would throw her silk scarf around her neck and clap her hands together just like my mother did. My grandmother looked like *Snoopy* from the Charlie Brown cartoon, when she danced. But her all-time favorite song in the whole wide world was "Silent Night" by *The Temptations*. She would play that song, all day long, from Thanksgiving to New Year's Day! I laughed out loud in my head.

When my son heard the music from his mobile, he smiled up at me from his crib. I loved him more than life itself. I would count his perfect fingers and toes, every night before I went to bed. All my life, I had been looking for someone to love and someone to love me.

When I held my son in my arms for the first time, all I could think was that he was all mine! I now had someone to love and someone who would love me back, unconditionally!

I was not like my mother at all, and she was no longer a part of my life. As happy as I was, thoughts of getting out of my grandmother's house never left my mind. She never let a day go by without reminding me that she didn't want me and my baby there, especially after I told her that we would not live in her basement. Every day spent there was a constant reminder of my awful childhood.

Growing up in the environments that my mother subjected me to helped me to become a brave, little soldier. Even in situations where I was scared, I managed to throw caution to the wind and fight for my life. It was always do or die, kill or be killed. My mother had taught me to protect myself, by any means necessary. I wished she had followed her own advice.

Flashbacks of my childhood brought me back to reality. I didn't want to follow in my mother's footsteps. I saw a different vision and had a different goal. I often wondered if my mother had a dream, or a goal. I thought about her determination to get her GED after I was born and how she went on to get her associate degree from Rutgers University in Newark. I wondered if she had dreamed past then and whether, or not, she had given any thought to her new baby's life. Maybe, I wasn't perfect (like my son), but I was hers.

I continued to reminisce... I remembered how I watched my baby sleep. I remembered how there were always dishes in the sink waiting to be washed. Every time that I went into my grandmother's kitchen, I was reminded of the time my mother taunted me about "getting my ass whooped," while I was pregnant. Sadly, I was still with the boyfriend who beat me. I guess my grandmother was right in saying that I was following in my mother's footsteps. This only gave me more incentive to follow my own dreams and not to be like my mother.

Little did my grandmother know, I was concocting a plan to leave her house as soon as feasibly possible. My only wish was that I had my friends Karen, Egypt, and Amy to help me like they did— when we were younger. I thought about my school counselor at Rutgers. He had been helpful in getting me financial aid and seemed like he might be trustworthy. Since the time when my ex-boyfriend (my first love) and I broke up because he gave me an ultimatum and then cheated on me, I had not trusted anyone.

My school counselor was a young, tall, slim, and somewhat handsome Black man. I'm sure he would prefer it if I referred to him as African-American. I never really got into the whole "race thing", or hang-ups about the color of people's skin, until my mother accused me of loving my cute, sweet, light-skinned aunt more than her. I remembered how that whole conversation started—all because my White teacher thought I was a "special" student. My school counselor thought I was special too. He was actually the EOF counselor in charge of providing ongoing support and financial guidance for students in need.

I was definitely in need of some guidance! I wanted an apartment and needed a car. More than anything, I wanted to get out of my grandmother's house immediately! My EOF counselor told me about graduate and family housing and some other options that would help me toward my goal of becoming independent. We discussed various options, such as applying for additional funding, and filing as an independent student rather than a dependent. All I needed to do was get my mother's signature and consent. That's when I knew that my dreams of becoming independent would never come true.

I had a flashback of all the arguments and fights that me and my mother had. I hadn't backed down when she "mean-mugged" me from her bedroom window on my first day of kindergarten, and I wasn't going to back down now. I didn't back down when we received the eviction notice, and she pulled one of her "disappearing acts," and I wasn't going to back down now. I didn't back down when my mother and I damn near killed each other in the new "family" house in Irvington, and I wasn't going to back down now. I was not a quitter! I was determined to become a functioning adult. I headed back to the "family" house where I was told I would find my mother.

I told her my plans, and she laughed out loud—just as she did when she read the letter from the White teacher (when I was in third grade.) I couldn't understand why my mother always thought my success was so funny. I ignored her and slammed the papers on the kitchen table. I told her that I was not leaving until she signed them. She didn't sign the papers, and I remembered the last fight we had. I decided to walk away—suddenly realizing that I was already emancipated and no longer needed her anymore.

My beautiful son and I moved into our new apartment in August, three months after I gave birth to him. I had worked since I was fourteen, including all that summer, and every year after that. I saved up enough money for a new car. I bought a "leftover" from the previous year, with no mileage. It was red, my favorite color! I didn't want a used car because I needed something reliable and wanted my son to be safe. I wasn't able to buy new furniture right away. My great-grandmother gave me an old brown-and-white plaid couch. The mother of my ex-boyfriend, "my first love," also chipped in and bought things for my first apartment. She arrived with a broom, mop, bucket, iron board, and can opener in hand.

The rent was $795 each month, plus utilities. The apartment was located on the college campus. Students and nonstudents lived there. I was a full-time student with a full-time baby and a part-time job. I worked nights and weekends at Joyce Leslie in the nearby shopping plaza. My "baby's daddy" did not move in with us, but he was still around. I put my son in a local day care, and he got a severe diaper rash. That's when I knew that I needed more money to pay for higher-quality care. My vision of working with young children had resurfaced, and I was about to give birth to a new dream!

CHAPTER 19

AZ Flava

No matter how hard I had strived to reach my dream—life, somehow, always seemed to repeat itself. I had spent most of my life trying not to be like my mother. But, the older I became, the more I wondered about the people who were a part of my life and the influence they had over me. Thoughts of the next seven years consumed me. *Oh what a tangled web we weave, when we first attempt to deceive!* That's what I would say every day, twenty-four hours a day, and 365 days per year (for the next seven years.)

Here I was, in my forties, and I still couldn't seem to find a good man. *Was I turning out to be like my mother, after all?* I consoled myself by agreeing with most of the other women in my life. The consensus was that "they just don't seem to make good men anymore." In my eyes, a good man is a man who takes care of business. I wondered if I would ever find a man like that—a man who takes care of his family and his children. I wanted a man like my grandfather, who would take care of children that weren't even his own. That's the type of man my grandfather was. He loved my grandmother, unconditionally. He loved her children, and he loved her grandchildren.

I never had a problem meeting men. My only problem was meeting the right men. Short men, tall men, fat men, skinny men, lying men, cheating men, cheap men, trifling-ass men. You name it, and I dated it! I even had a few female friends who thought that they could turn me out. One friend became irate when I told her that there was no way in hell I wanted her because I'm "strictly dickly."

I remember the men I met around the way, in the hood. Those were the "cuties", hanging out on the corner at the bodegas (with the bald heads, or dreads.) They were so cute, so smooth, so suave. They had all the swag!

Then, there were the ones who you could catch a glimpse of while they were shooting hoops and rocking the latest kicks. Those were the roughnecks, who usually walked around displaying their six-packs, rocking their Timberland boots—with their jeans sagging. Most of them were too fine to be fine, or too cool to be cute. They had a special way of folding the brim of their caps and rockin' them to the side. Sometimes, they just let their caps hang from their back pockets. These were my Jersey dudes!

Then, there were my New York dudes. They were definitely too cool, always rockin' their caps to the front to represent their hood. They loved to let you know if they were from Brooklyn, or Harlem. It was important to them, but it didn't make a difference to me. They always wore gold chains and had a special way of walking, real tough-like, as if they possessed a very special gift in their pants. I laughed out loud in my head because they are too much! Most of the guys I've met in New York were from Brooklyn (Bed-Stuy, East New York, or Brownsville.) They had a "flava" all their own, hollering out, "Hey, girl!" "How you doin', beautiful?" "Whassup, Ma?" with that NY accent.

Dudes from Jersey just said, "What's going on, gorgeous?" and kept it moving. Unlike my Jersey and New York dudes, men from Arizona had another whole type of flava. They weren't actually "from" AZ. They were from anywhere and nowhere, and most of them had no swag whatsoever. And then, there was Reggie! We met at a mutual friend's fiftieth birthday party. My two best friends at the time, Kerri and Tasha, had dragged me out the house and convinced me to come all the way to Scottsdale. I had been traveling out of town on business for the past several months and hadn't been out dancing in a while.

I always had a good time when I went out with Kerri and Tasha. Kerri was a native of Arizona and had grown up in Phoenix her entire life. She was intelligent, Black, and a single mother. The one thing that we didn't have in common was that she had been married and divorced. She was ten years older than I was, but we connected on so many levels. Tasha, on the other hand, was ten years younger than me. She was from Louisiana, very cute, and was also Black. We too connected on so many levels.

The strange thing was that Kerri and Tasha hated each other. They never actually had a "beef"—but, whenever the three of us were together, you could always sense tension in the air. I was curious to know why my two best friends didn't get along, but decided to wait until one of them was ready to tell me the story. One night, we were hanging out and Kerri explained that she liked a guy who also hung out at the club we were going to. She said that he was cute and a good dancer. Kerri had set her sights on this guy and intended to make her move.

Apparently, the cute and "good-dancer" guy had his sights set on Tasha. I decided to confirm the story with Tasha, who explained that she had no interest in this guy whatsoever. She told me that Kerri was obsessed with him and mad at her for no reason. I adored both of my best friends and decided to stay out of it. Tasha sat at the bar, and I sat at the table waiting for the waitress to bring my food. When the waitress arrived at the table where Kerri and I were sitting, she asked if I wanted a glass of red Kool-Aid to drink. I laughed out loud in my head.

The dee-jay was playing one of my favorite "Stepper" songs, and I got up from the table. As I walked toward the dance floor, a six-foot, dark-skinned man walked my way. He introduced himself by name and asked if I wanted to dance. The dark-skinned man was dressed in a beige suit. It was a two-piece suit and was unlike the suits that most of the other "Steppers" wore. He had nice short curly hair and pretty white teeth. He wore expensive-looking dress shoes, and I noticed that he was a little chubby. He also had a unibrow and a very thick mustache, like men wore back in the 1970s. Clearly, I had some work to do.

As a new "Stepper," I began taking lessons in Phoenix. I stepped with my friends at The Legion, Bobby C's, and The Elks in Phoenix a couple of nights a week. Stepping gave me the chance to do two things that I love—dancing and traveling. Most of the annual stepper events were held out of town. Whenever I was back home on the East Coast, I "stepped" with the New York Steppers at the Ripley-Grier Dance Studio, the Rustik Tavern, and other local spots in Brooklyn.

That night, back in Arizona, Reggie and I danced to three songs in a row. The dark-skinned man walked me back to the table and sat next to me. He seemed very aggressive, but he was charismatic, and I liked his smile. We exchanged telephone numbers, but I explained that I would be traveling for business over the next couple of months. Driving home from the party, my cell phone rang. I didn't recognize the number and figured that the incoming call must be from the dark-skinned man who I met at the party. I was wondering why he was calling, after I told him that I had an early flight back to Jersey the next morning.

I answered the call and pretended that I didn't recognize the voice. I asked, *"Who is this again?"* Reggie repeated his name and asked if I would meet him at the after-party. I explained again that

I could not come to the after-party because I was tired and wanted to go home to prepare for my flight back to Jersey. We talked on the phone for my entire ride home from Scottsdale to Surprise. The after-party was in Phoenix and, even if I didn't have to catch a flight in the morning, I had no interest in going.

Kerri called me that morning at ten o'clock, and I told her that I had just finished packing and was on my way to the airport. She told me to call her when I arrived to Jersey. I called Tasha to let her know that I was okay and would be back in town in a few weeks. Whenever I traveled to the East Coast for business, a few weeks turned into a few months. Several months had passed, and I had been back and forth to Arizona a few times, but I hadn't spoken with or seen Reggie. It was Thanksgiving weekend, and Kerri and I decided to go to a party in Phoenix.

I met and danced with another cute guy at the party. We exchanged numbers and talked on the phone every night over the next six months. He was from Tennessee and had been visiting his older brother in Phoenix for the holidays. By the time I returned to Arizona from Jersey, my short-lived romance with the guy from Tennessee was over. He turned out to be jealous and insecure, and was always complaining about me traveling. Kerri welcomed me home by inviting me to a "First Fridays" party at The Legion in Phoenix. We were sitting at the table eating our fried catfish dinners, when Reggie walked over to greet us.

I didn't recognize him because a year had passed since we last spoke, on the night of the fiftieth birthday party, in Scottsdale. The funny thing is that I hadn't thought about Reggie one time. I was too consumed with the new cute guy, who I met during the Thanksgiving holiday. Although things hadn't worked out with him either, I pretended not to be too concerned about my single status because I was still in my early forties and fabulous! I was 5'9" tall and weighed about 145 pounds. I had long dreadlocks that flowed to the small of my back. I met men all the time and pretty much had my pick of them, like Tasha.

I had moved to Arizona from Jersey two years earlier and had since built my dream house. I also owned and operated my own childcare center. I was extremely happy and doing very well for myself. However, there was one thing missing. It had been two years, and I hadn't met the man of my dreams yet! I thought about Reggie. Aside from the two-piece beige suit that clearly was not a custom fit, my first impression of him was that he was also doing well for himself. I was attracted to well-dressed men who carried themselves a certain way.

On the way to my car, I made sure to ask all the right questions. I checked Reggie's fingers for a wedding band. I even asked if he was married, or "legally" divorced. I asked where he worked and whether, or not, he lived alone. I asked how many children he had and by how many women. Reggie gave all the "right" answers and told me exactly what he thought I wanted to hear. He said that he had been married for thirty years, but had been legally divorced for five years. He said that his "ex-wife" lived in Chicago and that they had two adult children. His said that his son was thirty and his daughter was twenty. I would find out later that he and his wife of over thirty years were very much married and living together in Arizona. I would also find out that he had three other children by three other women.

I would find out that Reggie was a habitual liar—a narcissist, who only cared about himself. He claimed to own businesses that didn't exist and bragged about jobs that he didn't have. He drove around in different cars; none of which were his. He was always borrowing money from people and never paid them back. He was straight up crazy—a psychopath! Besides the fact that he answered my telephone after being in my house only two times, I should have known Reggie was crazy when he told me on our first Thanksgiving that I didn't make candied yams like his mother.

He sat on my chocolate leather swivel barstool watching me cook a five-course meal. Then, out of nowhere, he blurted out that I didn't cut the yams up small enough! I attempted to explain to his spoiled, noncooking ass that I didn't like to cut my yams up too small because they would break up into little pieces when they start to boil. Reggie made a face like he was so disappointed that my yams might not turn out like his mother's. I never wanted to be like my *own* mother and was confused as to why he thought that I wanted to be anything like *his* mother, or anyone else in his family. They all seemed to be as crazy as he was.

One time, Reggie's younger sister called and asked if I was making sure that he was taking his daily vitamins. *He didn't need vitamins. He needed medication!* I immediately gave her the dumb look through the phone. She would always complain that her brother was not with her to help take care of her house over the holidays. Sometimes, I would come home from work and find that they had been talking on the phone for hours. She had the audacity to ask me why I was checking my own caller ID. I wondered about the nature of their relationship. They were a little too close, and it made me uncomfortable. I laughed out loud, as I thought about her poor husband and what his role in the family was. Shenanigans!

Reggie was eleven years older than I was and seemed to be well-mannered (most of the time.) He would standup, whenever I left the table. He would always make me wait until he walked around to open the car door. He would always hold the front door open for me every time I was entering, or leaving. I liked the attention he gave me, though he came on quite strong. One time, I went to "First Fridays" and was sitting at the table with my friends, Marcie and Greg. They were a married couple who had lived in Phoenix for the past twenty years. There were only three chairs at the round table, and we weren't expecting anyone else to join us.

Reggie spotted us and walked over to the table. He grabbed a chair from the table next to us and invited himself to sit down. Marcie and Greg gave each other a look. I knew that look and silently agreed that our uninvited dinner guest was not welcomed. Then, the strangest thing happened. Reggie, literally, lifted my chair up from the floor while I was sitting in it and put it directly next to his. I was practically sitting on his lap. Greg shouted, "Daaaamn!" and Marcie gave him another look. I should have known right then and there that "crazy" was not the word that best described Reggie. He was more like "crazy and deranged!" I had a real stalker on my hands!

One time, we went to a comedy show to see Bill Bellamy who had also graduated from Rutgers University and was good friends with my son's father. We were sitting close to the stage, and Reggie started playing with my hair. A woman, who was sitting behind us, leaned forward and commented that she adored the way he played with my dreads all through the show. Reggie had a habit of twirling my dreads around his fingers and putting them in his mouth, without me even noticing. I never knew who I was getting.

Reggie could be so sweet one minute and a total psychopath the next. One minute, he was the sweetest, nicest, most caring man I had ever met. The next minute, he was a lying, cheating, manipulating drunk who would do or say anything to get his way. He was like Dr. Jekyll and Mr. Hyde, but scarier. Still, something about him kept me drawn to him. I loved the way he took care of me, when he wasn't acting crazy. Wherever I went, he was there. When I came home from work, Reggie would coincidentally be turning the corner near my house. Whenever I went out with Kerri, Tasha, or one of my other girlfriends, he would "happen" to show up.

Whenever he wasn't at a party with me, it seemed like he had people watching me. It was starting to get really scary, but I couldn't seem to break away from him. It had been nearly two years since we first met, and Reggie had become a constant part of my life. One Friday night, Kerri and I went to Bobby C's, downtown Phoenix. In walked Reggie and "girls' night out" was over. The dee-jay played my two favorite *Aaliyah* songs, "Let Me Know" and "Rock the Boat" back to back. Arizona was really behind in their music and was always playing "old school" hits. That night, I didn't care because I loved *Aaliyah*.

As I walked toward the dance floor, Reggie walked toward me—the same way he did on the first night we met. Our eyes met, our lips locked, and our feet were still. We danced so closely together that we were hardly moving. It was as though we were the only two people in the club. It was then that I let Reggie know... We began to do everything together and he had officially become "my new man."

Reggie lived in the next town over, approximately twenty minutes from my house. He ate and slept at my house, six out of seven days each week. On Thursdays, he always went home to do his laundry even though I had a washer and dryer at my house. I didn't mind because I hated washing clothes. I had only seen the inside of his house on one occasion. We were on our way home from The Legion one night, and he suggested that we stop by his place to get some clothes. He invited me in for some juice.

Soon after that, he moved most of his clothes into the closet of one of my guest rooms. He started going home less and less. We began doing all of our chores together. Aside from grocery shopping, laundry was my least favorite chore. Finally, I asked Reggie when he was going to invite me over to his house again. I really didn't want to stay the night at his house because I had to take care of my dog, Cocoa, and didn't like leaving her alone at night. Reggie explained that he lived alone with his daughter, who was about to get married.

I remembered that Reggie told me he had been divorced for five years and that his ex-wife lived in Chicago, but he never mentioned where his "two" children lived. The plan was that I would be "allowed" into the house after Reggie's daughter had gotten married and moved back to Chicago. Reggie told me that I couldn't meet his daughter because of their religion. He was a Jehovah's Witness. At least, that's what he claimed. During our first year together, I never saw Reggie smoke or drink. Right around the same time that I had asked him if he was single, Reggie told me that he didn't smoke cigarettes or weed and that he only drank alcohol on special occasions.

This was important to me because of all the things that I had gone through with my mother. One day, Kerri and I were at "First Fridays" and I saw Reggie holding a small glass in his hand and smoking a cigarette. I couldn't tell what was in the glass and was more concerned with the fact that he was smoking. It was obvious that Reggie didn't know we were coming to "First Fridays." It was also obvious that he didn't see Kerri and I walk into the club. He was in the back of the club with his friend, Larry. Little did I know, Larry would become a thorn in my side. He had broken up with his girlfriend and had nothing better to do except ruin my relationship with Reggie.

Later that night, I questioned Reggie about what I saw. Reggie explained that he had not smoked or drank in years, and was only doing it because he was hanging out with Larry. I figured as much, and he promised not to smoke or drink again. This would not be the first lie that Reggie would tell. We were two years into our relationship, when I found out that our entire relationship had been a lie. I had gotten off work early and decided to go to Reggie's house "unannounced." I didn't see this as a problem because he had always come to my house unannounced and uninvited.

I parked the car and rang the bell. I saw the blinds move. Then, an older woman answered the door. We both seemed surprised, and I asked the woman if she was Reggie's aunt. I'm not sure why those words came out of my mouth, but they did. This woman looked way too old and grungy to be a "side chick." I stood in the doorway waiting for an answer. The older woman told me that she was Reggie's wife! I was in shock and attempted to correct her by asking if she meant to say his ex-wife. She corrected me by confirming that she was his current wife and had been so for the past thirty-five years.

The woman asked who I was, and I was happy to tell her that I was Reggie's girlfriend and had been so for the past two years.

As we stood in the front doorway giving each other the staredown, Reggie came to the door. He was shocked to see me. His eyes grew big and his mouth opened, but nothing came out. After what seemed like fifteen minutes of silence and the three of us standing there looking stupid, Reggie asked what I was doing there. *The nerve!* He stood there next to this old hag claiming to be his wife, and he thought I owed *him* an explanation. The woman and I stood with our arms folded and waited to hear Reggie's explanation. I wondered how he would weasel his way out of this one. Strangely, the older woman started to speak again before Reggie opened his mouth. She told Reggie that he owed me an apology.

Reggie grabbed me by the arm and walked me to the car. He whispered in my ear that he was sorry and would explain everything to me later that night. I drove twenty minutes to my house, sobbing like a baby. All of Reggie's lies were passing through my mind—the smoking, the drinking, and the wife. Now, I knew why I had only been to his house once in the past two years! I recalled that one night, on the way home from "First Fridays." Reggie and I had stopped at his house for a brief moment. He invited me inside for a glass of juice, while I waited for him to pack a bag for the rest of the weekend. I stood in the living room and admired his decorating taste. I didn't see anything that seemed particularly "girlish", or like it had been picked out by a woman.

The living room was decorated with a red leather sofa, a large wall mirror, and framed artwork. There were no family photos, and there were definitely no signs of a wife. Reggie returned to the living room of the one-story, three-bedroom house. He had his favorite brown suit, silk yellow dress shirt, and brown dress shoes. We walked to my car and drove home. My car had become "our" car, since his daughter had gotten married and moved back to Chicago. She had taken Reggie's car with her. At least, that's what he said. My house had become "our" house, except for the occasional change of clothes once per week. That's how our life had been for the past two years.

CHAPTER 20

Fatal Attraction

I laid in my bed—frozen. I couldn't move! Three days had passed since I found out about Reggie's "wife" and I felt like my life was over - again. It was as though history was repeating itself. I felt the same emptiness that I felt when "my first love" cheated on me with Goldie and when my fiancé got the stripper pregnant at his bachelor party. Once again, I wondered about the people in my life and what my life had become. My life had been full of so many disappointments—so much pain, and so many lies. I wondered when my pain would end.

Three days after Reggie's wife and I had our staredown at his house, he finally came to my house to explain. He stood in my doorway—ringing the bell, frantically. I had considered ignoring the bell and not answering the door. Instead, I opened the door and watched him sashay over to the chocolate leather chair in my living room. My leather couch and oversized chairs matched the swivel barstools that sat high at my island in the kitchen. From where I was standing, you could see the entire first floor. I was in the doorway between the daycare center and the kitchen. It was called the "Great Room," and it was fabulous (just like me!)

My house had two stories and was much bigger and newer than Reggie's. It also had a pool and jacuzzi in the back yard, as well as a full child care in the front part of the house. Reggie had to walk past the child care before he reached the living room. The child care was actually the formal dining room, which had been converted to a child care and was unoccupied at that time. I watched Reggie walk toward me, with all his swag. I couldn't help but notice that he was well-dressed, as usual. He wore a pair of brown dress slacks with my favorite yellow silk shirt, and his favorite brown dress shoes.

I wondered if he owned any raggedy clothes. Reggie asked me if he could sit down. It was obvious that we both felt awkward about what had taken place at his house the other day. I had so many questions and wondered where his wife was and how long they had "actually" been married. I wondered how he could lie to me for so long and hurt me so bad. He said he wanted to marry me…We planned to have a baby… He knew how important this was to me. I had convinced myself that this man had been made by God, especially for me. I thought that I was divinely favored. Then, Reggie would do something crazy (just like this) to bring me back to reality. I was often reminded of the scripture in 2 Corinthians 6:14 "Be ye not unequally yoked."

I sat in my favorite oversized leather chair—speechless—and waited for answers. He started by telling me that he was sorry he lied to me. Reggie attempted to explain that the reason why I had not heard from him that first year, after the fiftieth birthday party in Scottsdale, was because he was married and didn't want to hurt me. I asked him why he had approached me in the first place. *Why hadn't he continued to "not hurt me"?* After all, I hadn't contacted him and hadn't thought about him at all that year. As a matter of fact, I wondered if we would have even ended up together if he hadn't run into me and Kerri at "First Fridays" that night—two years ago.

Tears started to run down my face and I became furious, as I listened to the heap of lies coming from Reggie's mouth. It had been three days since we last saw each other and two whole years that he had been coming "home" to me. I wondered where his wife had been all the nights that he slept at my house. *Where had she been on the six days out of seven that he spent with me each week for the past two years?* Reggie continued to explain his relationship with his wife. He told me that she was a registered nurse who worked back-to-back, twelve-hour shifts. Her only day off during the week was Thursday, which explained why he always went home to do his laundry on Thursdays.

I felt like such an idiot. Reggie had been cheating on his wife while playing me the whole time, and I was in no mood to be married to another married man. The irony is that Reggie didn't have a whole lot to offer. I paid the bills and he spent most of his time trying to make it up to me in other ways. He wined and dined me, and spent most of his time trying to make me happy. Every morning, he left little Post-it notes on my mirror to let me know that he loved me. Sometimes, he would lay his head in my lap while I read to him. He didn't help pay many bills, but Reggie would rub my feet when I came home from work every night. He cooked dinner and breakfast, and even prepared my lunch to take to work. He went grocery shopping with me and helped with the laundry (except on Thursdays.) More importantly, Reggie seemed to love my precious Cocoa as much as I did.

I sat uncomfortably in my favorite chair in the "Great Room" of my dream house. Once again, my dream had come to an end. Life as I had envisioned it was no more. I was tired of listening to Reggie and wanted him to leave. I walked him to the door and slammed it behind him. I remained numb for several weeks, as I continued to live through each pain-filled day. Then, the most surprising thing happened. Reggie's wife called me on the telephone.

At first, I wondered how she got my number. Then, I realized that she must have gotten it from Reggie or from his cell phone. Once again, I contemplated whether or not to answer (like I did when Reggie stood outside ringing my bell, frantically, on that dreadful day he decided to tell me the truth.) I continued to stare at the phone, like I did when I got that dreadful call at 12:30 a.m. from the wife of "my other married man." I answered the phone and asked who was speaking. Reggie's wife identified herself by name and asked if we could talk. I started to change my clothes, but decided to go and meet her just as I was—in cutoff jean shorts and a tank top. *Why not show off my fabulousness?* I was still mad, but I laughed out loud in my head.

I parked my car on the corner near their house and walked toward the front door. Flashbacks of my previous conversation with Reggie's wife went through my head, as I approached the doorway. If I was in Jersey, I would have had my "Club" in hand. But I was much older now and more mature. I hoped that Reggie's wife was as mature as she looked. The older woman opened the door and stepped out of the house. She closed the screen door behind her. She started by saying that she hoped we could have a civilized conversation and that I wouldn't start acting crazy. *The nerve!* I told her that I wasn't the crazy one.

Reggie's wife wanted to know when and where I met her husband. Her eyes grew big as I told her the events that had taken place over the past two years. I asked her about the other six days of the week. I explained that Reggie spent every waking moment with me outside of work, except for Thursdays when he did his laundry at their house. We both sighed with disgust, as we listened to each other's story. Reggie's wife asked if he had contacted me since the dreadful day that I found out about her. I told her about the day he came to my house (three days later.)

She folded her arms and shook her head. Reggie's wife claimed that he had not been home all week and wanted to know if he had been with me. I told her that he had called a few times, but I hadn't answered and let the call go to voice mail. I thought it was ironic that she was asking me where her husband was. I told her that I had an idea of where he might be. She attempted to call his cell phone and then tried a different number. She seemed proud that she had the number of one of his close friends, even though there was no answer.

I offered to call Reggie's number and leave a voice message. I assured his wife that he would return my call. We stood outside of the front door and, within minutes, my cell phone rang. It was Reggie! I asked him where he was. Reggie explained that he was staying with a friend because his wife had been "walking around the house with an attitude." He had a lot of nerve expecting anything different. I told him to come to his house because we all needed to talk, but Reggie refused. Little did he know, I had him on speaker phone, and his wife could hear everything that he was saying. I told his wife that I did my best to get him to come back home to their house, but that I was done.

I left their house and drove home. Reggie's wife and I agreed not to contact each other again. I assured her that I would not be contacting her husband again either! As I reached my house, Reggie pulled into the driveway. He begged me to listen to him again. I was not interested in hearing his sob stories and all his lies. Truthfully, I just wanted to be left alone so that I could go on with my life. Over the next couple of months, Reggie continued to stalk and harass me. Sadly, his wife was doing the same. She was constantly calling me to ask about her husband's whereabouts, and he was constantly calling to try and keep me in his life.

Reggie's wife claimed that he had not been home and, when he stayed at their house, they had not slept together. He claimed the same and said that he was suicidal. His wife agreed and finally moved back to Chicago. Before leaving, she gave him an ultimatum. But Reggie told his wife that he would not leave with her because he loved me. I tried to go on with my life. I began traveling back and forth to Jersey, more and more. Every time that I was out in the limelight with my friends in Phoenix, Reggie continued to stalk me. He had become a real-life fatal attraction! I was granted a restraining order, but it didn't seem to help.

Another two years had passed since the dreadful date in court when I had to listen to the ridiculous lies that Reggie told. I always knew that he was a habitual liar, but I had no idea that it was truly his gift. He had already served nine months in Arizona's "jail tent," but that hadn't stopped Reggie from stalking me. I always thought that you could tell something about a person by the way they dressed. That just goes to show that you can't judge a book by its cover. The harassment would go on for three more years, before I decided to travel back to New Jersey and stay for a while.

I couldn't believe my ears, as Reggie told the judge how I was the one "stalking" him! Years earlier, Reggie had resorted to getting a job right down the street from where I worked and would wait on the corner to jump on the hood of my car every morning (every time that I stopped at the red light.) I was convinced that he had gone insane. The judge placed Reggie on probation and ordered that he pay a fine and attend domestic violence classes. The harassment never seemed to stop because the problem was that I never seemed to have enough proof. He had even faked a heart attack to get out of serving more time. Shenanigans!

I had no proof of him following me into the parking lot of my workplace and showing up at local events that he knew I attended. Then, one day, he finally slipped up and lost his cool in front of everyone. I attended Marcie's and Greg's wedding anniversary party, and Reggie was there. I was told that he was not invited and that he had been asked to leave. I proceeded to dance with a man, who I met at the party. Instead of leaving—like he was asked to do—Reggie made a "B-line" for the dance floor and grabbed the guy I was danc-ing with by the arm. He told the man that he could not dance with me. He then grabbed me around my waist, ripping the belt to my silk jumpsuit, and threatened the both of us!

The new guy was in no mood for Reggie's shenanigans and wanted to leave the party. I walked him to his truck and went back inside to grab my pocketbook, and say goodbye to my friends. Reggie hid in the bushes and waited for me to walk to my car. I had asked Greg to walk with me. Reggie waited until I was alone. He did his usual charade of jumping on my hood and falling down in front of my car. He would get up and kneel on his knees, begging and pleading for me to take him back. I called the police that night, but they didn't arrest him.

I later found out that he knew one of the officers. I had wondered why they didn't arrest him, even though I had a restraining order. They claimed it was because he was at the party first. Greg and I explained that Reggie was not invited to the party and had been asked to leave. Shortly after this incident occurred, Reggie attacked me at my home and dislocated my shoulder. I went to Urgent Care following the attack, and the doctor determined that the injuries to my arm and shoulder were a result of domestic abuse.

That day, Reggie had kicked my front door in like he had done many times before. One time, he broke into my fuse box on the side of the house and turned off my electricity. He had also set off my sprinkler system and then shut off my water. He was always long gone by the time the cops came. This time was different because I had let him in, after he continued to kick the door. As usual, I was already embarrassed and didn't want to cause a big scene. He was supposedly there to pick up the last bit of clothes that he had left behind. He asked if we could talk and, against my better judgment, I agreed.

I hoped that we could sit down, as two mature adults, and have a civilized conversation. I told Reggie that I didn't love him anymore and that our relationship was definitely over. He had lost his house and his job. He continued to drink heavily and lost his license. I was done with the drinking and the smoking. I was also done with all the lying and cheating. Reggie didn't have an honest bone in his body. Other than shining shoes, he couldn't get or keep a full-time job. He had gotten caught driving without a license in the HOV lane, and his license was suspended. He had to be driven everywhere. On top of that, he got a DUI. He rode around for one year with a stupid contraption rigged to his steering wheel so that the cops could test his blood alcohol level on a regular basis. I was done with his shenanigans and done with him!

When we finished talking, Reggie asked if he could use the bathroom. He locked himself in the guest bathroom and wouldn't come out! I could hear running water and didn't know what to expect. I put Cocoa in my bedroom because I knew she would be scared with all the commotion. She loved Reggie! I grabbed my mace from my pocketbook and put it on the kitchen counter. It looked like a little pink tube of lipstick. Ironically, Reggie had bought me the pepper spray to protect myself against perpetrators. I had no idea that I would be using it on *him*! Oh well, if the shoe fits…

I dialed 911 on my cell phone and told the operator that my ex-boyfriend refused to leave. I explained that he had locked himself in the bathroom and that I could hear the water running. Reggie came out of the bathroom, with a strange look in his eyes. Both fists were balled, and he lunged at me. He grabbed me by the shoulders, as I stood in the doorway of the guest bedroom across from the bathroom. I tried to block the blows to my face and fell back against the wall. Reggie picked me up and threw me across the room like a rag doll.

When I came to, he was kneeling over me. There I was, lying on the floor with his hands around my throat, wishing I was already dead. I wished *he* was dead. *Why couldn't he use his words?* Reggie had a bad habit of putting his hands on people no matter who they were. He would shove, push, hit, or slap. He would even grab someone's hand extra hard, if he thought he had good reason. That reason would be if someone was trying to "steal" me away from him. He had disrespected so many of my friends. He had even choked me once before.

It was around the time (after I found out about his wife) that he jumped over the masonry wall in my back yard and broke into my fuse box on the side of the house. That's when he turned off my electricity. Then, he went to the front of the house and banged on my door for hours (like an idiot.) When he began ringing the bell like a maniac, I disconnected it and called the cops. Then, he turned my water sprinklers on. By the time the police came, he was running around the corner. They caught him and locked him up for two weeks. I couldn't believe that the police actually had to call Reggie's wife to come and pick up her car.

Now, here I was again, wondering when someone was going to put me out of my misery for good. I wondered if this was the way my mother felt when Will choked her. At least, I was there to rescue her. *Who would rescue me?* It had been more than twenty-five years. I would have never guessed that I would be going through this again—First, with my son's father. And now with Reggie!

I decided at that very moment that the cycle of abuse would not continue with me. The room was spinning, and I was still thinking about the time when Will was sitting on top of my mother and choking her. In that moment, I knew it was going to be my life or Reggie's. I kneed him in the groin and managed to free myself from the tight grip that he had around my throat. I ran to the counter and grabbed the pepper spray. I maced Reggie in the face. There was a knock at the door. It was the police! This time, I had all the proof I needed.

CHAPTER 21

Déjà Vu: Life Has Come Full Circle

It had been more than twenty-five years since I had been beaten by a man. I was starting to feel like all my hard work and efforts had gone down the drain (again.) All my adult life, I tried to be a good woman. I had tried to be a good daughter. I tried to be a good mother. All of my efforts were in vain. My life was coming full circle - And it felt like déjà vu. I sat back and thought about the times when my life changed the most. I remembered the time when I decided that I would never drink and do drugs like my mother. I remembered when I first fell in love. I remembered all the times, after that, when I *thought* I was in love. I remembered when I gave birth to my son.

Everything that I had done, I did for my son. My recent trips back and forth to Jersey were because my son and his girlfriend brought two beautiful girls into this world. My first granddaughter was born not long after I moved to Arizona. I wasn't there, when she was born. I started traveling back and forth to Jersey and staying for "extended stays" just so that I could spend more time with her. I made it my business to be in Jersey, when my second granddaughter was born. My son's girlfriend texted the time that she was scheduled to have the C-section. I was working in Brooklyn, New York, as an instructional coach. I took a half day and got off work early that day.

I jumped on the subway to Manhattan and then caught the #114 bus to Jersey. I got in my car and drove to Beth Israel Hospital in Newark, where everyone else in our family had been born. I was so excited! I couldn't wait to see my son's second child come into the world. I was proud of him, proud of them! I ran into the hospital room and hugged his girlfriend. She seemed nervous lying on the bed. I asked if she was okay, and she said, "Yes, I'm just waiting for your son to get here." Just as I went into the hallway to call my son, he came walking down the hall. He seemed surprised to see me, but not happy. We went into the room, and I watched him put a boom box and CD player on the chair next to his girlfriend's bed. It reminded me of "my first love" and how he always made special tapes for me. The doctor came in.

My plan was to wait in the hallway area with all the other people who were anxiously waiting for the new addition to their family. I saw my son's girlfriend whisper in his ear. My son walked me to the hallway and asked what I was doing there. I was surprised, and I told him that his girlfriend texted me while I was at work. We had talked about me coming to the hospital all week. She knew how excited I was. I wanted to be there when the baby came. I wanted to be there when she opened her eyes for the first time, looking through the glass. I wanted to see the nurses put her name on the little bed and the booties on her little feet. My son asked me to leave. I didn't understand. *Did he mean leave the room, or leave the hospital?* With tears in my eyes, I stood still (frozen)—listening to my son tell me that his girlfriend didn't want me at the hospital. I walked to my car sobbing like a baby. I was so confused.

Again, I thought back to when my son was born. The doctor had asked my grandmother to leave the room because only one person was allowed. I had asked her to come with me that Sunday, on Mother's Day, but she went to church instead. On Tuesday, I called my "soon-to-be" son's father instead. It was only right that he see the birth of his son. After all, my grandmother and I never got along, and she didn't even want me to have the baby! Here I was, more than thirty years later, anxiously waiting for the birth of my second granddaughter. *Had life come full circle? Was this déjà vu?*

I decided that there was no good reason for their behavior. This was just like the time when I invited them to Arizona. Summer was ending, and I said that it would be great if they could all visit, before my oldest granddaughter started school. My son's girlfriend agreed, and we talked about airline tickets and flights. The tickets would cost less than four hundred dollars for each of them. Everything was set, and they were all coming on the last weekend in August. Then, my son's girlfriend called and said that they couldn't come because her mother's birthday was coming up. So we changed the visit from Labor Day weekend to Thanksgiving weekend. I checked flights and agreed to give them $1,100.00 to help pay for the costs of the tickets. My son's girlfriend said that she could come up with an extra hundred dollars, "with no problem, if need be." When the date grew nearer, I started getting excited and asked my son if he was excited too. He said that he didn't know anything about it... I got the dumb look.

Didn't they talk? I told him to talk to his girlfriend and get back to me because it was time to purchase the airline tickets. He called and explained that his girlfriend said that she never told me they were coming. *OMG!* This was just like the time when my son said that they were all moving to Arizona to be with me. Then, out of the blue, he changed his mind and claimed he never told me that. That was almost ten years ago! *Had life come full circle again? Was this déjà vu?*

When I moved to Arizona, I had no intention of asking my son to live with me. I was ready to put everything behind me and start the next chapter of my life. But God had a different plan. In 2011, the year after my mother's death, my son called and told me that he was being evicted. He said that he and his girlfriend were having financial problems and needed a place to stay. I was surprised because I didn't think he would ever want to "stay" with me again - at least not in Arizona (of all places.) He would be away from everyone - my grandmother - his father! And I was curious about how his girlfriend would adjust to life away from her family. I sent my son the money he asked for, helped him draft a letter to his property manager, and decided to call her personally to see if I could help them keep their apartment. After the woman explained that my son and his girlfriend were already two months behind in their rent and she was concerned about how they would make their payments moving forward, I thought long and hard and decided that this would be a new beginning for all of us.

My son and I could rekindle our relationship, and I would get to know my granddaughter. I spoke with one of the preschool directors that I worked with to see if she would give my son's girlfriend a job. It was a great school, and I could get my granddaughter a tuition discount. I knew that my son had good customer service skills and was good with his hands. I figured he could get a job at the Verizon Wireless store near my house, since he had already informed me that he did not want to be a System Technician like me.

A few weeks had passed since my son and I last spoke about him moving to Arizona, but I continued to make the necessary arrangements. My house had two spare bedrooms for him to choose from. He could choose the "Red Room", or the "Purple Room", for him and his girlfriend. The other room would be for my granddaughter. There was nothing else to do except make travel arrangements and get their car shipped. I was starting to get excited, but I knew from past dealings with my son and his girlfriend never to get too excited.

That summer, I was home in Jersey and ran into one of my son's uncles at the Italian hotdog store in Newark. He told me that he heard the exciting news. My son had told him that he was moving to Arizona. Two weeks later, I was back in Arizona, and my phone rang. Not only was my son not coming, but he denied that we ever discussed him moving to Arizona. I later found out that my grandmother asked him to be her caretaker. I guess money does buy love, along with a rent-free apartment and a car!

What had I ever done except be nice to them? I paid for a hotel and had taken them on a boat ride around New York. We enjoyed several Red Lobster dinners together (just like I did with my son - when he was a young child.) I always bought them Christmas gifts and helped them out in whatever way I could. But I never knew what to expect from them. For my fiftieth birthday, I practically had to call and beg them for a card. Then, out of the blue (on my fifty-first birthday) my son's girlfriend texted me that "they wouldn't mind" going to the beach with me. She had previously asked me what plans I had. I merely mentioned that I was going to spend my special day at my special place - Seaside Heights, of course. It certainly wasn't an invitation. She was acting like they were doing me a favor. But I didn't mind since it gave me a chance to be with my granddaughters.

Of course, they posted it on Facebook. Later that day, my son texted me and said, "See! Look how many followers you have." *What did that even mean? But that's how they always seemed to be— always putting on a show to make people think something other than the truth.* His girlfriend was shady from the first time we met. When he introduced us, she called me by my first name. Then, she literally laughed out loud when I told her that most of my son's friends call me *"Ma", "Miss Phillips", or "Miss Rahimah".* Then, I had to practically beg for her to let me see my oldest granddaughter. At the time, I was staying with my ex's mother in Vailsburg for the summer. My son was in jail. When I spoke with him on the phone, I told him that his girlfriend was always coming up with excuses why I couldn't see my granddaughter.

He had me call her on three-way and told her, "If my mom wants to see the baby, let her see the baby!" He later told me that she said that I intimidate her. Shady boots from the start! One minute, she was being disrespectful. The next minute, she was claiming that I intimidate her. *Next-level Shenanigans!* I thought back to when my son first introduced me to his new girlfriend. He seemed so excited. She wasn't his first love, but I could tell that there was something special about this one. When I first saw her, I thought—*Wow! My son hit the jackpot!* She was stunning—young, thick, and light-skinned, with hazel eyes. More importantly, she adored my son.

That's why I was so confused, when we first met. *Why was she being shady from the start?* She needed to stay in her lane because whatever was going on between me and my son had nothing to do with his girlfriend. Besides, I would be leery of any man who disrespects his mother. And regardless of anything, she brought my two beautiful granddaughters into the world. So, no matter how we felt about each other, I tried to focus on that and all the other positive things. I remembered the time that she fed and walked Cocoa for me, while I had to go on a business trip to Atlanta. I remembered when I saw my first granddaughter for the very first time.

The year was 2006, and I was so excited to meet my new grand-baby! I stayed with my son and his girlfriend at their apartment in New Brunswick. They had gone on a date night, and I watched the baby. While she slept, I cleaned the apartment, fried chicken, and made lasagna. His girlfriend claimed that she couldn't even boil water. So, I was more than happy to teach her how to cook my son's favorite foods. The next day, I had some errands to run and planned to visit a friend in Irvington. It had just started to get dark, and I was on my way back to my son's apartment. I made a right turn onto Mill Road. I saw lights flashing behind me. Then, sirens.

I wasn't sure why I was being stopped. I hadn't run any traffic lights, or a stop sign. I wasn't speeding. This was not going to be one of those DWB cases… *You know… Driving While Black!* I heard the police officer call my last name. I hated when my friends who were cops used to do that, but this voice was unfamiliar. The officer got out of his police car and walked toward my door. He seemed surprised, when he saw my face.

He took another look at the car I was driving and walked back to his car. I knew that he was running the plates on my son's car. He walked back over and handed me the license and registration that he had retrieved earlier. He said, "Sorry, Ms. Phillips. I recognized the car and thought you were someone else." He went on to explain that the car shouldn't be driven and should "technically" be towed to the impound. The police officer apologized again and let me go. I drove back to my son's apartment.

After that, things seemed to be going okay. Still, I kept wondering why things were the way they were. Right before my second granddaughter's baby shower, my son's girlfriend told me that her mother and sister would be calling me because they wanted me to help with the shower. I never got a call, and I had to text my son to get the time and location of the baby shower. At the shower, I asked my son to read my card out loud because it had a cute little poem. He said that they weren't reading cards and would just be opening the gifts. Then, he read a card from my cousin!

The straw that broke the camel's back was on the day before my second granddaughter's first birthday. I received a text from my son's girlfriend. She said that I could come by, if I wanted to, because they were "throwing a little something" for the baby. I responded and said, *"Of course, I would love to come!"* I asked what they were doing the night before and if they needed help with anything. I later found out that they had a party that night and didn't want me to come. The next day, I noticed that everyone else wore pink and purple. I didn't get that memo either. Truth be told, I could have cared less about going to the party. All I wanted was to spend time with my granddaughters.

I thought back to when my second granddaughter was born. I remembered leaving the hospital and sitting in my car. I was in shock! Thirty minutes passed, I looked at my face in the rearview mirror. I wiped my tears and took a deep breath. Just like always, I would shake this off and keep going. I continued to think about when things changed for good between me and my son. Just once, I wished he had said, "Thank you!" for all the sacrifices I had made. *Did he hate me as much as I hated my mother growing up? Had life come full circle? Was this déjà vu?*

I've tried and tried… I'm over the shenanigans! I'm not doing toxic relationships anymore. *Respect me, or forget me!* Maybe, one day, my son will realize that I was and am a good mother and I'm an even better grandmother! Still, I found myself thinking about when things went wrong between me and him. I thought back to the times when he had been in and out of juvenile detention, and the time when he had stolen a van and escaped. That day, I scrolled through the caller ID for the unfamiliar telephone number, just like I had done when he was kidnapped by his father. He was calling me from a pay phone in the area. I called the pay phone back, but no one answered. There were only a few corners with pay phones in Union. I jumped in my car and drove around the corner to Stuyvesant Avenue.

I asked the man at the bodega if he had seen someone using the phone outside his store. He told me that a young man came into the store to get change for a dollar. *I knew it was my son!* I drove down the street and rolled my car right up on the sidewalk. I dared him to run. I had found my son again! I convinced him to come home with me. There was a warrant out for his arrest, and he needed to turn himself in. I called his probation officer and begged her to let me bring him to the police station in the morning. Against her better judgement, she agreed. She warned me that, if he ran again, it would be on me. Once he was back in jail, my son decided to put me back on his "visitation list." Oddly, things seemed to be back on track. After nine long months, he would be released on "good behavior" and his record would be expunged.

I later found out that my grandmother visited him on all the days that I wasn't there. Strangely, my grandmother had always been in competition with me for my son's affection. But my son was coming home to me in a few weeks, and my life was coming full circle. It hadn't been long before that—that my body and mind had completely shut down. I didn't know whether I wanted to live, or die. I remembered feeling really tired. I remembered feeling fed up. I couldn't remember everything, but I remembered the pain I felt the night before. I remembered wanting to sleep forever. I remembered wanting my pain to end. I remembered going to the drugstore. I remembered the call that I got from my ex-fiancé's pregnant stripper.

I remembered the betrayal I felt from my grandmother when she showed up in court with my son's father to testify against me. I remembered being tied down to a chair, like I had been when I was in nursery school. The only thing that I couldn't remember was where I was. I remembered waking up to find my son and his father standing over me with balloons. They both had the dumb look on their faces, like they had nothing to do with the reason why I was in the hospital. My son hugged me like he loved me.

I could tell that I was in a hospital room because I recognized the small TV mounted on the wall and the IV machine attached to my arm. I recalled the slew of doctors asking me strange questions, trying to determine if I knew who I was and where I was. I knew my name, but I had no idea why I was where I was. I had gone into cardiac arrest, and my heart stopped beating. I slipped into a coma. I was told that I had been in a coma for five days and would spend the next two weeks confined to this bed in this unfamiliar place. I hadn't been in a hospital since I had given birth to my son.

I spent twenty-four hours under "suicide watch." I was locked in a room; tied to a chair. The room was spinning. I felt nauseous. I could see people watching me through a large glass window. I saw my grandmother and her sister, I saw one of my coworkers. *What was she doing here? Why was everyone staring at me?* The next day, I woke up in a regular hospital bed. Doctors and psychiatrists came through my room like a revolving door. They gave me drugs that made me forget why I was there in the first place. They wanted me to say that I was depressed, suicidal, and sexually abused. All I knew is that I was tired!

When I refused to answer their questions, the doctors explained what had happened to me. My son found me on the floor next to my bed. He said that he was on his way to school and told me "goodbye." When I didn't answer, he knocked on my bedroom door. Apparently, he called my grandmother and 911. Between my son's sudden hatred for me, all the back-and-forth court shenanigans, and the situation with my ex-fiancé and his pregnant stripper, my life was going in circles and had spun into a downward spiral. I didn't realize it then, but that's when things between my son and I changed forever. That's when I put my plan to move to Arizona into motion. My dreams would come to fruition.

In the midst of everything else that was going on in my life, over one thousand system technicians were getting laid off from work. After seventeen years of service, my name was on the list! NJ Bell had become AT&T. AT&T had become Lucent Technologies. Lucent Technologies had become Avaya Communications and offered us one full year of pay, with benefits, as part of a nice severance package. I had worked with computers since I was in elementary school, but I wasn't sure what I wanted to do with my life anymore. Over the years, I had enjoyed working with children.

I could have panicked like some of my coworkers. Instead, I looked at this as an opportunity to take a much needed rest. I wanted to think about my future. I decided to explore my options. In addition to the severance pay, the company was offering full tuition assistance for employees who were interested in continuing their education. I took advantage of the opportunity and went back to school.

My son was locked up, again! I was struggling to overcome my depression, but my grandmother couldn't wait to let the judge know all about my recent "suicide attempt." Surprisingly, my son's father seemed appalled at my grandmother's accusations. When she accused me of drinking and doing drugs, he actually told the judge that my grandmother was lying. That was only one of the many lies she told. My son's father added that he had known me since high school and had never seen me drink, smoke, or take any drugs.

I was surprised. I was used to him beating up on me, and I had never heard him take up for me before. This reminded me of the time when my youngest and eldest aunt came to my defense and told my grandmother the same thing. My grandmother was always trying to make me out to be a bad person even though I had always tried to live up to the person she wanted me to be. I wasn't sure why this was so hard for her to believe, but she insisted on believing what she wanted and telling lies about me anyway. When all else failed, she told the judge that my son was in a gang. That's when my ex-boyfriend's mother stood up in a rage and told the judge that my grandmother was lying.

My ex's mother loved me and my son like we were her own, and she was not about to let anyone hurt us. This gave my ex's sister even more reason to hate me. That day, when we arrived from court, she claimed that her mother had never taken off work before and would never miss a day of work for her own granddaughter. I shook my head and told her that she was delusional, if she really believed that about her mother. Suddenly, I had flashbacks of me standing in front of the judge. I continued to try and recall the events of my life. I remembered that my son kept a journal with all sorts of strange names and codes in it. The journal was a black-and-white composition notebook, like the one that I used to have when I was a young girl. *Had life come full circle? Was this déjà vu?*

I had no idea what I was looking at, and everything in my son's journal looked foreign. My son's behavior began to change around this time, and he started acting more strangely than usual. Red had always been one of my favorite colors. It seemed as though my son had suddenly taken a liking to the color as well. He began to wear a red headband, red wristband, and red shoe laces in his boots and sneakers. He also wore a red T-shirt to school every day. Before I could even talk to our counselor about what this all meant, my grandmother was telling the judge all sorts of stories.

Fortunately, my son's "red phase" was short-lived. As life went on, I hoped he would graduate to "bigger and better" things. I had high hopes for him because, like my mother, I only had one child. In as much as she never received credit for it, I truly believe that my mother tried to be a good mother - in the best way she knew how. It is very hard to show love, when you have never received love. As a young mother, I began to understand the complexity of a love-hate relationship or the so-called tough love between a mother and her child. I would try to love my mother differently, if only I had the chance.

Thinking about the relationship between me and my son made me think more about the relationship between me and my mother. The drugs, the alcohol, the tough love—*It was like déjà vu!* It is still hard for me to think about the abuse and all the things that I went through because of her addiction. My mother and I reconnected shortly before her death. The plan was for her to move to Arizona to be closer to me. I promised her that she could move into my "dream house" with me, if she completed a drug rehab program.

A friend had given me the name of a drug counselor in Phoenix, whom I contacted and made arrangements for my mother to meet with. I wanted to attend the initial meeting with my mother to be sure that she went, but the counselor insisted that my mother attend the session alone. Needless to say, that meeting never took place. In the interim, I had been flying back and forth to Jersey to meet with her drug counselor in Newark. We discussed her progress since she had recently been hospitalized. He too expressed that he normally would not meet with anyone other than the patient because of doctor-patient confidentiality.

The counselor in Newark agreed to meet with me because he was very concerned about my mother's recent acts of paranoia. I remembered the first day she called me in Arizona. It was early in the morning before work. I was standing in my kitchen and received a strange phone call. I didn't recognize the phone number, but I recognized the New Jersey area code. It was a 973 area code, which I knew was in Newark. I would have never guessed that the call was coming from my mother.

I was curious as to why she would be calling me, but glad that I always kept the same telephone number after all these years. After answering the call, I wondered what made my mother call me out of the blue. It had been years since we had spoken, or seen each other. I had only been in Arizona for a few months and had just gotten settled in my new home. I was renting a nice small house, while my "dream house" was being built.

My realtor and the builders assured me that my house would be move-in ready in nine months. It had already been eight months, and I was ecstatic! However, it took an additional three months before I could move in, and I had to extend my lease on the rental home. I didn't care how long I had to wait because I was finally going to have my very own "dream house," and it was even nicer than my grandparents' house in the Weequahic section of Newark.

I took a deep breath and placed my cell phone down on the kitchen counter. I hit the speaker phone button and listened to my mother's voice. She was telling me that she heard I moved and she wanted to know how things were going in Arizona. I told her that I was very happy and couldn't wait to move into my new house. I never in a million years would have dreamed of having a home built. My new custom home was not my only dream come true.

I was also in the process of building my own childcare center. This was a lifelong dream that I had shared with my son and his father, and everybody else that I knew. I had always talked about how I would someday make this dream come true, and it was finally happening! Despite some of the other things that I had gone through (when I was…)—I felt like life had come full circle and I was on top of the world!

Somewhere in the middle of the conversation, I heard my mother say that she was very sick. She had been in and out of the hospital. I didn't ask why. I was relieved that she sounded okay and asked her why she was calling. She began telling me that my grandmother—her own mother—was trying to drive her "crazy," literally. Listening to my mother's story reminded me of the story my son told me when he was in the hospital, after he had stolen my grandmother's car and crashed it. He too had tried to convince me that my grandmother was crazy. *It was like déjà vu!*

My mother explained that she was on medication, but the pills made her feel psychotic. My mother's doctor explained that she might be developing psychological issues from fear, stress, and anxiety. I didn't want to believe that she could have a mental illness. My mother was so smart, beautiful, and funny. And she always seemed fine—as long as she wasn't around my grandmother, drugs, and men. However, the conversation with her doctor reminded me of my own experiences of feeling overwhelmed—and how those feelings of anxiety lead to panic attacks. I refocused my attention toward the phone and continued listening to my mother's story, as I recalled the first time that she claimed to hear voices and started to show signs of paranoia and other "suspicious" behavior.

It was when I was in high school and we lived on Prospect Avenue (in my grandmother's three-family house in Irvington.) My mother would always accuse me of calling her names under my breath. Maybe, I called her names under my breath when I was six years old. But when I was a teenager, I was no longer afraid of her. I remembered that I had seen a dramatization on *Lifetime* and thought that my mother might be displaying symptoms of having schizophrenia.

The Lifetime story starred Diana Ross (one of my favorite people in the world) and was about a woman who became a drug addict. She suffered from mental illness and reminded me of my mother because of the psychosis. I became intrigued about how this mother's addiction affected her life, as well as the lives of her daughter and other family members. *It was like déjà vu!*

Oddly enough, the movie also reminded me of some of the good times that my mother and I had together. I thought about the times when we would stay up late on Friday nights and watch Diana Ross in *Mahogany* and *Lady Sings the Blues*. When I was young, I hated listening to Billie Holiday sing and often wondered why my mother would listen to such depressing music. Today, *Lady Sings the Blues* is one of my favorite movies, along with two of my mother's other favorite movies - *Claudine* and *Uptown Saturday Night*. Although the movie characters were fictitious, the stories rang very close to home—the welfare lady, pimps, prostitutes, church, and drugs.

I remembered how I had begun to watch my mother's actions closely over the years. I noticed that her behavior became worse, whenever she was around my grandmother. As I listened to her story, I also listened for the sincerity in her voice. I could always tell when my mother was lying, or high on drugs. Over the years, her drug of choice had changed from marijuana to crack. One day, my grandmother found crack vials on the kitchen floor and accused my son of leaving them there. I was aware that my son had started to smoke weed, but he did not smoke crack! It was just like when she accused me of smoking, when I was younger. *It was like déjà vu!*

At that very moment, on the phone, I knew that my mother was not high and that she was telling the truth. I also knew that she must have really needed my help because I had not heard from her in years. Her story of how my grandmother was "holding" her money and trying to control her life sounded all too familiar. It reminded me of the time that my grandmother convinced me to let her "buy" me a car with my own money. *It was like déjà vu!*

The plan was for me to give my grandmother the money that I had saved up and intended to use to purchase the car. She said that it would be better for me to pay her on a monthly basis, instead of paying the car dealership. I later found out that she was charging me more than the dealership by including a monthly late fee and higher annual percentage rate. Shenanigans!

My two best friends at the time, Kyle and Hope, enlightened me about the fact that my grandmother did not even extend me a grace period like the actual car dealership would. She just assumed that I would pay late and included the penalty in my monthly payments. The trick was that, at first, she wanted all the money upfront. I laughed out loud in my head. *How the hell was that helping me?*

I continued to listen to my mother tell me her story about how she received over $700 each month from the state, plus food stamps and medical coverage. She said that my grandmother would pick her up and take her to the bank each month to retrieve the funds from the ATM. She convinced my mother that it would be in her best interest to let her "manage" the money so that she could pay my mother's bills for her.

At first, this didn't sound like a bad idea to me. After my mother explained that my grandmother paid the rent (which was a little more than half of the $700), bought a few groceries with the food stamps, and kept the rest of the money - I fully understood what was happening. My grandmother had a knack for making people think that she was doing them a favor when, in actuality, she was the one reaping most of the benefits.

I thought about the time that she invited herself on one of my business trips to Detroit. Even though I had already made travel arrangements for me and my son, my grandmother convinced me to drive instead of fly. She said that she would help me drive and that her "tagging along" would be beneficial so that she could watch my son.

I ended up driving the whole trip (thirteen hours.) When we arrived to Detroit, my grandmother didn't spend any time with me or my son. It turned out that she wanted to visit her cousins, whom she hadn't seen in a long time. We argued, and I left. I checked myself and my son into the hotel. She gave me one of her usual "You'll be sorry" speeches. Whenever my grandmother's manipulation tactics failed and you didn't do what she wanted, she would make threats about how "you would be sorry!"

As my mother continued her story about how my grandmother was manipulating her, I thought back to all the times that I had seen her. Each time I saw my mother, she was either on the street corner begging or lying on a hospital bed. Sometimes, my mother didn't even know that I was there. I thought back to the time when she stayed with me for a short while at my house in Union.

Thinking of my mother's short stay reminded me of all the good times my son and I had at our house. I thought about all of the times we celebrated his birthday and Mother's Day by having a party at our house. He would invite his friends and I would invite mine. I always cooked barbecue chicken, potato salad, tuna macaroni salad, and macaroni and cheese—all of which were my grandmother's recipes. Of course, I made my "famous" lasagna and would order a cake to top it all off!

I thought back to the drug counselor in Phoenix and how he told me about a residential treatment center in Flagstaff. I called and spoke with the program director, who told me that she had one available bed and would accept women with HIV. The cost of a six-month stay could be covered by my mother's and my insurance plans. My mother was not happy about the idea of living with complete strangers in a new house and in a new state for the next six months. I reminded her that this was a new beginning for us and that she had lived in worse places.

I also thought back to the day I had come home from work and saw that my mother left. I never went to look for her, like the time she had left me abandoned on the stairwell. Now that I had her on the phone, I decided that I was not going to let her go again. My mother needed me to take care of her, just like I had done when I was a young child. *Life had come full circle - And it was like déjà vu!*

CHAPTER 22

Déjà Vu: Growing Up Newark

Finally, I moved into my brand new, custom "dream house." My mother continued to call me, every morning, before I went to work. Then, the phone calls stopped. She had disappeared - again. I asked one of my old high school friends to check "around the way." My mother hung out around Valley Fair and Wendy's on Chancellor Avenue. She was also known for frequenting the crack houses "around the way," on Leslie Street and Wainwright Street—the very same streets I grew up on until the third grade. I wanted to put the memories of my childhood behind me. I wanted to forget all about "growing up Newark"—But combing the streets of Newark—looking for my mother felt like déjà vu.

I couldn't believe my luck when my old friend, Priscilla, called to say that she had actually found my mother. The challenge would be getting her to the airport in Newark. She had never been on a plane and had seldom left Newark. The streets of Newark were her home, her solace. Unfortunately, I had become all too familiar with the goings-on that occurred around the way, late nights in the streets of Newark. The events of my mother's latest shenanigans brought back some old memories.

I thought about memories with another old friend. His name was Bernard, but most people knew him as "Dirty Bird." We actually dated for all of four months. He lived on Goldsmith Avenue, down the street from my grandmother. I would run into him, whenever I was in the neighborhood. One Friday afternoon, he pulled up to my car and asked me if I wanted to go to the movies. We went to the movies a couple of times, and I cooked him dinner once. He had asked me to make him a lasagna dinner, which was my favorite thing to cook and one of his favorite things to eat.

One day, I stopped by his apartment "unannounced" and one of his boys opened the door. Bernard and I had gotten pretty close— and I knew all of his friends. Terrence opened the door and gave me a hug. I threw my brown leather jacket on the couch in the living room and walked to the bedroom. Bernard was surprised to see me and seemed upset. He gave Terrence a strange look and finished counting the money on the table. A few minutes later, Terrence and another guy left the room and never came back.

Bernard asked if I wanted something to eat. I told him that I didn't, even though I was hungry. I could tell that something was on his mind, and he wanted to talk. He walked to the kitchen and came back with two cans of Coca-Cola. I moved from the chair to the bed, and he sat next to me. I sat patiently—waiting, like a child, to hear what he had to say. Bernard asked me if I recalled the number of times that he had told me not to come by his apartment without calling. I didn't respond. I knew that, no matter what number I said, he was going to be unhappy with my answer.

I moved closer to Bernard and wrapped my arms around his neck. I kissed him gently on the lips. I loved kissing him because he had the softest lips, and his breath always smelled like Juicy Fruit. I promised to never come by again without calling, and we fell back on the bed. An hour later, I got dressed and gave Bernard a kiss goodbye. As I grabbed my leather jacket on the way out, I made up my mind that I would not see him again. Months later, I heard that he was in jail. His sister told me that he had gotten set up by one of his "boys."

I recalled the last time that I was in his apartment and the strange look that Bernard gave Terrence.

I decided to pay Bernard a visit. Before then, I had never been to visit anybody in jail. I baked Bernard a chocolate cake, with chocolate frosting. It was his favorite (and mine too.) The guards used their hands to tear my cake to pieces. I was crying by the time I got to the visiting area. I wiped my face and walked slowly to the table where Bernard was sitting. He said my eyes were red and puffy—and asked if I had been crying. I said, "*No!*" He called me a liar. I told him about the cake. We laughed out loud, together.

Years later, I saw Terrence slangin' on the corner of Lyons Avenue and Leslie Street. I kept driving and didn't bother to roll down my window to say, *"Hi."* The next time that I saw him, he was kneeled over on the ground in a fetal position. Bernard was home from jail and was kicking the crap out of him, while Terrence tried to protect his stomach and face with his hands. His lip was busted, and blood covered the ground. I could see that Terrence did not stop Bernard from kicking him in the mouth. I guess they were no longer "boys," like I was no longer his girl. Bernard had two rules—don't come by his apartment without calling first and don't get high on your own supply! Some people and some things never change.

Bernard wasn't my only thug-love, or "roughneck." I met Lennox a few years later, and he also was "infamous" in the streets. Lennox was tall, bald, and light-skinned. He had *all* the swag, and his jeans sagged like nobody's business. He had a Black baby momma and a White girl on the side. He was "hella" cute and always made me laugh. We met when I accidentally ran over his foot, backing out of the parking lot of the laundromat. He bent down to grab his knee and told me that I had to be his girl, or he would sue me! I laughed out loud.

Like Bernard, Lennox never thought twice about knocking somebody out over his money. He too had an issue with me coming over "unannounced." He and his family lived in Hillside, not far from my grandmother's house in the Weequahic section of Newark and not far from where I met Bernard. I had gotten pretty close to his family and spent most Sunday afternoons with them—when I was doing my laundry. One day, I got a call from his cousin. She said that the White girl had set him up and got him shot, and just like that—Lennox was gone!

I remembered how Lennox would pull up to my apartment complex blasting his music. He would always play, "Flex—Time to Have Sex" by *Mad Cobra.* I laughed out loud in my head. Bernard was a true "thug", but Lennox was a real "roughneck" - a *Bad Boy.* The love that I had for them wasn't real. It was a "thug love."

It was more like an infatuation. It was a need—the need to feel secure. Every *good* girl needs a *bad* boy! It was that same need that I had when I met "my first love." Lennox would say that he only loved and needed two things—sex and money. He would then admit to doing just about anything to get either one. I thought back to my mother and remembered that I *needed* money to purchase an airline ticket for her online. Deep down, I knew that my mother would refuse to get on the plane. I knew that she had not flown before, but I wondered how she thought I would get her from Jersey to Arizona. Deep down, I knew that she would never come.

Just as I suspected, Priscilla called to tell me that my mother refused to go to the airport with her. They were sitting on Priscilla's porch in Newark. She too lived in the Weequahic section, not far from my grandmother's house. I spoke to my mother over the phone. Then, I told Priscilla to abort the mission—And I made arrangements to fly home. I was going to get my mother. When I arrived back home, I ran into one of my mother's first cousins who was also "in the life" and accustomed to running the streets of Newark. Our cousin told me that she saw my mother on the corner of South Orange Avenue and Bergen Street, near University Hospital.

This was a known drug area and was also where I would meet with my mother's counselor. I drove the rental car to the familiar area in hopes of finding my mother. I went to the two crack houses on the corner of the block. There was no answer at the first house. At the second house, a man came to the door and said that my mother hadn't been there in days. I waited for her across the street in the parking lot of Pathmark.

I sat in my car for over three hours. I had just decided that I would come back the next day, when I spotted my mother stumbling through the lot of a gas station across the street. She was on her way to the crack houses. I rolled up on her and yelled her name. It reminded me of the time when I rolled up on my son at the corner bodega, after he had escaped from jail. *It was like déjà vu!*

My mother turned and looked at me in shock. I walked over, grabbed her by the arm, and walked her toward my car. We sat in silence for about twenty minutes. I had to catch my breath. Now that I had her, I wasn't sure what to do. She said that she was hungry. Before driving off, we stopped at the Jamaican store on the corner to get something to eat. Then, we sat in the car for another hour and talked. I decided to rent us a room at a hotel in Newark. That night, it made me so happy to hear the joy in my mother's voice as she took a long (and much needed) bubble bath. I laid in my hotel bed and looked around the room to take everything in. Once again, I wondered how I would get my mother on the plane to Arizona.

The next morning, we went to breakfast at IHOP on Bergen. The manager claimed that my mother had been soliciting there and would not let her in. I told my mother to wait outside, while I paid for our food. We went back to the hotel to eat. Surprisingly, my mother told me that she had a boarding room downtown Newark. She said that she had a few personal belongings that she wanted to pick up. I wondered why she was outside begging. We went to her room to get her things, and she seemed proud to introduce me as her daughter. To tell the truth, it made me feel good too!

I never thought I would see the day when I was proud to be my mother's child because I had always been a motherless child. It felt good to hear her brag about my accomplishments. She told everyone all about my new "dream house" in Arizona. I laughed out loud in my head, as I listened to her brag about me "flying" my car to Arizona. After a few visits with her "friends," we grabbed her things and went back to the hotel. I prepared myself for the disappointment of hearing her tell me that she was not coming back with me to Arizona.

We sat on the edge of the bed. Moments later, I listened to my mother tell me that she could not leave Newark. Once again, I had taken care of her needs, but my mother could care less about my needs. She was adamant about not coming to Arizona, and there was nothing I could do to change her mind. It was then and there that I decided this would be the last time that she hurt me. It was the same way I felt after my son came home from jail. I was so tired of being hurt. *It was like déjà vu!*

I never thought that sitting on the hotel bed with my mother would be one of my last memories with her. I wished that I was dreaming, when I heard about my mother's death. This time, she was gone forever! The superintendent of her apartment building found her dead in the bathtub. She had been dead for nine days. The odor and overflowing water from her apartment led the superintendent to open the door. Someone had tried very hard to make it look like she drowned, but there was no water in her lungs. The police tried to convince me that there had been an "accident," which resulted in my mother's death.

My mother's life was no secret. Everyone knew that she drank and did drugs, but drowning—that was a stretch! For one thing, she had just gotten out of the hospital and couldn't walk. I had flown home to visit her at East Orange General Hospital. She used a walker to help her get around. When the superintendent found her in the bathtub, there was no walker to be found! *How had she gotten to the bathroom from the kitchen, or bedroom?* I remember screaming in the elevator at work, when I first heard the news. Then, I went numb. I made arrangements to fly home—again.

When I arrived in Newark, I immediately went to my youngest aunt's house. Then, I went to the mortuary to identify my mother's body. The mortician refused to open the bag with my mother's body. She said that the body was in no condition to be viewed and would not be recognizable. I insisted. There was no way in hell that I was not going to see my mother one last time. The mortician unzipped the thick gray bag, and I saw my mother's face.

I couldn't speak and ran out of the mortuary. My grandmother and her sister, along with my youngest aunt, were waiting for me in the car. When I got inside the car, I heard them arguing about whether to eat at Wendy's or Burger King. They hadn't even bothered to come inside. I drove the car to the next corner, pulled over, and got out. Without a word, I jumped out of the car and left them sitting there like idiots!

No one cared that my mother was dead! No one even thought to ask if I was okay after leaving the mortuary. Just once, I wished that my family could act normal. That's what I was thinking, as I walked down Martin Luther King Boulevard toward South Orange Avenue. I would catch the first cab, or bus, that I saw. I just wanted to get away from them. Several hours later, I returned to my youngest aunt's apartment. She told me that she understood why I did what I did, and we didn't speak another word about it.

When I arrived back to Arizona, I began to contact the Newark Police Department to see if they had any new information about my mother's death. I called every day (sometimes twice.) While I waited for a copy of my mother's death certificate, I requested a toxicology report. The results showed large amounts of prescription medications, combined with illegal drugs and alcohol.

Finally, the lead detective told me that the FBI had become involved. They confirmed that there was foul play, and my mother's death would remain "unsolved." I could remember clear as day sitting at the police officer's desk, several months earlier, and listening to him refer to my mother as an "unimportant person!" He hadn't actually called her that, but I saw it on the manila folder on his desk. When I asked him what the bolded letters on the folder stood for, that's what he told me!

It reminded me of all those episodes of *Law and Order: SVU (Special Victims Unit)* that I watched on TV. "Hos" and prostitutes always got killed and blamed for their own rape. But this was real life (not a TV show), and my mother was a real victim! I had heard about and seen so many victims throughout my lifetime. I thought back to the time that I heard a young girl screaming in Green Acres, across from Untermann Field. She sounded very young and scared. I was also young, scared, and didn't know what to do. It had been a long time since I heard someone cry "rape." I remember crouching down below the window in my grandmother's bathroom and shutting the light off so that no one could see me. I covered my ears and cried.

After my mother's death, my youngest aunt and I stayed in touch. We spoke on the phone almost every day. Then, the calls stopped. I had heard that she too was "in the streets." This was a breaking point in our relationship. She had always been there for me (for the most part.) She was the one person, other than my grandfather, who I looked up to. I had heard about her drug use. I chose not to believe the things I had heard. I chose to believe that she was the young, cute, and sweet aunt that I had always known and loved. I guess—deep down inside—I always knew that she was about that life—just like my mother. Growing up Newark—*Life had come full circle, and it was like déjà vu!*

Thoughts of my youngest aunt and my mother consumed my mind. In 2011, on the one-year anniversary of my mother's death, I almost became a victim (myself.) I decided that I wanted to follow up on my mother's murder. I went to talk with the superintendent again. There were pieces of yellow tape on the door that had not been there before. My mother's apartment was still vacant, and the superintendent let me in with his key. The tub was clean. Strangely, the rest of the apartment had not been cleaned. There was a two-liter bottle of Schweppes Ginger Ale on the floor in the corner. A pack of cigarettes, three crack vials, a large spoon with residue, a lighter, and a crack pipe were spread out on the kitchen table.

I was determined to find out what happened. I wanted to know who was responsible for my mother's death. I wanted to know if she was actually murdered. Whoever was responsible was going to pay! The superintendent told me that he had seen two other tenants in my mother's apartment that week before her death. My mother lived on the first floor. The superintendent said that one of the other tenants lived on the second floor. Coincidentally, he moved out of the building right after the incident. The other tenant lived downstairs in the basement.

I banged on the basement door, frantically. No one answered. I could hear movement. Someone was looking through the peephole. Then, the knob turned. A woman opened the door. She looked like she was in her early thirties. She stood in the doorway, holding onto the handle of a stroller. The child in the stroller looked about two years old. I looked down at her and smiled. I looked back up at her mother. I wasn't smiling. I wore sneakers, and my small pocketbook was across my shoulder and chest. My fists were clinched. I was ready to pounce, if she even flinched wrong. One thing I knew is that you can never trust a crackhead.

The woman who lived in the basement admitted to doing drugs with my mother. She also told me that the young man who moved was also in the apartment on the day that my mother died. It made me wonder. *Had the three of them been doing drugs together, when things went terribly wrong? Or was my mother killed, murdered tragically at the hands of drug dealers?* There was a bank receipt for $700 on the floor near the table. That's a lot of drugs. I figured that my mother either got a bad patch, or she overdosed. They must have panicked and taken her to the bathroom. Then, they put her in the bathtub and left the water running to make it look like a suicide. The money was gone, the drugs were gone, the young boy was gone, and my mother was gone!

Looking around her apartment confirmed that it was a good idea that I had taken a leave of absence from work. I was happy that I had packed up most of my things and put the rest in storage. I wasn't sure how long I would be staying in Jersey, so I brought my dog (Cocoa) along for the trip. One night, I decided to take her for a walk. It was very late, and I had no business being outside alone. It was a bad area. Just before moving into the apartment that I rented, the landlord told me that crackheads had stolen some pipes and plumbing from the bathrooms.

I had barely gotten settled in, before two guys jumped over the fence and stole Cocoa's new doghouse from the back yard. But I was staying in Newark, and these things were not that unusual. That night (the night that I was walking Cocoa), she was doing her usual "horse trot" and taking extremely long to handle her business. I heard a noise and looked over my right shoulder. I saw a white unmarked van cruising down the street. As the white van drew nearer to where we were standing, the headlights were shut off. Without another thought, I grabbed Cocoa's leash tighter and started walking as fast as I could (toward the block of my new apartment.)

A young Black guy, in his early thirties, jumped out of the passenger side of the van and started walking really fast behind us. By this point, I was dragging Cocoa and running for my life. Cocoa, on the other hand, was not in her "typical" Doberman role and clearly thought the strange man chasing us wanted to play. The white unmarked van continued to cruise down Chadwick Avenue toward the corner of Hawthorne Avenue, with its lights off.

The apartment that I was renting was two houses in from the corner, one block from my mother's building. I let out the biggest sigh of relief when Cocoa and I turned the corner. I saw a familiar face on the steps waiting for us. The young man, who was chasing us, slowed his pace and walked down the street past my apartment. The white van turned the corner and went in the other direction toward my mother's old building.

I knew this was a dangerous area, but I just wanted to be close to my mother again. I had no idea how close I was about to become! When I returned to Arizona, I never told anyone about the mysterious white van or the shenanigans behind my mother's death. After her death, I thought about all the times we missed—all the times that I hoped and prayed I would *not* be like her.

At the age of six, when I first saw her get brutally beaten by her boyfriend, I knew that I did not want to be like my mother. At the age of seven, when she offered me a sip of her wine cooler, I knew that I did not want to be like my mother. At the age of eleven, when she missed my valedictorian speech, I knew that I did not want to be like my mother. Sitting on the stairwell waiting for two days after we had been evicted, I knew that I did not want to be like my mother. At the age of seventeen, when she missed my high school graduation, I knew that I did not want to be like my mother. At the age of twenty-two (when she missed my college graduation) I was reminded that I did not want to be like my mother. Now, there were only memories (good and bad.) Now, she was gone. Now, I wished that she was alive to see that I struggled to be a good mother (just like her.)

Several years had passed since my mother's death. I was back in Jersey for work, when my cell phone rang. I immediately recognized the 973 area code. At first, I thought it was my youngest aunt's number, but it looked different. I thought about the time when she called to tell me about my mother's death. I had settled into my new "dream house" and was on my way to a business meeting with my boss. We were in the elevator, when my aunt called. Now, my mother was dead and I wondered who was calling me from this mysterious number. I took a deep breath and stared at the phone with fear.

The voice on the other end of the phone belonged to the man, who I often referred to as my favorite uncle. He was the father of my three first cousins (the ones that I had grown up with.) He was the one, who my youngest aunt hadn't married. He had been her high school sweetheart. She, indeed, was everybody's sweetheart. She had been the glue that kept us all together. She had been there for my mother (when I was born) and there for me (when my son was born.) She was the one, who had called me (when my eldest aunt died.) She was the one who was full of life (the cute, sweet, and light-skinned one.)

I thought about all the good times I had with my aunt. She might have been the cute, petite, sweet, and light-skinned one, but she had the loudest whistle anyone has ever heard. She could hail a cab from blocks away. I thought back to the two times that I had asked my aunt if she was doing drugs. The first time was after my eldest aunt's funeral. She avoided the question. The second time was after my mother's funeral. She told me that she "had some problems and was working on them." I remembered all the times that I had seen her act just like my mother. She had always been more functional, except for the time that she and my mother acted like two buffoons on the day of my grandfather's funeral.

I had always adored and admired my youngest aunt. I loved her like a daughter loves her mother. I loved her like a little sister loves her big sister. She promised to love me back. She promised that she wouldn't do drugs. She promised that she would always be there. She promised that she wouldn't leave me the way my mother did. I wondered what made her start doing drugs. *Was she in pain like my mother? Was she hurt by the fact that she found out she had a different father than her sisters?* I hadn't seen my aunt since my mother's funeral.

I had been mad at my youngest aunt since my mother died. More than six whole years had passed, when she walked into my son's apartment on Thanksgiving Day and demanded a hug. She said, "You actin' like you don't know nobody." I didn't *know* her anymore. She had stopped calling, and she had stopped answering my calls. I stood up and hugged my aunt. I hugged her and whispered, *"I'm sorry"*—in her ear. I wanted to tell her that it wasn't her fault. None of this was any of our fault. We all came from the same woman—my grandmother! We were each desperately searching for someone to love, or someone to love us.

I wondered if things would have been different, if we were from someone else—from somewhere else. I knew that my aunt was running and ripping in the streets of Newark. But I wanted to be wrong. For a quick moment, I closed my eyes and thought about the times that I sat on the edge of my youngest aunt's king-sized bed. We would listen to one of her favorite songs, *"A Song for You"* by Donny Hathaway. When I was young, we listened to music together all the time—just like me and my mother did (whenever she was around.)

On Thanksgiving of 2016, I knew that it might be the last time I would ever see my youngest aunt. I wasn't going to miss out on the chance to say goodbye and tell her that I loved her, like I did with my mother. Two months had passed since that Thanksgiving Day, and I was staring at my cell phone. For a quick moment, I had a flashback... I thought back to the holidays that we spent as a family - back when I was growing up - back in Newark (on Goldsmith Avenue.) I wished we could go back. My cell phone was still ringing. I answered it. It was my "favorite" uncle calling to tell me that my youngest aunt was gone—dead. *Once again, life had come full circle... And it was like déjà vu!*

CHAPTER 23

Closer To My Dream

I never expected life to stand still, or to be perfect. But my life always seemed to be changing. As I continued to strive to get closer to my dream, it seemed like everything and everyone in my life was disappearing. My grandfather, the Dobermans, my eldest aunt, my mother, and now my youngest aunt were all dead—gone, just like that! I thought back to my son's brush with death. Although this was a very difficult time in our lives, it seemed to bring us closer. My son and I had always been close—but, right before he was diagnosed with cancer, we began to grow apart. I thought about how I had lie in his hospital bed with him for months.

The hospital had become our solace, our "special" place, our sanctuary. In the midst of pain, we would laugh together at all the funny things that had happened in our lives. Since then, I have come to the realization that everything happens for a reason and everyone has a purpose. Lots of bad things have happened, but I know that there are still good days to come. I know that I have a purpose in life, a dream to fulfill. This is not the life that I have chosen. It is the path that was chosen for me.

I thought that having a baby would change my life. I was born minutes before Independence Day, "a firecracker"—always have been—always will be. My mother was born an Aquarius—free spirited, eccentric, and independent. The birth of my son would forever remind me of Mother's Day and how proud I was to become a mother. My grandmother was the matriarch of our family—a leader—born on the same day as the great Martin Luther King Jr. Between the four of us, we should have been able to create a most powerful union. Instead, we lived our lives with such hatred and dysfunction. Life just don't seem fair…

I needed to remain strong. I needed to have courage. It would be that same courage that I had mustered up when my son's father kidnapped our son from the babysitter and took him to his mother's house. That same courage was needed the second time he kidnapped my son and I had no idea where they were for over a week. I was determined to get my son back. I would need to muster up that courage again to identify my mother's body, after reading the police report.

When I think about my mother's death, I become fearful because I don't trust what has been told to me. All of the facts remain *unknown* and I still don't know! When I first started writing this book, I was scared of the unknown. I was scared that it might bring up old feelings of hurt from my past. I didn't want to relive those feelings. I was also scared that it might cause other people to feel hurt. My intention was only to tell the truth and not to hurt anyone.

As I thought about my fears and insecurities, I began to think about ways that I had conquered some of those fears. My first fear has been conquered. From the first time that I stood on stage and gave the sixth-grade graduation speech, I knew that I would grace the stage again. It didn't matter if I was in a fashion show, or giving another speech. Flying was my other fear. When I was a little girl, I was deathly afraid of flying. I thought that my feet would never leave the ground. Besides, I had no interest in ever leaving Newark. The next thing I knew, I was on a plane. I flew to Canada to give my very first oral presentation, when I was twenty-five years old. Although my training skills didn't begin in education, I've been flying back and forth across the country training ever since.

I started tutoring other students, when I was in elementary school. Tutoring students in math, English, and computer science helped me follow my dream of becoming an early childhood specialist and an instructional coach. Growing up, my teachers took a special interest in me and it actually made me feel special—like they loved and supported me. Throughout my career, I've been able to make other teachers feel special. I love spreading the love, especially to the children. Although I've never really had the love and support from a father or a mother and a sister or a brother, I gave birth to a beautiful son—a son, who from the first time I looked into his eyes, I loved and adored. I love spreading the love to *all* children.

Growing up without parents has made my life extremely hard. I wouldn't wish that on my worst enemy. I wish my mother was still alive so that I could tell her that I love her. Love, especially a mother's love, is something that should never be taken for granted. I've always loved my son and wanted the best for him. I've always wanted for him whatever he wanted for himself. When he was younger, I longed to see the days when he would become a man. I wanted to experience our lives together as adults, with me as the woman I am; and him as the man I raised him to be.

Although the people closest to me and who I trusted the most tried to bring themselves up by tearing me down, I know that I am a good mother. I've struggled along the way and I've made some mistakes, but I love my son. It hurts my heart that he doesn't see the sacrifices that I made. He doesn't show appreciation for all my struggles. But it's hard to do that, when everything he has was given to him. Like most young people these days, there is a sense of entitlement. It would be hard for anyone to appreciate someone else's struggles, if they haven't had to struggle themselves. I know what it means to struggle and I know the value of hard work.

Some people might think that my life has been easy and I have never had to struggle, but I am a true hustler for real… Always on my grind and never wasting time… I never miss an opportunity to make a special connection. I don't just talk about it. I *am* about it. Whether it was growing up on the streets of Newark or the streets of East Orange, whether it was washing people's cars or washing their clothes… I saved my pennies every day until I had hundreds of dollars in a glass jar at the end of the month. Sometimes, I gave my mother the pennies and dollars from my jar to pay the electric bill when she couldn't afford to pay it herself. It didn't always get paid—but, at least, I gave her the money. I've always been about my business. Always doing what I gotta do to make it happen. Whether we like it or not, life happens. Life always throws us a curve ball. There will always be hardships. But I'm a firm believer of these two things—If you believe it, you can achieve it! And love conquers all!

I was still in my "hustle state of mind." I finally found a way to do what I love doing. I found a way to turn my dream into a reality. When you're good at what you do and you love what you do, it's easy to do it. Every day, I get to wake up and share my passion. I get to share my passion with some of the most exceptional school leaders in the country, some of the most dedicated teachers, and some of the most amazing children in the world! Each night, before I go to sleep, I smile because I know that I've made an impact. I've made a difference in a child's life, like my teachers did for me. One of my proudest moments was when I made a connection with a child who has autism. Before I enter a school; a classroom; or do a presentation, I reflect upon the words on the front cover of my notebook, "*Be the change you want to see!*"

Right now—I am who I want to be! People are always saying that I am always smiling, showing all of my teeth. Sometimes, I just can't help it. Even when my days seem bad, the children I work with make me smile. But, sometimes, it seems like my happiness makes other people sad. It's a shame that people have to come for you when you're on your way up. But that's when you brush your shoulder off and tell them, in your Kenya Moore voice, "*Don't come for me unless I send for you!*" Only losers sit around talking about other people to make themselves feel better. Because, if you have a problem with me and I don't have a problem with you - then, your problem is probably with yourself. But I always say that you're no one, if no one is talking about you.

It's time for everyone to grow up! But when we grow older, the child in us never leaves. I still do some of the same things that I did as a child. I still save my pennies. Except now, I have hundreds of pennies saved in my car (instead of a jar.) I can't remember wearing red shoes since my ex's mother bought me my first pair, but I still wear high heels to make my arches higher and my calves bigger. Cheerios and Shredded Wheat are still my two favorite cereals - And I still love applesauce with milk. I still apply my makeup, just like my eldest aunt taught me on the night before my junior prom. I use a razor to shave under my arms, but I don't shave my legs - and I use baby oil to slick down the hair on them, just like my mother taught me. Most men love it, just like she said they would.

I'm still scared to watch horror flicks! But, on October 31, you can bet your last dollar that I am somewhere watching *Halloween* (the one with Jamie Lee Curtis.) Whenever the thirteenth falls on a Friday, you know that I am extra careful to avoid any shenanigans. And I am definitely watching "Jason" in *Friday the 13th* on TV. I'm definitely a creature of habit. I still like my peace and quiet. I still cook a big dinner and do my laundry on Sunday. I still order Chinese food (shrimp and broccoli, or shrimp egg foo young) from Amin's on Chancellor Avenue, whenever I'm in Newark. Wednesday will always be spaghetti day! I always use Colgate and Listerine, never Crest and Scope. I still chew ice like it's going out of style.

Some things stay the same and, sometimes, there's a need for change. When I decided to change my life and my career, I moved across the country to follow my dream. Things might not have gone the way that I would have liked as a child and they definitely haven't gone the way that I would have liked with my *own* child, but the joy that I get from working with young children is such an indescribable feeling! I have dedicated my life to helping young children and teachers reach their full potential so that they are successful in life. My only other dream is to speak on "TED Talks." I am moving onward and upward, as I get closer to my dream.

After everything I had gone through, I just wanted to get away from everything and everyone. I needed a place of solitude. A place where no one knew me. A place where I could reinvent myself. A place where I could start a new life. Surprise was just the place. *Surprise! Surprise!* It was perfect! When I moved to Arizona in 2005, I heard a remix of *Marvin Gaye's* "Let's Get It On" on 104.3 and I knew Black folks were in the building! I laughed out loud in my head. Then, I fell in love with a song called "Closer" by *Goapele*. I listened to that song day in and day out, as *Goapele* sang the words "closer to my dream." The song seemed so appropriate. It was one of the first songs that I danced to, as I learned to do "Chicago-style stepping." One of the first things that I did—besides learning a new dance, opening my child care center, and deciding where I wanted to have my house built—was get a tattoo. My butterfly tattoos would be a symbol of my newfound freedom. A symbol of my transformation...

I remember how I had begged Sherrie to come with me to the tattoo parlor. She didn't have any tattoos because she was afraid to get one, but her husband had a tiger on his right shoulder. I liked tigers too. They always reminded me of the scene in *Scarface*, when Tony Montana got married and had a chained tiger in his back yard. I also like tigers because they are fierce and beautiful—like me! Sherrie was beautiful, but I don't know about fierce. I laughed out loud in my head.

We met at church and shopped at the same grocery store—Fry's. Sherrie was White and had beautiful, long, flowing hair that fell down her back. She was absolutely gorgeous and we became best friends, almost immediately. After we left the tattoo parlor that day, she handed me two Motrin and drove me back home. The stupid lady, who was supposed to do my new tattoo, had forgotten about my appointment and booked someone else. Sherrie tried to comfort me by saying that we could come back another day. I didn't want to come back another day. I had gotten up all my courage on *that* day. I grabbed my Motrin and came back the next day, alone. I finally got my tattoo!

I thought back to my fears and my insecurities. Suddenly, I felt liberated and elated! But there is nothing worse than trying to get to a specific place in life, without first acknowledging where you've been and knowing from where you came. I am a Jersey girl. Most people from New Jersey just say "Jersey." I was born in Newark and raised on the streets of the tri-city area (Newark—Irvington—East Orange.) I can never change that. No matter where I live, I'll always be from Newark. I am born of my mother, who came from her mother (my grandmother.) I can never change that.

I gave birth to a beautiful son, who is a father to two beautiful daughters. We intermingle and our relationships are intertwined. Although we seek to understand, we may never fully appreciate the struggles and the relationships that came before us. Past relationships are a precursor for building new ones. Each person we meet helps us to make a connection to yet another person, so forth and so on. We are responsible for how we choose to interact with the people in our lives, and we hope to have some control over the people who we allow to remain a part of our lives.

This culmination of brief interactions and ongoing relationships helps shape us. I know now, like I knew then, that my elementary school teachers are a significant part of my life. At the time, I didn't know what the future held. But I was pretty sure that I would be special, just because my teachers deemed it to be so. Each day that I work with young children, I think about the time when my fifth-grade teacher patted me on the shoulder and told me that I would be successful in life.

She believed in me more than anyone else. She knew and always told me that I would be special. My third-grade teacher, the one White woman in an entire school of Black students, made me realize that a strong belief is all that is needed to achieve my goal. Although I was always encouraged to go to school, I never really had a support system. I will always remember the courage and persistence my third-grade teacher showed by coming to my apartment in the "hood" to talk to my mother that day. She and my sixth-grade teacher are the ones who taught me about courage. They taught me to conquer my fears. They helped me find my voice!

Never in a million years did I think that a little Black girl from Newark—raised around drugs and alcohol, entangled in a life of abuse, addiction, and dysfunction—would become valedictorian. Standing up on that stage, in an auditorium full of over three hundred students, I realized that I had a gift. My gift became clearer to me when I began working for AT&T as a global customer service representative. The vice president of our organization had chosen me to represent the company. She accompanied me for my first oral presentation. We flew to Toronto, Canada. She accompanied me, the first time… I was on my own after that.

I had always been afraid of flying. But this time, I was deathly afraid. My eldest aunt had just died in a plane crash. She worked as an elementary school teacher during the week and often worked as a flight attendant on the weekends. My youngest aunt called me and said that my grandmother would only trust *me* to identify the body. There was nothing else for me to do except fly home. TWA Flight 800 had crashed. It was July 17, 1996. I was training in California. There was a three-hour time difference. For some reason, I had woken up extra early that morning and put on the news. I never watched the news! I remember watching the names of all the victims scrolling down the television screen. I saw my last name. I was in shock. *What was happening?* Then, I saw my eldest aunt's first name.

My mouth fell open. There were over two hundred students. Then, the phone rang. It was my youngest aunt. The next thing I knew, I was standing over my eldest aunt's dead body with her ex-husband. We were looking at her severed limbs and trying to figure out what went where. The mortician handed me a large Ziploc plastic baggie. It contained one black Nine West shoe. I immediately knew the shoe belonged to my aunt. She loved Nine West shoes! There was also a black leather wallet and checkbook, which I also knew belonged to my aunt. I had given the wallet to her years ago for her birthday. The only other identifying mark was the mole on her chin. We didn't agree on which side of her face the mole was, but my uncle and I both knew right away that the woman lying on the table was my eldest aunt.

That year, I was asked to travel to Virginia, Atlanta, Detroit, and Texas. Lastly, I was asked to train in California. The trip was originally supposed to be for two to three months, but I ended up traveling back and forth from Cali to Jersey for almost a year. I became a frequent flyer. I was no longer afraid to fly and I no longer had stage fright. The audience grew bigger and bigger, as I attempted to perfect my newfound talent. I knew my gift! My educational background and work experience began to pay off, and I was earning a pretty nice salary. That's when my son and I moved from our apartment in Irvington to our new home in Union. The house was old (built in the1940s) and needed some work. I had it remodeled, but it was not as beautiful as what would later become my "dream house." Nevertheless, it was my first home and the place where I raised my son.

As determined as I was to succeed in the workplace, I was equally determined to succeed in my personal life and give my son a good upbringing. I wanted to stay clear of Newark, Irvington, and East Orange. There were too many bad areas of which I was all too familiar. Reflecting back on my childhood and growing up Newark—I remembered a saying, "the apple doesn't grow far from the tree." Thinking back, I often wondered how true that statement was. I was nothing like my mother, and my son was nothing like me.

There are some things we don't like to admit, but we know that they are the bane of our existence. The life lessons that my mother taught me will live with me forever. The educational foundation that my grandmother, eldest aunt, and my mother laid for me helped me to become the educator that I am today. When I got laid off from Avaya, I had no idea that I would relocate across the country and end up living in Arizona. My initial plan was to remain a trainer and continue working in California, for at least one year.

After my coworker bragged about his trip to Sedona and told me how beautiful Phoenix was, I had to see for myself. *Who knew that a two-week vacation would turn into a lifelong journey?* The Spanish palm trees, mysterious saguaros, clean sidewalks, fresh air, and big, beautiful houses were a welcomed change from the dirty, loud, and congested streets of New Jersey and New York—not to mention the calmness. I was captivated by the quiet and knew that Arizona was where I wanted to be. It was the perfect place for me to live out my dreams. This is where I would build my "dream house" and my "dream business."

Before I left New Jersey, I decided to go back to school and pursue a degree in early childhood education. Once I moved to Arizona, I began volunteering as an assistant teacher at the church that I joined in my new neighborhood. Working at the preschool reminded me of when I was a teacher and taught dance at my son's school. I taught "Music and Movement" to toddlers and preschoolers at five different schools in Jersey. Prior to moving to Arizona, I began teaching "Jazzercise" to adults.

I was excited about my new move, my new life, and my new church. It was a Southern Baptist church with six classrooms and an afterschool program. The pastor of the church was extremely nice and offered me a job right away. The pastor's wife and the school director didn't seem as nice and only offered me minimum wage. I wondered how I could go from making $50 an hour in Jersey to $8 an hour in Arizona. Even with the cost of living being lower, it would take a miracle.

The assistant director and I hit it off and became very good friends. She, like my fifth-grade teacher, became a mentor and encouraged me to continue following my dreams. After six months of working at the church, I took heed to the assistant director's advice and applied for a management position at another school. I was soon hired as the assistant director at a Sunrise Preschool. Soon after that, I applied and moved into the position of center director at a private Christian academy. Now that I had worked as a school director for two years, I felt that it was time to put my managerial skills to good use. Prior to leaving Jersey, I had taken courses at the Small Business Association and applied for a business loan to open my own childcare center. I received a grant and started working with the zoning department and an architect in Surprise, Arizona.

Everything—the house, the business, and my classes—seemed to be going along as planned. My son and I seemed to be getting along, and he came to Arizona for a few visits. During one of his visits, I came into the kitchen to find him going through my mail. A few weeks later, I received a letter from the court in New Jersey requesting my presence at a hearing that involved his father. I asked my son if he knew how his father got my new address, and he claimed that he had no idea. Once again, I was hit with the realization that some people and some things never change.

Once again, I was on my way up and my son's father was trying to bring me down. Despite his new tactics, I continued to pursue my dream. I applied for a license to operate as a LLC, which meant a Limited Liability Company. It also meant that I was the sole proprietor. I owned and operated my childcare center for over two years. Then, the economy plummeted, and I had to close my business.

Parents were losing their jobs and couldn't afford to pay me. I could no longer afford to pay salaries for myself and my head teacher. I was living beyond my means and had begun to use my savings. Eventually, I had to file for bankruptcy. I was able to keep my home and car, but needed to rebuild my credit. It was like starting all over again! It turned out to be a blessing in disguise because I had become business partners with someone who had no liquid assets, and I wanted to dissolve our contract. The other silver lining was that closing the childcare center gave me the opportunity to get back into the "field."

I became a coach and training specialist for other early childhood providers. The pay wasn't the greatest, but I loved the benefits and the flexibility of the job. Once again, I was able to work and travel while doing what I loved and did best. Attending National Association for the Education of Young Children (NAEYC) conferences, Zero to Three, and Birth to Five early childhood summits gave me the inspiration that I needed. It had been over twenty years, since I first taught as a preschool and dance teacher at my son's school in Irvington.

It had been over ten years, since I became a center director and owned a childcare center. Those opportunities gave me the skills, background, and experience that I needed to continue following my dream of becoming an educational leader. When I first became a training specialist in Arizona, the same stage fright came over me as when I was delivering my sixth-grade graduation speech. Similar to the words spoken to me as a young student, I remember the words that my manager spoke to me as an adult. She said, "You have the presence. Now, demand attention and command respect. Your knowledge is your power. Speak with confidence and people will listen!" These were words to live by.

Although my role over the years has changed from student to teacher, from trainer to coach, and from educator to early childhood specialist, I will never forget the encouraging words of the educators who came before me. I am older, wiser, and no longer afraid. I am no longer in a daze! I want to be an inspiration to others. I want to inspire young girls who look different and who think that they will never find love. I want to inspire young children who think that they don't have a chance, or a choice. I want to help them find *their* voice! I want to inspire teachers who think that they do not make a difference. Most of all, I want to inspire young mothers because their lives matter. No one should ever give up on their dream.

It was May 2005, and my dream was coming true. This is how it all began… I bought a one-way ticket for myself and my cat, Shana. I would call my "first love's" mother, as soon as I arrived to Phoenix. It was her birthday and I had never missed calling her on her special day. It was also the week before Mothers' Day and I was excited about going to a new church. After springing my big news on her, I looked around my new home. I was proud. I was ecstatic! I laughed out loud, as I thought about how I had called 411 to ask if there was a Pathmark and ShopRite in the area. The operator told me that she had not heard of those grocery stores, but assured me that Fry's and Albertson's would suffice. I also needed to know if there was a nail salon, a Red Lobster, and a Bed, Bath, & Beyond. There are just some things a girl can't live without!

I remember hearing a man curse a cashier out at the Walgreen's near my new house because they didn't sell Hellmann's mayonnaise. Looks like I wasn't the only crazy one in the area. After arriving in Arizona, I knew three things—I wanted to have a house built, I wanted to work with children, and I also wanted to work with elders. Working with elderly people reminded me of working with babies because they both need lots of love and care. I volunteered with a hospice organization, soon after I arrived in Arizona.

I smiled, as I thought about my ride from the airport. I had taken the SuperShuttle and had already made a new friend. She was an older White woman, who was coming back from visiting her son and daughter in California. I listened to her talk about her husband, who had recently passed away. Since his death, she lived alone and visited her family in Cali on holidays. Then, the strangest thing happened. The woman wrote her name, address, and telephone number on a piece of paper and handed it to me. She said that she would be my "new family", since I didn't have any family in the Phoenix area.

My ride from Phoenix International Airport was enjoyable and interesting. Remembering the incidents that followed, I don't know which was funnier. Soon after I got on the SuperShuttle, another older White woman got on with a million bags. She had luggage for days! She started asking the driver a million and one questions. I could tell he was annoyed. He answered the first three questions and then began to turn his head in the other direction. The woman continued to talk, as he ignored her. Then, she whipped out her cell phone and put it on speaker. That's when all hell broke loose!

Before I could even start rolling my eyes good, the driver turned his head back in her direction. He literally pulled the blue van over to the curb. He threatened to throw the woman off the van, if she did not end her conversation immediately. The driver and the woman argued back and forth, as he pointed to the sign that read - *No Cell Phones!* The woman hung up and pouted, until he got to her stop. *The nerve!* I laughed out loud in my head. I didn't want to get thrown off the van for laughing too loud. That's when I started talking to my new friend.

It's a good thing that I kept my sense of humor because the first thing I saw when I got off the SuperShuttle was a cotton field. What the *hell?* I almost lost my mind and started to tell the driver to take me right back to the airport. *I wasn't about to pick nobody's cotton!* About three weeks had passed, and I decided to give my new friend a call. We met at Arrowhead Mall the very next week. We decided to have lunch before shopping. She ordered a pastrami and provolone on rye with spicy mustard. It was the exact same way that I ate my pastrami sandwich. She ordered me not to get a sandwich. She said that they were too big and too expensive, and she would split hers with me. After that, we ate and shopped together every weekend.

Sometimes, I would shop while she got her hair done in the mall. I visited her several times at her home. We would look through photo albums full of pictures of her and her husband. When I hadn't heard from her in a while, I called her number. A man answered the phone. I knew it wasn't her husband because he was deceased. The man asked who I was and told me that my new friend passed away. At the funeral, the man introduced himself to me as her son. He then introduced me to the rest of their family.

He told me that he was glad that I called and was able to make it to the service. After a lot of hugging and crying, he and his sister said, "We thought you were our mother's imaginary friend!" I laughed out loud in my head.

I remembered how I told my new friend all about my new dream. She had listened intently and shared in my excitement, as I described my new home. I had even described and pictured the way I would arrange my furniture. I had ordered my chocolate leather chaise sectional from IKEA before I left Jersey. I also ordered a ten-piece chocolate entertainment unit, with a matching coffee table. I had read books on how to create an in-home daycare and ordered all the necessary children's furniture. I planned to save decorating *that* room for later. I wanted to finish school and run my business from my new house that was being built, before I moved into a larger facility.

I thought about how I had chosen the lot for my new home in the "lottery." I had never done that before. I had never even played *any* type of lottery before. I chose to have my home built near a corner lot, where no other houses would be located in front of or behind my house. I would have the privacy that I always dreamed of. I handpicked every detail. I chose the knobs on the cabinet doors down to the shape of the pool. I laughed out loud at the thought of actually having a pool boy. I had a landscaper, who cut the grass in my front yard and back yard in Jersey, but this was different. My new landscaper and pool boy turned my back yard into my own personal resort. It was like a spa vacation—an *oasis*!

Before I left Jersey, I sold my house and was able to get more than double what I paid for it. I bought the house for $140,000 and sold it for $325,000, less than ten years later. I used the proceeds from the house, along with money that I had saved up over the years, and a very generous income tax refund. I walked away with almost $200,000. I put half of the money down on my new "dream house." A portion of it was designated for opening my new childcare center. But, more than anything else, I wanted to walk into a Lexus car dealership and slam $50,000 cash down on the table! I had always dreamed of buying the SC430 hardtop convertible.

It was my "dream car" and it would be my favorite color—red, with tan leather seats. The salesman said it would cost $53,000 fully loaded. I laughed out loud in my head. *Did it come any other way?* I didn't get the car. But it would only be a matter of time… I decided that my new home and business were more important. It had been almost ten years since I bought my first home in Union. Now, I was buying my second home. Except this time, it wasn't an old house that was built over sixty years ago. No one lived in my new home except me! I would be the first one to use the bathroom and the first one to lie in my new beautiful bathtub. The only other thing I was waiting for was my new Doberman puppy to arrive. She too would match the chocolate furniture that I had chosen. I laughed out loud in my head. I was following my dream and everything was perfect!

CHAPTER 24

A New Chapter Of My Life: Finding The Truth

Sometimes, things may seem perfect from the outside. But those looking in really have no idea. I am still in search of the truth. We all {most of us} are searching for something. Some of us are searching for love. Some of us are searching to find the truth. Part of my journey was me learning to love myself—as I learned the truth. Sometimes—we often feel insecure and jealous, threatened by others who are on the same journey. My move to Arizona reminded me about the importance of finding one's truth and knowing one's worth. My journey continues…

As much as I want to forget, the truth is that I can't. I can't forget my past because it makes me who I am. No matter how much my mother hurt me, the truth is that I still loved her. No matter how much my son hurts me, the truth is that I will always love him. They're not a part of my past. They're a part of me! *But was my son a part of me?* You think you know someone—especially your own child. But he was a complete stranger. I thought back to all the lies. It's like my son had been brainwashed. This wasn't the child I gave birth to. This wasn't the child that I raised. I wanted to get to the bottom of things. I wanted to find out the truth.

While I continued to read my "well-loved" Bible every day and have faith, I was reminded of the scripture from 1 Corinthians 13:6,

"Love does not delight in evil, but it rejoices in the truth." I have always wondered why most people tend to believe what they want to believe. Maybe, it is easier for them to believe a lie than to believe the truth. I can think of several instances when someone has tried to bait me into having an argument about my own life. Life is too short to spend wasting time arguing over who is telling the truth and who isn't. And my time is too valuable to spend trying to convince people of the truth.

During one of Joel Osteen's messages, he talked about how eagles soar high over crows. He went on to read a scripture from Luke 6:29, "Simply ignore insignificant insults or losses and do not bother to retaliate—maintain your dignity." I laughed out loud in my head at the number of times that I have wanted to tell certain people to "shut up, mind your business, and get the hell away from me!" Actually, I am pretty sure that I have said those exact words to a few people. I learned a long time ago that it is important to take the high road, in order to reach my highest potential. I would not be where I am today, if I allowed others to take me off my course.

I will continue to turn the other cheek and take the high road. I will continue to soar like an eagle. Some people might perceive backing down, or walking away, from an argument as weakness. The truth is that no one has any idea of what went on in my life behind closed doors. The truth is that no one really cared. The truth is that, although I learned many of life's lessons from them, I didn't learn how to become a mother from watching my own mother—or my grandmother.

No matter how far I had come, somehow, life seemed to continue repeating itself. But I've learned many of life's lessons just by living life—itself. All the same shows from the 1980s and 1990s are back on TV. I often think back to the "good times" when my son and I watched *Family Matters, Full House,* and *Boy Meets World*—together every Friday night. I crack up every time I think of my son doing the "Jerome dance" from *Martin*. I would join in the fun and pretend to be "Sheneneh". I was never a big fan of *The Facts of Life*—but, as I scroll through the TV Guide channel, I am reminded of all the life lessons that I learned. Most of the things that I know are things that I learned growing up. I learned how to cook from my grandmother and how to live from my mother.

Ironically, I learned about etiquette and the importance of education from my grandmother, eldest aunt, and my mother. I learned (on my own) how to become independent and take care of myself, as a single woman (as a mother.) The truth is that I thought by doing the opposite of what I saw and heard, I would be a better mother than they were. The truth is that by choosing not to drink or smoke, I was choosing not to become an addict. The truth is that I cleaned up after my mother when she came home from being in the streets for days because deep down I loved her, and I knew someday that I would become a different type of mother.

Every now and then, I think about the time when my grandmother dropped me off at Rutgers. It was my first day at the college. She dropped me off and handed me a check to cover my books. She helped me to my room and said, "Goodbye." That was it. No hugs and no love—and just like that (just like my mother), she was gone! In fifty years, I have not seen a picture of my grandmother holding or kissing me. As a matter of fact, I don't ever recall her telling me that she loved me.

I don't ever remember being loved by my grandmother. The only time I can recall her expressing any type of emotion toward me was the one time she told me that she was proud of me. It was right after I bought my first house. She told me that she was proud because I was the only one in the family who had not asked her for money. Everything with her was about money. My mother wasn't much of a hugger either. But, at least, I had seen pictures of me sitting on her lap. I've never seen pictures of my grandmother hugging me, when I was a baby. The truth is that she hated my mother for having me, and she hated me for being born.

The truth is that my son never had to wonder if I loved him, or where I was, because I was never missing in action. The truth is that I had dinner on the table every night (mostly) by 6:30 p.m., so that my son would have a stable life. The truth is that by reading to my son every night, from the time he was in my belly until he was about twelve years old, I was hoping to create the bond of a lifetime. The truth is that I often stayed up until midnight and watched my son sleep, while I worried about how to pay the bills, because I loved him more than life itself and hoped that *he* would never have to worry. The truth is that I have worked nonstop since I was a young child and have busted my butt for the past thirty years so that *he* wouldn't have to bust his.

The truth is that, from the time that I was ten years old, people said that I wouldn't make it. I would have believed that to be true, if it weren't for my elementary school teachers. I have graduated three times during my adult life, and each time was harder than the time before. High school was a breeze, but thoughts of my mother made life hard. The truth is that if it weren't for the words of the sixth-grade teacher who told me to "stay focused on one thing or one person" while I was up on that stage, I would not have been able to stay focused at all.

The truth is that I almost lost focus. I started college with a bang! I was an honor student with a 4.0 GPA, and I almost lost everything after I became pregnant. I got caught cheating on a final exam. I was pregnant and anxious. I had studied so hard and memorized every answer, but I wanted everything to be perfect! My grades dropped from an "A" to a "C" minus in almost every subject, and I was placed on academic probation. I talked to the Dean of Students. I talked to my professors. I talked to my guidance counselor. I talked to myself. I had a baby, and I had a job. More importantly, I had a dream. I hadn't come this far to lose the battle now! I encourage all young mothers to follow their dream and stay focused on "the goal." Don't ever let someone tell you that you are something that you're not.

Find your truth. "Above all else, to thine own self be true" (Polonius/Hamlet.) Stand up for yourself and be your true self. *Remember… If you don't stand for something, you'll fall for anything!* Find something that you enjoy, something that will keep you focused and give you the incentive to keep going. After everything you do, ask yourself—*What is my goal?* The truth is that it had always been my goal to figure out a plan to raise my child, finish school, and get a job that would help me get where I am today. Each time that I walked across the campus, with my son on my hip, I hoped he would remember my struggles and would appreciate them.

The truth is that walking across the college campuses and receiving my degrees, my only hope was that I would one day see my son walk across the stage with his cap and gown. Thanks to the shenanigans of his father and my grandmother, the last time that I saw my son graduate was after his near-death experience. Prior to homeschooling him for two years, I was constantly getting him tested—working with tutors and counselors to make sure that he would not fall behind. The doctors told me that my son had Attention-Deficit/Hyperactivity Disorder (ADHD) and should be on medication. But, now, he was battling cancer and I was pleading with Burnet Middle School to let him graduate with his class. They agreed! My son walked across the stage with a white suit that he asked me to buy for the special occasion. As he held onto his cane, I remember him looking so weak. I could tell that he was struggling to get across the stage, and I went up to help him. Seeing him get his diploma was one of my proudest moments.

The truth is that I didn't truly understand everything my son was going through, when he had cancer. I didn't know exactly what the chemo was doing, but I knew that it was saving his life. I knew he was in pain—and I'm glad I was there. Fighting cancer is something that no one can truly understand, until one has actually had to live with it.

The truth is that no one knows *my* pain and my struggle because they have not walked in my shoes. It's really not funny, but I laugh out loud in my head when I think about some of the "truths" that people say they've heard about me. After my youngest aunt's funeral in 2017, one of my relatives told me that she had heard about all the accusations my grandmother made about me. She was referring to the allegations made by the "anonymous caller," regarding the alleged neglect of my son.

I asked my relative, who has known me for my entire life, why she hadn't reached out to me back when she first heard the allegations. That situation was over fifteen years ago. I wanted to know why, if she had become aware of such vicious lies, had she not tried to defend me. She claimed that she knew what type of person my grandmother was because she had seen her do the same thing to my mother. She went on to say that she didn't want to get involved because she too had been threatened by my grandmother in the past. Shenanigans!

That same day, after my youngest aunt's funeral, another relative claimed she "heard" that I had gone crazy. *Here we go again!* I reminded her that I had heard the same about her and, just like my other relative, she too has known me all our lives. I didn't argue with her, but reminded her that we've spoken several times over the years. I asked her, "*Did I sound crazy any of the times when we have spoken?*" I also asked her, "*If you thought that there was the slightest possibility that I had gone crazy, why didn't you offer to help me?*" Crickets... Then, she said that it was none of her business since it involved my grandmother. She too admitted to having seen the wrath of my grandmother. Shenanigans!

I thought back to the day of my mother's funeral, in 2010, and how one of my younger cousins accused me of "deserting" the family. Besides the fact that this was a totally inappropriate time, I reminded him that he was the one who had "gone away." He had been arrested and had gone to jail for several years. I also asked him to name a time when he, or anyone else in our family, needed my help and I wasn't there. Crickets... It just goes to show that most people choose to believe what they want to believe. These are the same people who stand by snickering and sneering, just like they did at my mother (when she was alive.) These are the same people who have a lot to say, but never actually *do* anything.

My son is no exception. He and his father have come down with a case of "selective amnesia." I have tried to instill in my son and my oldest granddaughter some of the same family values and life lessons that I learned over the years. I laugh out loud in my head, whenever he says that I am trying to relive my childhood. There is no way on God's green earth that I would want to do that! I want my son to appreciate family traditions, and I want my granddaughters to know that their grandmother loves them. I want my son to know that I was the best mother that I knew how to be. I want his life to be different from my life. I want him to know and understand the truth about my life.

Just once, I wish my son would take responsibility for his own actions. He has never said "sorry" for all the things that he's taken me through. All these years, I never knew why exactly he's been so angry.

Then, as I was looking through the scrapbook that I put together for him, I saw it… I created a scrapbook for our family and his friends to express their love to him (during his near-death experience.) I had decided to use the same scrapbook to combine our journeys. One day, while flipping through the pages, I saw a letter in the scrapbook. It was an apology for all of his wrongdoings. He said that he was sorry for hurting me and disappointing me. I cried, as I read the letter. I've waited all these years to hear those words. It reminded me of one of my favorite scriptures: "Train up a child in the way he should go: and when he is old, he will not depart from it." (Proverbs 22:6—KJV)

I hope that my son will find his truth. I hope that his truth will bring him peace. All my life, I tried to protect him from the truth. *How do you tell your only child that his grandmother is a drug addict? How could I tell my son that his own father was hurting me? What could I do to protect my son and myself when his father showed up at a friend's house, after following me?* Those are the times when you pretend that everything is okay.

No one ever believes you anyway—especially when you're supposed to be a strong, independent Black woman. I often think back to all the times that my son's father threw me against the car, or talked to me like a dog. He didn't hurt my face. He hurt my heart! But no one could see my heart. If you've ever been in an abusive relationship, you know… First you're in shock. Then you ask yourself, *"Did this fool just hit me?"; "What did he just call me?"* Once the initial shock wears off, you begin to blame yourself. *Why did this happen? How could this happen to me? What did I do wrong?* Then, you wonder if you should tell anyone. Then, you decide to keep it a secret.

You decide to stay because you "love" him, or you've convinced yourself that he "loves" you. Or he's your "baby's daddy"… So you fix your face and go on with your life, as if nothing happened. That is, until it happens again. Then it becomes a pattern and, before you know it, you're in an abusive relationship. No matter what he tells you—No matter how smart, or how strong you think you are—He will probably do it again. You, and only you, can be the only one to decide when you've had enough. I've had enough… It is time for me to turn the page and start a new chapter in my life. I continue to search for love, but I am no one's victim. I am no longer searching for my place in the world. I have found my truth and my peace.

The sad truth is that I can't change the past, and I can't predict the future. I have spent half of my life remembering things that I wish I could forget. Life is what we make it! I have taken complete control of my life. I know that everyone of us has gone through, or is still going through, something. Thinking back to one of my NY subway rides, I felt proud and confident. I stared up at the woman standing over me and realized that every person has a story to tell. I wondered what *her* story was.

She held the metal pole with one hand, as she tried to brace herself on the crowded train. Her nails looked like mine, except they were coated with an acrylic pink gel and a black French tip. I stole my French tip idea from Sharon Stone in "Casino". I prefer to have my natural nails painted with a light pink gel polish and a dark brown French tip because it matches with almost everything I wear. I have always had long nails, like my mother. My grandmother always said that nice girls wore light natural colors. She said red was for whores! I laughed out loud in my head.

I am as particular about my nails as I am about my shoes and boots. Anyone who knows me knows that I'd rather call in sick than go to work with a chipped nail! When *life* is hard—because *work* is hard—because *raising a child* is hard—because *getting an education* is hard, you have to do whatever you can to make yourself happy. Sometimes it's just a little thing like buying a new pair of shoes, or getting your nails done. Then comes that day when you walk past a mirror and catch a side glimpse of yourself "looking all kinds of good"… And suddenly the annoying email you received earlier that day doesn't seem to matter so much.

On special occasions, I have the tips of my nails painted purple or black and lined with silver or gold. My toes always match my fingernails. I laughed out loud again, as I thought about one of my high school girlfriends who only got pedicures in the summertime. She would say, "There's no need for pretty feet in the winter because we always where boots, and no one is looking at our feet!" I continued to look up at the woman on the train, trying not to stare.

The train was crowded, and there were more people standing up than there were sitting down. I was lucky to get a seat because I got on at Winthrop Street, and most of the other people got on the train at Borough Hall. I was impressed by the number of people who still read books. Most of the people were on their cell phones, but many of them were reading an actual book. I am one of those people who enjoys reading an actual book because I like placing a bookmark between the pages so that I know where I left off.

I have always liked reading and wondered if I might see my book in the hands of a stranger sitting on a train. I can only hope that, one day, I will look up and see people reading *my* book! I always read the highlights and my horoscope in the "amNewYork" and the "Metro" daily paper, while I was riding the train. I was surprised that only a few people were reading from Kindle. I never really liked Kindles because I prefer to turn the actual pages of my books. I thought about how I would lie in the bathtub of my "dream house" in Arizona and read a good book to candlelight.

I still like to read, but the only problem is that I would often miss my stop (if I was reading something really good.) I laughed out loud in my head. I thought back to the times, when I was a young child. My friends and I would catch the train to New York to pick our mothers up from work. My mother only had two jobs that I can actually remember. She worked as a data entry clerk at the Prudential Building downtown Newark and, later, at the Twin Towers in Manhattan. Back then, it was much safer for young children to be alone in the streets and on the subway trains.

As I continued to watch the woman standing over me, I wondered why so many people were on the train in the middle of the day. It was almost 2:00 on a Thursday afternoon, and I was on my way home from work. I usually caught the #2 train from Brooklyn to NY Port Authority. Sometimes, while on a local train, the conductor would suddenly announce that the train had become an "Express" train and wouldn't be making the next four stops. That day, I decided to catch the #5 Express to Grand Central Station and take the shuttle to Time Square—42nd Street. My office was on Riverside Drive, but I was working "in the field."

I had another fifteen minutes before the #114 bus would arrive at Port Authority to take me back to Jersey. New Yorkers always called it "across the bridge," but it was more like through the tunnel for me. On the weekends, I didn't mind driving through the Holland or Lincoln Tunnel. I laughed out loud in my head, as I thought about the number of times I told my son that the Ninja Turtles lived in the Lincoln Tunnel. After all, they did come from the sewer and were combatting crime in New York City!

During the week, I found it best to let the bus driver handle the traffic so that I wouldn't trigger my road rage. After I left the subway, I was trying to walk as fast as I could. No matter how much my feet hurt and no matter how late I was running, I always found time to stop at the boutiques and pick me up something nice. In the summertime, I got off the train at the Herald Square Station and walked from Bryant Park to 42nd Street and 8th Avenue. It was better than walking through that dreadful subway tunnel, where some people actually wore "germ masks" over their nose and mouth to avoid spreading or catching something.

I loved to walk down 8ᵗʰ Avenue and see all the stores, food trucks, and people yelling on the street. I found the cutest off-white summer leather top for my trip back to the AZ. I laughed out loud in my head because that's what my oldest granddaughter always calls it—"The AZ." I laughed out loud, again, as I thought about the scene from *Waiting to Exhale* when Lela Rochon called her boyfriend (Troy) a "leather-wearing in the summertime…" I planned on wearing my black leather dress with my three-inch red-and-black Steve Madden strappy sandals that tie around the ankle to the masquerade ball. I am definitely a shoe person. My shoes and boots are *everything!* But I keep it cute and comfortable…

I let out a deep sigh, as I thought about my trip back to Arizona. I recalled that the first time I had ever laid eyes on the beautiful sights in Arizona was when I watched *Waiting to Exhale*. I continued to think about my upcoming trip back to Arizona, as I counted the ten cops that I passed on my way to the Port Authority bus terminal. It's no wonder that the police are never around when you need them. They're all at Port Authority! They were all dressed in navy blue from head to toe, with black boots and guns to match. When I arrived at NY Port Authority, I looked out of the large glass window that went from the ceiling to the floor.

The bus usually arrived on time, but I overheard the guy in the little booth tell another worker that the bus was running late because of heavy traffic and snow on the side of the road. I couldn't believe that there was eight inches of snow on the ground, and spring was only five days away. I thought back to the crowded trains (the #2 and the #5 Express.) I wondered where each person was going and what stories they had to tell about their day. On the bus ride home, I drifted off and reflected on the stories that *I* could tell.

At fifty-one years old, I was a single Black woman and my life had come full circle. I decided that I want to work smarter, not harder. Things may not have worked out exactly like I planned, but life was good, and I was happy—until I got the news! I was ready to wrap it all up and start the next phase of my life—a new chapter of my life! It had been exactly thirteen years since I first stepped foot in Arizona, on Christmas Eve of 2004. It was seventy-one degrees that day. Now, it was the year 2017. It was the eve of Christmas Eve, and Monday would be Christmas Day!

The sky was clear. The very first time I arrived in Arizona (thirteen years ago), I stayed at the Pointe Hilton Tapatio Resort. I remember looking out over the cliffs, as I ate my dinner. I stared out at the stars, in a daze. An older couple asked me if it was my first time visiting the resort. They said that they came every Christmas. The stars were so bright. The couple was so nice. Everything was so beautiful. It was at that very moment that I decided to move to Arizona.

Now, I was sitting in the Surprise Public Library - as I attempted to finish writing my book. I looked out over my computer and saw ducks walking across the sand, toward the man-made lake. Two men were fishing. Parents were playing with their children. The temperature was sixty-four degrees that day. I could hear other people typing away at their computers, as I thought about the things that happened in the world around me.

I continued to reflect on my life and the things that mattered to me. I smiled, as I thought about the fact that we finally had a Black president. I smiled again at the thought that a woman ran for office. I let out a sigh of relief, as I thought about the things that I had gone through with my mother. I laughed out loud, when I recalled my beautiful red dress and the showdown that my mother and I had on my first day of kindergarten. I am tickled pink by my affinity toward dark-skinned men and all the hang-ups my mother had about the color of people's skin. At first, I was in love with Michael Jordan (with his smooth, dark skin and bald head…) But after "Boyz in the Hood" came out, I would always dream that my baby had a different daddy. *Morris Chestnut…??? Yes, please!*

I laughed out loud, as I thought about all the good times, as well as the bad times—and all the other people who have come in and out of my life. I remembered the friends that I had, as a young child growing up. I remembered how I always chose my friends wisely (just as I do now) so that I wouldn't get hurt.

When I was ten years old and my mother left me, I thought I would die… But I managed to survive. When my grandfather passed away, I wished it was me… But I kept on living. When my son was diagnosed with terminal cancer, I didn't know how I would go on… But I stood strong (for him.) All of the times that I've had my heart broken by the men who I thought I loved and have claimed to love me—Nothing could have prepared me for the pain I had felt over the past fifteen years.

I guess the truth is that the truth hurts! My life and my quest for love seemed like a series of bad movies, in which I starred as a lonely and desperate woman starving for love and affection.

Then, there was that "thug love" and my "homie lover friends." The "homies" are my close friends (some of whom are my best friends), who I kick it with and who just happen to be male. At some point, I decided that I would rather be "friends" than lovers with these men. I am still friends with most of them and I have never since regretted my decision. My friendships with men seem to last a lot longer than my friendships with women. Shout out to all my Jersey and Brooklyn dudes, who showed me some love.

And shout out to all the haters smiling and profiling—showing fake love. *So disingenuous!* Shout out to all the people who try to love, but don't know how. Shout out to the young boys, who actually knew how to treat a young lady back in the day, but we were too young and dumb to realize their potential. Shout out to all of the brothas, over six feet tall, with six-packs and more than six inches (who think they are God's gift to women.) It's a good thing that I can now sit back and laugh out loud about these stories and the men who "claim" to have loved me.

Shout out to all my freaks. I remember there was this one dude who kissed and sucked my eyelids. *Who does that?* Then, there was the guy who told me to stick my tongue out. When I did, he sucked on it until I almost choked. I couldn't even breathe. I wanted to scream, but I couldn't! Then there are always those freaks who think they're porn stars, trying to make me act out their every fantasy. *Boy, please! I might call you "Daddy", but I'm not breaking my back or my headboard for nobody!* I laughed out loud in my head.

I could tell so many stories about "love" and the men in my life, but I would have to write another whole book! Of course, the book would be titled "*Shenanigans!*" It would feature "first loves," "baby-daddies," "married men," "ex-fiancés," and of course, "the abusers" and "stalkers." The book would include the various men that I have met in my travels and all the men who I have met in the NYC subway. Let's not forget about all the "dregs of society," as my grandmother so often called them. These were the men "from around the way" that drifted in and out of my mother's and my life. I am so glad that I love myself now more than any man could ever possibly love me.

Over the years, "my first love" and I have kept in touch, and I still love his mother as if she were my own mother. At my high school reunion, "the love of *his* life" Goldie walked over to me and said, "I remember you!" Crickets... Then, she said, "You use to go with "what's his name.'" She knew good and well what his name was. She continued to smile devilishly and said, "I could have had him if I wanted him, but he wanted *it* too bad!" I rolled my eyes and walked away. *She better take her "it" and get the hell out of my face!* Shenanigans!

CHAPTER 25

Something Different

Once again, everything in my life was changing and things seemed very different. I was told by a mutual friend that Goldie keeled over at her desk where she worked. No one knows what the cause of death was, and we haven't spoken a word about it since. My infatuation with the high school basketball player has long since warn off. My ex's sister and I are not BFFs, but we're cordial. We have spent many Christmases together at her mother's house and, some days, we even laugh at the times (when I was head over heels in love with her younger brother.)

After several years of being apart, my ex-stalker remained obsessed with me. While I tried to maintain my dignity, he continued to try and slander my name. He thought that he could ruin my reputation, by defaming my character and spreading vicious lies. He's never apologized for the hurt that he caused me. In spite of it all—I have continued to live my best life!

After everything (and all my convictions about love), I still don't know which hurt more—the fact that my mother chose her love of drugs, alcohol, and men over her love for me or the fact that my grandmother didn't love either one of us. Somehow, the constant pain that I felt from the long, drawn-out court process of my son's father trying to kidnap our son and gain custody didn't hurt as much as I thought it would. I guess the reason for that is because I expected something like that from such a cruel, conniving, and vindictive person. I tell myself that my son's father did those things because it was the only way he knew how to love.

After all the trials and tribulations—and weekends waiting with a bag packed only for his father to never show, my son now loves his father more than anything—more than *me*. It's amazing how life has come full circle. My son's father came to Phoenix a few years ago for a business meeting. He called me and we met for dinner. I was cordial, but deep down—I still hated his guts! I still hated his guts for all the things he had taken me through—For all the sleepless nights I spent wondering where my son was—For all the time wasted in court—For all the lies he told—For all the tears I shed—For taking away the only "real" family that I ever had—And for never once telling me that I was a good mother!

He always knew that he couldn't take away my independence. He couldn't take away my intelligence. So he took the one thing that mattered the most—he took my son away from me.

The feelings that I shared for my son's father and my grandmother were different than any other feelings I had ever felt. I was never a trusting person because that always seemed to get me hurt. The lack of trust that I had for my son's father was the same as that which I felt for my grandmother.

They were the two people, of all people in the world, who knew the things I had gone through with my mother. They knew all the things that I had gone through in my life. They knew how much I loved and adored my son. They should have been the last two people on earth to try and take my son from me. It always amazed me that my son's father found the time to take me to court, but he could never find the time to spend with his own son until the court finally determined visitation rights.

Shame on him and my grandmother for plotting against me to take away the one person that I truly loved and who loved me back. During one of the custody battles, I remember laughing out loud in my head when the judge asked my son's father to name any of my son's doctors—any of his friends—any of his teachers. Crickets… He didn't know. When asked, "What type of cancer does your son have?" - More crickets… Shenanigans!

I recalled the time when the fortune-teller told me that "an older woman to whom I was very close would hurt me very badly, later in life." Looking back, I can't say that I was surprised to find out that the woman she was referring to was my grandmother. I guessed, a long time ago, that the "older woman" was my grandmother. Unfortunately, no one believed me. I remember telling people that she was trying to take my son from me. I tried to tell them how conniving and manipulative she was. She was so calculating and malicious, but no one would listen. They thought I was paranoid and had gone crazy. When shit hit the fan, no one was there. No one wanted to know the truth.

Unfortunately, most of the people who know the truth about my grandmother are deceased or too old to do anything about it. The others just don't care, or are too scared to say anything because it might affect their livelihood. I guess money really *can* buy love. My grandmother is preceded in death by her four brothers, her only sister, two husbands, and her three daughters.

We hadn't spoken since we had words on the steps of the courthouse, over fifteen years ago. But, during her short stay at a nursing home a few years ago, I stayed in contact with my son daily to comfort him and to make sure that they were both doing okay. In 2016, she spent Thanksgiving at my apartment in Jersey (along with my son, his girlfriend, and my granddaughters.) In 2017, I spent Thanksgiving at her condo (along with my son, his girlfriend, and my granddaughters.) So many people, who don't know the truth, often ask me if I will ever speak to my grandmother again. I wonder if it had happened to them, would they be able to forgive so easily.

These days, I try to stay focused on the things that make me happy. My precious baby, Cocoa, makes me happy and is still hanging in there. She is much older, now. Two years ago, she had to have her front nipples removed because they were badly infected. She also has cysts growing all over her body. The vet said that it would cost approximately $1,100.00 just for a biopsy to see if they were cancerous. The surgery to have them removed cost $1,200. I paid about $300.00 for her medicine, alone. I had the surgery done over the Christmas break, so that I could be home to take care of her. She could barely walk and I couldn't carry her up the stairs. I was quickly reminded that dogs are like children. They're expensive and need lots of love, care, and attention. But I wouldn't trade my Cocoa for anything in the world! A friend stayed with us during the first week to help me with Cocoa.

Everyone Cocoa meets loves her! When she first arrived in Arizona, she loved to play with all the children at the childcare center. When we are in Jersey, I walk her to the corner of the school—near my apartment. It always reminds me of the times when my grandfather came to pick me up from school with the Dobermans. She loves to play with the children and the crossing guard. They say Dobermans are one of the most loyal creatures on earth. I thank my grandfather for allowing me to trust him, for loving me, and for sharing his love of Dobermans with me. Cocoa is loyal to the core and always right by my side.

In 2015, when we left Arizona to go back to Jersey, I drove across the country by myself. Of course, Cocoa was right by my side. She sat in the front seat because the backseat was filled with bags of clothes. We rode from state to state, only stopping to eat and use the bathroom. Cocoa went right outside the car, when I couldn't find a proper place for her to pee and poop. I had plenty of plastic bags to clean up the mess. We left on a Sunday at 10:30 p.m. and arrived in Jersey on a Tuesday at 12:00 noon. When we arrived back home, in Jersey, the property management office staff was out to lunch. Waiting in the car for another hour wouldn't hurt us. I laughed out loud.

I leaned my chair back and remembered when I first got Cocoa. I asked the veterinarian, who worked next door to the childcare center where I worked, if she could recommend a good breeder. I had seen the vet with a Doberman and knew her reputation. That same month, I contacted a breeder in Florida, who referred me to a breeder in Pennsylvania. Soon afterward, I went to pick up my new puppy from the airport. She was caged and cute—and still reminds me of the color of deep, rich hot chocolate. That's how she got her name. She will always be my "hot Cocoa." Since my mother's death, Cocoa and I have traveled back and forth between Jersey and Arizona several times. Jersey will always be home, but Arizona is my "second home" and where I plan to retire.

Four months after returning to our Jersey apartment, it caught on fire. It was an electrical fire from the stove, which happened the week after Thanksgiving. It was the first time I had used the oven. No one was badly hurt, and nothing was badly ruined, but we couldn't stay in the apartment for a week because of the smoke. We stayed in the car on the first night. Cocoa and I had become pretty accustomed to doing that. We spent the next day at the shelter. Then, we were given a Red Cross voucher to stay in a local hotel on Route 22. I was so glad that they allowed dogs! We stayed there for five whole days. They also had continental breakfast, which was great!

The fire, though nowhere as fatal, made me think about my neighbors' fire in college. My son and I had to evacuate our very first apartment. The shelter made me think of my mother. I missed her and wished that she was still alive. While at the hotel, I thought about how much I loved Cocoa and our Arizona "dream house" more than anything. Thinking back, I remember that I was about thirty years old when I bought my very first house in Union. I loved that house because it was my first home. I was about forty years old, when I bought my second home—my first "dream house." I loved that house because it was my first "custom" home and the first house that I had built from the ground. I am making plans to build my next and final "dream house."

After everything, I am thankful for all the blessings that I've had (including the chance to travel.) These opportunities have allowed me to see another part of the world and brought me to Arizona. They've also given me the chance to meet new and interesting people. I even got a chance to sit right behind Ice-T and his wife, Coco, on a flight from Los Angeles. I also met Tim Gunn, the fashion consultant from *Project Runway*, on a flight from Phoenix to Newark. I asked Ice to tell "Olivia Benson" that she is the baddest chick alive. Thinking back, I wished that Tim had asked me to sashay down the airport runway in true fashion (like the model that I am.) I laughed out loud in my head. Some things never change. Now *that's* the truth!

I remember when I thought that I would never leave New Jersey—never leave Newark. I remember when I was that awkward little girl who tried to fit in and look like the other girls in my neighborhood. I remember when Karen and I ran away from South Clinton Street to Main Street in East Orange. I remember when my mother nearly beat me to death, after we returned home from our adventure. I have not heard from, or seen, Karen since college.

The days of combing the streets looking for my mother are over. The endless days of sitting on the hallway steps, or waiting on the front stoop of our building, for my mother to return are no more. The sleepless nights spent worrying and praying for my mother to come home safely will never happen again. I used to do the same for my son. There will be no more visits to the hospital and no more sessions with the drug counselors. I will never have to hear my so-called family members snicker about my mother's wayward life ever again. Most of them are gone anyway and my mother is up in heaven, smiling down on us!

Thinking of my mother has always helped me to put my life in perspective. As far back as I can remember, I have always had a plan for my life. At first, my only goal in life was "not" to be like my mother. I wanted to be *someone* different and have *something* different. I've heard it said that a goal without a plan is just a dream. When I first moved to Arizona, my dream became a reality. I fell in love with the wide streets, the clear skies, and the mountains that surrounded the beautiful state. The vibe in Arizona was very different from that in Jersey and New York. I had grown up to believe that *I* was always different. It turns out that the people in Arizona were different. The clothes in Arizona were different. The food in Arizona was different.

The weather in Arizona was different. There are only two seasons—*hot and hotter!* The houses were also different. Most of them were big and beautiful. Strangely, they were all different shades of beige. It also seemed strange that the houses in Arizona did not have porches, or basements. People laughed out loud at me when I referred to my front step as a "stoop" and the side of my house as the "alleyway." My neighbors also laughed at me, whenever I referred to my purse as a "pockabook." My next-door neighbors were originally from New York and welcomed me with open arms. They told me that they saw my car arrive with Jersey plates and decided to gather all the other neighbors to welcome me to the cul-de-sac. I felt like I was starring in a *Lifetime* movie, as fruit baskets and pies were bestowed upon me.

I didn't see many apartment buildings in Arizona and there were no fire escapes. There were no hissing radiators and kids playing in the street while jumping through fire hydrants. South Phoenix reminded me a little of Newark, except there were no projects. I laughed out loud in my head, whenever I heard people in Phoenix refer to their two-story apartment buildings in the hood as "the projects." The first time that I had actually gone to "the hood" in Phoenix was when I asked Sherrie, my White girlfriend from church, to take me there. She agreed, but told me that she would drop me off and leave me because her husband didn't want her in "that type of neighborhood." I laughed out loud.

Several of the houses that I saw in South Phoenix were run down and beat up. The clubs were even worse. I'm not sure that I can even call them clubs because they looked more like outhouses from down South. Some of the men dressed liked country pimps and the majority of the women looked a hot mess. Prior to moving to Arizona, I had never heard of an HOA and didn't know what it meant. I later found out that HOA stood for Home Owner Association and referred to the people who managed the homes within a residential subdivision. I don't think I had ever heard the term "subdivision" either. Most of the homes outside of Phoenix seemed brand new, and I often wondered if they existed before I moved there. The roofs were made of Spanish tile and reminded me of the houses in California.

The culture in Arizona was also different. After I arrived, I only counted ten Black people in my neighborhood. There were six Black people in my church, which included an usher, two older women, a young man, and his two children. I spoke to a young Black woman at the grocery store, who looked a little younger than me and clearly wanted nothing to do with me. The young woman looked to be in her early thirties. She wore a teeny-weeny, natural afro like my mother and youngest aunt. She also wore big hoop earrings and an

African-print wraparound skirt. As I attempted to tell her that I was new to the neighborhood, she rushed to her car and said, "Good luck, sister!" I was expecting her to call me "sista" rather than "sister." I guess that I should have been happy that she spoke at all. Some of the Black people in Arizona also proved to be a little different.

There was the guy who delivered Pepsi to the Fry's grocery store on the corner. Then, there was another guy who I also met in the same grocery store, and a third guy who I ended up going on a date with. We went to Red Lobster and he wouldn't let me get a word in edgewise. He bragged and bragged about how all the women in his church wanted him. I was bored to death! There definitely were no cute guys in my neighborhood and it seemed like the rest of the Black people lived in South Phoenix, or Mesa.

I remember standing in the dressing room at a store in Fashion Square Mall, one Saturday afternoon. Scottsdale was beautiful, but I never had any reason to go there outside of shopping. Two young Black girls were cackling, like hens, as they admired their figures in the mirror outside of the dressing room. I couldn't believe my ears, as they planned and plotted to seduce the pastor of their church. *Yikes... Not the Pastor!* My mouth fell open and I tried hard not to breathe loud so they wouldn't hear me. I had waited six long months to venture out of my neighborhood and found my way all the way from the West Valley to the East Valley.

I was desperate to meet other Black folk, but there was no way on God's green earth that I wanted to befriend these two creatures. I was definitely out of my element. Other than the months that I spent in California, I had never been to the West Coast. Arizona was considered the Southwest, a little country and a little Western—and I liked it! The first time that I went to the grocery store, a young White man (who was extremely bowlegged and wore a cowboy hat) tipped his hat to me. He smiled and said, "Well, howdy, ma'am. You must be the Halle Berry of Arizona!" I, literally, laughed out loud.

It seemed like there were very few Black men in the entire state of Arizona. So, I decided to taste other flavors. I decided to get my feet wet by dating a Mexican man and a White man. I had never dated a Mexican before and he referred to himself as a "real" Mexican.

He didn't want to be referred to as a Mexican-American, or anything else, and he hated "Tex-Mex" food. He was very proud of his culture.

Unfortunately, my Mexican man wasn't open to learning about other people's culture. Besides, he was ten years younger than me. Although he was quite yummy, I knew the relationship wouldn't last. He was a cutie and very sweet. My friends adored him, but I knew that it was time to move on.

Then, I met this White dude online. He too was very cute and very sweet. He was also very funny, very charming, very old, and very White. I laughed out loud in my head. He was fifteen years my senior and had absolutely no rhythm. He could spend an entire day at the farmers' market. Strangely, he loves him some Black women. We never actually had *relations*, but he could put a smile on any woman's face.

I also met a cute Italian man. Our first date was nice. We met at a Sport's Bar near Arrowhead Mall for dinner. I wore a pair of skinny jeans with my pointy-toe ankle-high black boots and a little black sweater. I came to win. He must have fallen in love with me that night because he kept calling me every five minutes. After that, I told him that I had to fly back home to Jersey for the Christmas holiday and would be in touch. Clearly, he didn't get the memo because he kept calling me. I had to cancel his contract *real quick!*

Finally, I decided to venture out and find what I was used to. I needed a *Black* man. Clearly, the three Black men that I had already met were not going to do. Since moving to Arizona, I had met a lot of interesting people. I wasn't quite sure of the culture in Arizona because everyone kind of did their own thing. Most of the people that I met were White and Mexican, and I wondered if I would fit in. I laughed out loud in my head, when a four-year-old Mexican girl referred to me as a "Chocolate Girl." She said that I looked just like her!

Later, that same year, two other preschoolers (who happened to be White) asked me if I had a tan! One day, I caught them watching me wash my hands to see if the brown would come off. I worried most about the parents of the children, who I provided care for, and wondered if they would accept me. I was still at a point in my life where I needed approval and validation. I was insecure and wanted to belong. After all I had been through, I still wanted to be accepted!

When I went to church, I saw people in shorts and khakis. When I arrived dressed in my "Sunday best," people would call me "New York City", like in the movie—*Life*. I learned to look more casual at church and didn't spend a lot of time dressing up other times because I mostly worked with children. When I became a center director, at a Christian academy in Phoenix, I would dress up in work clothes and the owner would always comment on how nice I dressed by saying, "She got on her New York City clothes."

All types of people moved to Arizona for different reasons. Arizona was a step up for some, while it was simply a change of pace for others. Originally, I hadn't planned on staying—but went for the peace and quiet. Little did I know that Arizona would become my home! I started to fall in love with Arizona—its culture and its people. But for the first time in a long time, I realized that I missed the hustle and bustle of city-life back East.

I missed the fashion. I missed the food trucks. I missed the Steak-n-Take and Italian hotdog trucks on the corners of Newark. I also missed the 24-hour bodegas in Brooklyn and the Bronx, and the big cheesy slices of pizza in Manhattan. No disrespect to New York, but the biggest and best slices of pizza that I've ever had in my entire life were on the boardwalk at Seaside Heights in Jersey. There's nothing like the boardwalks and beaches at Seaside Heights and Atlantic City. The Jersey shore is where it's at!

I thought about the times that my grandmother took me and my two cousins to the beach in Asbury Park on Saturdays, when we were younger. My cousins and I would crowd in the car and fight over who would ride in the front seat. My grandmother always parked ten blocks away from the beach because there were no meters, and parking was free. It would take us almost thirty minutes to walk to the boardwalk. We didn't mind, until it was time to go home. Then, we would have to pack up all the bags and walk thirty minutes back to the car. Of course, we had to shower in cold water on the beach, before getting in the car. My grandmother didn't want any sand in her car, and the bathroom stalls cost a whole quarter!

Things have changed, since the days when my cousin and I were like sisters. We no longer spend weekends together at the beach. There is no ocean in Arizona, but I have learned to appreciate the calmness as I stare out at the man-made lake surrounding the Surprise Public Library. Although I appreciate its beauty, I've come to find out that Arizona presents its own challenges—such as scorpions and snakes. Basically, it's a constant reminder that I am and have always been deathly afraid of all things that scurry.

Needless to say, I will never miss the life-sized subway rats and the heaping pounds of garbage on the streets of New York. But there's more to New York than the dirty sidewalks, crowded subways, and gigantic rats! After all, it's New York City! The city that never sleeps! Home of the yellow cabs! Although I worked in New York for many years, I've never taken full advantage of the beautiful things that "the City" has to offer. I had been to a few plays, when I was younger. I've been to the Brooklyn Museum. I've eaten at a few restaurants and I've strolled through Central Park, on occasion. But there's so much more to see and so much more to do. I often wonder if most people, who live or work in New York, take it for granted.

As I reminisced about my work in New York, I couldn't decide what I hated more about the subway—the fact that it always smelled like a dirty toilet, or the fact that someone was always trying to squeeze into the seat next to me—on the train (knowing full well that they couldn't fit.) One day, a man was standing in front of me and literally fell right onto my lap. I wouldn't have minded him falling onto my lap if the stranger had made my "cute list."

In addition to not being cute, I'm always so grateful when someone decides to share their bad breath and germs with me by yawning or coughing bacteria right into my face! I especially love it when someone sneezes right into their hand and uses the same hand to grab the pole that everyone else is holding onto. *That's the best! And it was definitely something different!* That's why I wear gloves on the subway trains, in both the winter and the summer. Shenanigans!

I used to be thankful that I hadn't caught any terrible disease and hadn't been diagnosed with any chronic health illnesses. Aside from a few minor aches and pains that came along with turning fifty, my doctor said that I was as healthy as the horses that I've grown to love. I laugh out loud in my head, every time I think of the men—who think they are complimenting me by calling me a "stallion." I wonder if they know that a stallion is a male horse. My doctor suggested that I exercise, eat healthy, and maintain a stress-free life. I laughed out loud in my head (again.)

My blood pressure elevates, whenever I get stressed. I like reading the Ladders.com news articles, which gives me tips about things that I should do to stay focused, positive, and healthy. It also tells me what kinds of people to stay away from, such as toxic people, and which people are a good influence in my life. My doctor says that I will have to take medication for high blood pressure, if I don't eat better, exercise, and avoid stress. Therefore, my new goal was to avoid toxic people and toxic foods. So I decided to stay away from the things and people who bring stress into my life. I started to work out a couple of times each week, and I continue to eat turkey bacon. I only eat beef bacon, when I eat at King's Halal Restaurant—in Newark (of course.)

But my stomach had been hurting for months. It was January 2, 2018 (one day after the beginning of a brand new year) and I had just returned from my Phoenix trip. Then, I got the call... Something felt different - First, I was constipated. Then, I had diarrhea. Then, there was the blood and the migraines. I couldn't sleep, and I couldn't eat. My chest hurt. Something was wrong. My blood work showed the same things it had always shown—high cholesterol and anemia. At least, my pressure was back to normal. But the CT scan showed something abnormal. There was a mass, a tumor, in my colon. A colonoscopy and an MRI confirmed a second and third tumor, one on each side of my liver. There were polyps in my esophagus and lungs. I had a kidney infection. The biopsies confirmed that I had stage four colon cancer that had spread through my body. I was devastated!

Once again, all my dreams and hard work seemed like they were going down the drain. I wanted to die, but I had to live. I had work to do! Listening to people tell me that I'll get through this, hearing the doctors describe my chemo treatments and upcoming surgeries, and thinking about the portacath in my chest—all these things reminded me of when my son was diagnosed with cancer. His brush with death happened twenty years ago. Only, it wasn't the same because I don't have a mother to take care of me.

I wish that I didn't have cancer! But since I do, I wish that I had a mother to lie next to me and hold my hand, to watch over me while I sleep, to wipe my tears when I cry, and to tell me not to be afraid when I get scared. I remember the countless times that I drove my son back and forth to the hospital for chemo treatments, and whenever he got a fever. I remember the countless times that I fell to my knees and prayed for God to spare my son's life. I remember being my son's mother, the only one there when no one else was there.

There I was... So scared... So alone. I didn't remember having the colonoscopy. I remember crying, during the first biopsy and the first surgery. I remember the questions that ran through my mind. *What did stage four mean? How many stages were there? What did met-astatic mean? How did I get this awful disease? Was I going to die? Had God left me?* I remember a nurse holding my left hand, while a tech-nician held my right hand. She was praying for me and I remem-bered that I had seen her earlier in the hospital hallway. She smiled. I tried to smile back, but it hurt. They rolled me down the hall to the operating room. Everyone else had family members there. I was the only one—all alone. I would make sure that I was not alone the next time. I would be surrounded by love!

The truth is that, even if my mother were still alive, she would not have been there. She would never be here to do any of those things. So all I had were the tears that ran down my face, trickling down my chapped lips, as my body glided through countless MRIs, CT scans, and x-ray machines - as the doctors pushed needles into my arm to draw blood and into my spine to draw fluid - as the chemo continued to run through my body to kill the cancer. Right then, at that very minute, before the doors to the operating room shut - I just wished things could go back to normal. But I never knew what nor-mal was. My life had never been normal. I had begun to live my *new* normal. One time, I was at the cancer center and a volunteer asked me how to pronounce my name. She proceeded to say that she didn't want to mispronounce it because she was "White and uncultured." I laughed out loud. I was diagnosed in February and had been on chemotherapy since March. My tumors were shrinking and in August of 2018, I prepared for my next surgery.

This time, I was not all alone! They removed the primary source of my cancer, which came from my colon. I didn't remember counting backwards, as I had done before and seen my son do (when he had cancer.) I was alive! I survived the surgery! When I woke up, the tumor in my colon and part of my liver had been removed. The surgeon explained how the next surgery would involve removing my gallbladder and the rest of my liver, once the other part had regenerated. I was tired and in pain.

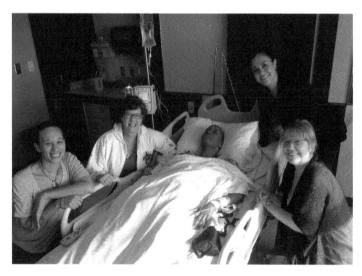

The surgeon joked about how he kept my butterfly tattoo intact. I stayed in the recovery room for hours, before going up to my own private room. My AZ friends made sure that Cocoa was taken care of and they were each by my side, on each side of the hospital bed. I remember them taking a picture. I tried to smile, but I couldn't. About a week in, I was told that I would be transferred to a rehabilitation facility. This is where they would help me learn to stand up by myself and begin to walk, all over again. This is where I would learn to walk up and down the stairs, all over again. This is where I would learn to dress myself, all over again. This is where I would gain back my independence, all over again!

Two months later, I had to prepare for yet another surgery. The majority of my liver was removed. I woke up in the intensive care unit. An oxygen mask covered my nose and mouth. There was a large tube down my throat. I couldn't breathe on my own. I continued to drift in and out of consciousness for days. My speech was slurred and I felt funny - sleepy. My friends said that they had been talking and singing to me - but I couldn't seem to remember... *Had I been in a coma?* I was happy to be alive and couldn't wait for things to be normal again. But things weren't normal... *They were still different.*

EPILOGUE

It was December 2018. I had been fighting for my life all year. All of my surgeries had been successful, but I had some complications. I was finally going home from the hospital. My phone rang over and over. There were several missed calls from a 973 area code. I spoke with my cousin. I spoke with my ex-boyfriend (my first love). Then, like my grandfather, my eldest aunt, my mother, and my youngest aunt—I found out that my grandmother was gone. She was dead. I didn't know how to feel. I didn't know what to feel. I had felt numb since my diagnosis. After all the chemotherapy and after all the surgeries, I felt dead inside. But I was still alive. I was a survivor. I was a cancer survivor.

As I tried to recover, so many feelings and thoughts consumed me. I couldn't sleep. I couldn't think. I couldn't even do a simple normal thing like eat. I thought about how, when I was younger, I could eat whatever I wanted. And I never gained weight. Everybody knows that I love to eat. Not only do I enjoy my food, but men also like to watch me enjoying my food. Some men actually love to buy food and feed me so that they can sit back and watch me eat. It must be that whole "happy wife is a happy life thing." The only problem with eating all of my favorite foods is that I start to *look* like I eat all of my favorite foods.

In elementary school, I wore a size 3–4. I thought that I was doing something because my youngest aunt only wore a size 0. She was all boobs. At least, I had hips with my little boobies. In high school, I wore a size 5–6. In college, I wore a size 7–8. When I was in my thirties, I wore a size 9–10. By the time I turned forty-five, I was wearing a size 11–12. By age fifty, I was wearing a size 13–14 and bought my first size 16.

I remember how the salesgirl took one look at me and started walking me back to the "plus" size rack. *Excuse me! The nerve!* After that, I remember how I started eating grilled chicken and salad like crazy. Let's just say that I went back down to a size 12, in no time! Last summer, one of my Brooklyn dudes called me "plump." Thank God for the block feature on my iPhone. Now, with the cancer, I've lost forty pounds in four months. I continued to work with my physical and occupational therapists to regain my strength and endurance.

That's okay. I'm still a "foody"—as long as I can keep my food down. No eating salad and drinking water on a date for me, unless they come with the rest of the meal. I laughed out loud, as I thought about how I have always loved food, fashion, and dancing. I have always loved the arts, and I still have an eye for fashion. I still have my own sense of style. They say that a person can learn fashion, but one cannot learn style. I look at each day as an opportunity to "cat-walk" down the runway. I can still recall when I coordinated my first fashion show in Arizona a few years back. My rule of thumb is that I always keep my hair nice, my nails right, and my body tight! I'm over fifty years old, and some people say that I look like I'm in my thirties (okay, maybe my early forties.) *Even so, I'll take it!*

My motto is, if something makes you smile, keep doing it! I recently watched a pastor preach a sermon on TV that talked about the "Ls" of life. The "Ls" that he referred to included learning, laboring, loving, living, laughing, listening, leaving your burdens behind, and longing for your dreams! Basically, the key to living a happy, healthy, and prosperous life is to be kind to others and to yourself. As we struggle through our everyday lives, it is important that we treat others the way we want to be treated. At the end of the day, I truly believe that we are all sinners in the eyes of God. It's hard, sometimes, but we must accept the fact that we don't have the right to judge anyone else and how they live their life.

I remember a time, not long before my mother's death, when I brought her to the church in Newark that our family grew up in. It was the first and only time that I can remember us being in church together. When my grandmother saw me walk into the church with my mother, she gasped. She was standing in the aisle, ushering. She walked up to us. Then, she grabbed my arm and told me that we better not embarrass her. When my mother died, my grandmother didn't even come inside the mortuary to identify the body. At the funeral parlor, my grandmother refused to pay for my mother's burial and did not want to get a headstone for her gravesite like she did for my eldest aunt.

This was the same aunt whose body I had identified more than ten years earlier because my grandmother couldn't bring herself to do so. I had flown all the way from California to be there for her! I wonder if my grandmother has ever thought about how she made me and my mother feel, throughout our lives. When I told my son that my grandmother wouldn't buy my mother's headstone, he didn't believe me. A few weeks later, he called me at work in Arizona and told me that he took care of it. I felt so proud! It was one of the nicest things he had ever done for me.

Now, my mother's name is there. It will always be there! At least once a year, whenever I'm in Jersey, I visit the cemetery. Sometimes— on Mother's Day, Father's Day, Christmas Day, or on my mother's birthday—I drive to the cemetery in Kenilworth and talk to my mother and my grandfather. A few Christmases ago, I bought my oldest granddaughter a locket. Inside was a picture of me and her at my youngest granddaughter's baby shower. I had the locket inscribed with the words, "I will always be here!" On her tenth birthday, I gave my oldest granddaughter a photo album with pictures of us over the past ten years. I bought my youngest granddaughter a snow globe carousel that reminded me of the one I bought when I first moved to Arizona. My hope is that she too will one day remember the times we've shared together.

Shortly before her death, my mother told me that she loved me. It may have been the first and last time… But, at least, she said it. I no longer have the locket that my mother kept of us from my first Easter, but I keep a 2010 calendar with a picture of our favorite Halal and soul food restaurant on my refrigerator (in memory of my mother.) Eating at King's reminded me of the times when my mother would take me to eat at Stewart's on the corner of Lyons Avenue and Clinton Place, in Newark.

Whenever I hear the song "No Diggity" by *Blackstreet*, I am reminded of my mother's smile and the good times that we had dancing together. For her funeral, I asked that the following be printed on the front of my mother's prayer card, "*A mother holds her child's hands for a while...their hearts forever!*" The life lessons that my mother taught me have all come to fruition.

I still think that I look different, but my height no longer bothers me. I embrace my tallness. It makes me stand out in a crowd. Most men seem to love my full lips and long, hairy legs, just like my mother said they would. My mother's baby oil trick still works to this day. It's a "Black" thing!

I remember a conversation that I had with my eldest granddaughter (when she was younger.) One day, she just came out and said, "We got the tame kin!" That's how she compared her skin color to mine. She couldn't pronounce the letter "S" yet, but she was beginning to recognize the color of people's skin (just as I did, when I was a young child.) She went on to say, "My mommy and daddy got the tame kin too, but it's different than ours." She knew that there was a difference in our skin colors and that she and I were brown-skinned, and her daddy and her mommy were light-skinned. When she was older, I asked her what made her unique. She answered, "My hazel eyes!" I smiled as I thought about her baby sister and how she too had hazel eyes, but she was light-skinned. My two granddaughters reminded me of my mother and her younger sister.

In the world we live in today, some pale-skinned White people use tanning lotion to darken their skin and some dark-skinned Black people bleach their skin so that it appears lighter. I am just happy to be in the skin I'm in! To each his own... With all the injustices in the world and so much hatred, one of the most valuable life lessons learned is that we all should "look to a day when people will not be judged by the color of their skin, but by the content of their character."—(Martin Luther King Jr.)

My life has definitely come full circle, with all of its shenanigans and déjà vu. Most people look at me and think my life has been good. No doubt, life *is* good, but that's because *God* is good... *All the time!* Trust and believe... I've had to face many challenges, and

I've struggled to overcome many obstacles. Sometimes, I feel like the little boy riding "The Mystery Horse" with no hands, at the end of *The Black Stallion* movie. Other times, I feel like giving up. So many people have asked me if I would do it again. Move to Arizona and start a new life... My answer is "absolutely!"

I am reminded of a scripture in the Bible that says, "It is not the wants of man, but the wishes of God that prevail." (Proverbs 19:21 NIV) As adults, we should reach for the hands of our children and guide them through life. We should keep and hold them tight, teaching them not to make the mistakes that we did and as our parents did before us.

Teachers, educate your students. Mothers, love your children. Fathers, love and respect the women in your lives—your mothers, sisters, daughters, wives, girlfriends, and baby-mamas, because *all* lives matter!

Within the past fifteen years, I've started my life all over and have gone from making minimum wage to earning a six-figure salary. But my greatest success comes from working with great people, who thrive by helping others and who strive to make a difference in other people's lives. As I reflect upon my personal growth and my financial struggles; my losses and my gains - I am reminded of a quote from the former First Lady and the wife of our first Black president, Barack Obama: "Success isn't about the *money* you make, it's about the *difference* we make in people's lives"—(Michelle Obama.) Pastor Joel Osteen once said, "Material things may increase your net worth but not your self-worth."

I work hard, I play hard, and I love hard. I treasure the things that I have, and I respect the way other people live their lives. I wish people would do the same for me. I know that some people believe in karma. They believe that "what comes around goes around" - and "bad things only happen to bad people." I believe, if that were true, a lot more people would be a lot worse off than they are. I believe that, if we sow good seeds, God will bless us with good things in return. I know this because through each of my struggles came a blessing.

Until a person is able to say, "I am perfect...I am a perfect person. I am a perfect wife, or husband... A perfect mother, or father...

A perfect son, or daughter… A perfect brother, or sister… A perfect friend… And I have never lied, cheated, stolen, said a bad word, or had a bad thought. I have never lusted, or yearned. I have never treated anyone unfairly, or unkindly. I have never done any of these things, or anything else to hurt anyone—ever in life—Until we can say these things, we should worry about ourselves and should not judge others. None of us are flawless—And it would be unfair to judge someone, without having walked in their shoes.

Sometimes, I wish that I could erase my life. Instead, I've learned to embrace change. I'm a change agent. But I know that I can't change my past. It makes me who I am. I'm sure there will be more things to overcome, but I'll be ready. *It's what I do!*

I have learned so many lessons… But I'm grateful that I've lived, I've laughed, and I've loved. I am a mother and a motherless child. I am a child of God. I was chosen by God; Made by Him, and God doesn't make mistakes! I am Rahimah—*Merciful* and *Compassionate.* I am amazing!

I've come a long way and I have a long way to go. I stand by my truth. Everyone has a story. This is *my* story. This is my life—*The Life Of Rah.*

Blessed is the one who perseveres under trial because, having stood the test, that person will receive the crown of life that the Lord has promised to those who love him. (James 1:12 NIV)

ACKNOWLEDGMENTS

While I have lost some old friends and gained some new ones-I thank *God*, first and foremost, for allowing me to be my authentic self, for always loving me, and for being my very *best* friend!

Thank you, Reverend Joseph L. Napier, my pastor. I was the first person you baptized at *New Point Baptist Church* in Newark. You have continued to pray for and with me. Your words; your voice; your prayers have comforted me. You encouraged me to stay in faith.

Thank you, to my elementary school teachers! You told me that I could become anything that I wanted to become. You told me to always believe in myself and never give up. You planted a seed…

I want to thank everyone who has said at one time or another, "*You should write a book!*" Over the years, you've allowed me to share so many stories with you about my life. In 2015, I finally got up the nerve to gather all of my Post-it notes and express my thoughts through writing. Thank you for listening and encouraging me to share my life with the world!

Thank you, Deanna, for being one of the first to encourage me to write a book! You have been one of my biggest supporters through my journey with cancer. I will never forget the night that you worked tirelessly in the hospital lounge, as I slept. You snuck me extra sips of water, when the doctors said I could only have ice and only a few sips of water. You helped me shower and dress, when it was time to leave the hospital. You were there before, during, and after! Thank you for continuing to "check in" on me, as I prepared to fight this next battle. Words cannot express my gratitude!

To my primary doctors, oncologists, neurologists, surgeons, and caregivers—Thank you! To Dr. Ramasamy, Dr. Scopp, Dr. Naraev, and Dr. Choti, I am indebted to you for saving my life! A very special thanks goes to the medical team and nursing staff, at Saint Barnabas Medical Center, who showed so much patience as I began my fight against cancer. I am also very grateful to each of the nurses, schedulers, volunteers, physical and occupational thera-pists, at MD Anderson Cancer Center and Banner Gateway Medical Center, who took care of me for months on end.

Thank you, Beth, for your undying love and support during my battle with cancer. Thank you for worrying about me until I arrived to Arizona safely. Thank you so much for sitting with me during my chemotherapy treatments and doctor consultations. Thank you for picking up my prescriptions. Thank you for always buying groceries and dog food. Cocoa also sends her love and grati-tude for taking care of her while I was in the hospital.

Thank you, my Juli, for spending nights on the hospital couch and watching over me after my surgeries. Thank you for wash-ing my clothes and bringing cans of soup, after I returned home from the hospital. Although I was in a lot of pain, it brought me such joy to play with Sebastian and Baby Nicolas. Thank you to Sebastian for helping me walk again, and for noticing when I no longer needed my walker!

Thank you, Lori, for your love and support during my time of need; for helping me to prepare for surgery; for keeping every-one updated; for keeping up with the nurses to make sure my hospi-tal bathroom was clean; for staying up late to watch Lifetime movies with me; and for putting chapstick on my cracked lips!

A special shout out goes to my very special friends, Cindi and Julie, who took time out of their day to help proofread several chapters of this book. We worked, we fought, we laughed, and we cried. Four years in the making, and it's finally done! Thank you, Cindi, for visiting me in the hospital with George and for helping me pack up all of my shoes to go to AZ!

A special thanks to Milly Gonzalez and all of the early childhood coaches, teachers, school leaders—and everyone on the NYC Pre-K Explore Team at Bank Street College and the New York City Department of Education for their endless support.

Thank you, Raymond, for your generosity and support; and especially for taking me back and forth to the hospital for my chemo treatments in Jersey.

My sincere thanks to my Aunt Tiny, Nancy Chatmon, and all of my friends and colleagues who have sent cards, gift boxes, donations, positive thoughts and prayers. Thank you for supporting me during a very difficult time.

Thank you to my "little" cousin, Kareem *(aka Reemy Reem)*, for continuing to check on me every day. I know life has been hard, but I promise it will get better. Hang in there, cuz!

Thank you, Dr. Charles Stanley of *In Touch Ministries* and Joel Osteen of *Joel Osteen Ministries*, for unknowingly helping me to recognize the good in me and inspiring me to become an even better person. Your television broadcasts have provided me with so many messages of hope and inspiration, during some of the most trying times.

A very special thanks goes to the *American Cancer Society*, the *Colorectal Cancer Alliance* and the *Blue Hope Nation* for providing resources, financial assistance, and transportation in support of cancer survivors and individuals who continue to fight against cancer.

For my mother

Sunrise January 25, 1949
Sunset March 9, 2010

Also by Rahimah S. Phillips:

The Life Of An Addict

My Spoken Words

ABOUT THE AUTHOR

Rahimah Samira Phillips is a first-time author, with a second book in the works. She has one adult son and two beautiful granddaughters. Born and raised in Newark, New Jersey, she currently lives as a single woman in the Phoenix Metropolitan Area with her dog (Cocoa.) With great compassion for helping others, Rahimah began her career as a student tutor. She then became a preschool teacher, and later taught dance to young children and adults.

After relocating to Arizona, Rahimah continued her career in the *Valley of the Sun* by working as a hospice volunteer to help provide respite care for seniors. Many years prior to moving to Arizona, she helped take care of her grandfather until his passing. Growing up without a mother, or father, Rahimah grew very close to her grandfather. Her passion for caring for others also stems from growing up as an only child and the oldest grandchild, during which time she often cared for her younger cousins.

While in Arizona, she went on to volunteer at a local church, providing care to infants and toddlers. Rahimah also provided care to young children, while working at a crisis center in Scottsdale. Although she also has a background in telecommunications and information technology, Rahimah decided to follow her dreams and opened *ECAYA (Early Childhood and Young Adult) Learning Center*. *ECAYA* served as a place where children of all ages could learn and grow in a loving and safe environment. She later became an infant and toddler specialist and worked for various agencies, collaborating with Head Start, Early Head Start, United Way and other Birth to Five, and Zero to Three programs.

Rahimah has been nominated to join the National Society of Leadership and Success (NSLS), "the largest collegiate leadership honor society in the United States." Rahimah is dedicated to working with young children and continues to provide training and coaching to other early care and education professionals. She has hopes of reopening *ECAYA Learning Center*. Rahimah obtained her Bachelor of Arts from Rutgers University in New Brunswick, New Jersey. She also possesses a master's degree in education, with a concentration in Teacher Leadership, and plans to pursue her doctoral degree in Educational Leadership at Arizona State University.

On a more personal note, Rahimah became ill in 2017 and was later diagnosed with stage four colon cancer. She looks forward to becoming a cancer survivor and living her life to the fullest—and hopes to share her story on TED Talks! To learn more about Rahimah's struggle and to join others in the fight against cancer, please visit the following websites:

https://www.gofundme.com/Rahimah-fights-cancer
cancer.org
ccalliance.org
https://www.cancercare.org
www.stompthemonster.org